# The Child Psychotherapist

## And Problems of Young People

**edited by Mary Boston and Dilys Daws**

Routledge
Taylor & Francis Group
LONDON AND NEW YORK

First published in 1977
New Revised Edition 1981

Published 1988 by Karnac Books Ltd.

Published 2019 by Routledge
2 Park Square, Milton Park, Abingdon, Oxon OX14 4RN
52 Vanderbilt Avenue, New York, NY 10017

First issued in hardback 2019

*Routledge is an imprint of the Taylor & Francis Group, an informa business*



ISBN 13: 978-0-367-09955-8 (hbk)
ISBN 13: 978-0-946439-43-0 (pbk)

British Library Cataloguing in Publication Data
A C.I.P. for this book is available from the British Library

# *CONTENTS*

Papers by various contributors appear in the *Journal of Child Psychotherapy, The Psycho-Analytic Study of the Child* and other scientific journals. Other publications include the following:

**Dilys Daws** *Your One Year Old* (Corgi Mini Books, London, 1969).

**Martha Harris** *Thinking about Infants and Young Children* (Clunie Press, Perthshire, 1975); *Your Eleven Year Old, Your Twelve to Fourteen Year Old, Your Teenager* (Corgi Mini Books, London, 1969).

**Gianna Henry,** co-author with Lina Generali of *Strutture deliranti alla bae di sindromi fobiche: 2 casi di fobia della scuola (Delusional structures in phobic-syndromes: two cases of school phobia)* (Acts of the 3rd Congress of Child Neuro-psychiatry, Edizioni 'La Porziuncula', Assisi, 1968); co-author with Tim Dartington and Isabel Menzies Lyth of *The Psychological Welfare of Young Children Making Long Stays in Hospital,* (C. A. S. R. Document 1200, The Tavistock Institute of Human Relations, 1976) available for reference only at the Tavistock Library; 'Psychic Pain and Psychic Damage' in Box et al., *Space for Thinking with Families* (Routledge & Kegan Paul, London, 1981).

**Shirley Hoxter** 'The Residual Autistic Condition and its Effect upon Learning' in *Explorations in Autism: A Psycho-Analytical Study* (Clunie Press, Perthshire, 1975).

**Patricia Radford** Chapters on 'Transference', 'Countertransference', 'Principles of Mental Functioning' and 'Ambivalence' in *Basic Psycho-Analytic Concepts on Metapsychology, Conflict, Anxiety and Other Subjects,* vol. iv, Hampstead Clinic Scientific Library (George Allen & Unwin, London, 1970); Radford et al. 'Aspects on Self-Cathexis in Main-Line Heroin Addiction' in Monogram Series of *The Psycho-Analytic Study of the Child,* no. 5, 1975 (Yale University Press, Connecticut, 1975).

**Sara Rosenfeld** 'Some Reflections Arising from the Treatment of a Traumatized Border-line Child' in Monogram Series of *The Psycho-Analytic Study of the Child,* no. 5, 1975 (Yale University Press, Connecticut, 1975); *Collected Papers* (to be published shortly).

**Isca Salzberger-Wittenberg** *Psycho-Analytic Insight and Relationships* (Routledge & Kegan Paul, London, 1970); 'Primal Depression in Autism' in *Explorations in Autism; A Psycho-Analytical Study* (Clunie Press, Perthshire, 1975).

**Frances Tustin** *Autism and Childhood Psychosis* (Hogarth Press, London, 1972); *A Group of Juniors* (Heinemann Educational, London, 1951); *Autistic States in Children* (Routledge & Kegan Paul, to be published March 1981).

# *Preface and Acknowledgments*

The idea of inviting a number of child psychotherapists to contribute accounts of their work in different settings was initially conceived by Dilys Daws. She collected the first drafts from some experienced psychotherapists with varying backgrounds. Mary Boston joined her later, as co-editor, to help with the task of editing the material and integrating it into a hopefully readable book.

We have been helped in this project by a number of people, who have given their time generously to reading and commenting on the manuscript. In particular, we are grateful to Professor Brian Foss, Dr Robert Gosling and Mr Sidney Gray for their encouragement and to Dr Arnon Bentovim, Mrs Gianna Henry and Miss Dina Rosenbluth for helpful suggestions. Stan Gooch has done valiant work on the literary editing. Our thanks are due to him and to Zoë Richmond-Watson, to those involved in the typing and the final preparations, to Mrs Janet Halton for compiling the index, and not least to our publisher Dieter Pevsner, without whose confidence this book might not have seen the light of day.

Finally, we should like to thank our contributors, who have waited so patiently for their work to appear, and our long-suffering families, who have tolerated our preoccupation with editorial duties with considerable forbearance.

*January* 1977 M. B., D. D.

### *Preface to the Second Edition*

In this second edition, we are pleased to be able to include, as an appendix, 'Doubly Deprived' by Gianna Henry. This paper provides a further study of psychotherapy with an adolescent patient, and indicates the possibility of working with patients who have been exposed to very early deprivation.

*August* 1980 M. B., D. D.

# *REVISED FOREWORD*

When this book was originally published in 1977 it had a radical feel. The profession of child psychotherapy was relatively new and was only recently recognised by the NHS. The book was the first attempt to bring our ideas to the general public, and it was an exciting task. It helped to spread these ideas and putting them into print added to the growing confidence of a small profession.

Child psychotherapists have not only grown in numbers and in recognition since then but have also considerably expanded their field of work. This has been described in subsequent books, *Extending Horizons*, Karnac (1991) and the *Handbook of Child and Adolescent Psychotherapy*, Routledge (1999), however the practice of individual, in-depth work has remained the core of the profession.

Twenty-five years after its publication, the original book has changed its status. It now has a classic, historic value. The Association of Child Psychotherapists had its 50th birthday in 1999 in the knowledge that Child Psychotherapy is esteemed and influential throughout much of the country. The time has come to realise that we have a history, and our book portrays vividly the shape of the profession as we saw it at the time. Some of the chapters are examples of beautiful, original thinking by those who helped to create our profession. Several of these, Jess Guthrie, Martha Harris, Sara Rosenfeld and Frances Tustin have now sadly died. It is good to acknowledge their founding contributions to our way of thinking.

Child psychotherapy has flourished since the book was written and we think it has played a part in inspiring this development. However, one of us (D.D.) is somewhat embarrassed by her own naive chapter—it was the first time she appeared in print! We are also proud to have been involved with some of the changes in thinking and practice since this book first came out.

Mary Boston
Dilys Daws

# *Introduction*

## by Mary Boston

The psychological treatment of children with emotional or behaviour difficulties has been practised for some considerable time. The first child guidance clinics actually date from the early 1900s. Nevertheless, child psychotherapy is still a relatively new profession. Its parentage is on the one hand psychoanalysis, in particular the developments in child analysis during this century, and on the other, an increasing awareness of the importance and meaning of children's play.

The first child guidance clinics in Great Britain were established after the First World War. The pioneers were the East London Clinic and the Notre Dame Clinic in Glasgow, but others gradually followed. Then the problems of evacuation during the Second World War once again focussed attention on emotional and developmental difficulties in children. Following the war the provision of guidance clinics became the responsibility of the health and education authorities, and a rapid expansion in the service then followed.

From the outset child guidance clinics had been staffed by a team of three kinds of professional workers: a psychiatrist, an educational psychologist and a psychiatric social worker. This combination of a medical doctor specializing in problems of emotional disturbance, a psychologist trained in the assessment of the child's educational achievement and potential, and a social worker trained in understanding the psychological tensions in family relationships, at once underlines the importance of team work as a central concept in child guidance. For the child's disturbance was, and continues to be, understood as the product of a variety of social, environmental and family relationships, as well as of factors inherent in the child himself.

The early clinics offered mainly diagnosis and advice: any actual treatment of children was then largely the province of the psychiatrist. The psychologist might also give remedial education to individual children. However, as more and more children were referred, the pressure to provide psychotherapeutic treatment for them increased. Non-medical members of the team therefore, the psychologists and social workers, began increasingly to undertake this work. On their own initiative they obtained what specialized training they could. At this time there existed very little organized professional training in child psychotherapy for non-medical members of the team or, for that matter, for the medical workers, except psychoanalysis.

Margaret Lowenfeld, a pioneer in the field, had in 1928 established in London a children's centre, where play was observed and studied. In 1933, she set up training for a small number of child psychotherapists at this centre. In time the department was to become the Institute of Child Psychology, now discontinued. A general move to set up a professional body for the training of child psychotherapists was then interrupted by the war. Later, however, arising mainly out of Anna Freud's experience of war nurseries, the Hampstead Child Therapy Course was inaugurated in 1947, to train child psychotherapists on psychoanalytic principles. In 1948, under the auspices of John Bowlby and the inspiration of Esther Bick, the Tavistock Clinic launched its programme. Then, in 1949, the Association of Child Psychotherapists (Non-Medical) was established, incorporating the existing trainings and now including a Jungian course.

Since 1949 the member institutions of the Association of Child Psychotherapists have been responsible for the training of a small, but ever increasing, number of psychotherapists, whose primary function is to undertake the psychological treatment of children along dynamic, psychoanalytic lines. The traditional team of the child guidance clinic has been enlarged now to include the specialized child psychotherapist. Hospitals, too, since the establishment of the National Health Service in 1948, have increasingly set up child psychiatric departments, where team work between psychiatrists, psychologists, psychiatric social workers and child psychotherapists also flourishes. Child psychotherapists, incidentally, who work in local authority clinics as well as in hospitals, are (since 1974) employees of the National Health Service.

As might be expected with a relatively new profession, child psychotherapists are still few and far between, especially outside London. Their numbers are, however, growing and they are increasingly contributing to the general understanding and treatment of children's problems. More recently they have been extending their contribution into yet other fields.

The purpose of this book is to describe the nature and practical implications of the child therapist's work, including aspects of its theoretical basis and the nature of the professional training. It is hoped the book will interest a variety of readers concerned to know more of this field, not only those directly concerned in psychiatry, but also teachers, social workers, doctors and parents. The book may particularly interest the parents of children with difficulties, and students contemplating professional training for this work. Directed as it is to a wide readership, the text does not attempt to be comprehensive in all the detailed aspects of the field and the theories. Rather it is an introduction, which will hopefully arouse interest in the kinds of work that are being undertaken. Full references are given for those wishing to pursue further any particular aspect.

## General Plan of the Book

The first chapter deals with the incidence and causation of emotional disturbance in children. It discusses at the same time the nature of the child psychotherapist's contribution to resolving disturbance and outlines his basic approach.

The second chapter introduces the problem of disturbed children within the school setting.

Chapters 3 – 7 describe the child psychotherapist's work in a wide variety of settings – in the child guidance clinic, in day units, in a hospital, and in work with young people at university and at a young people's consultation centre. These chapters describe both brief and long-term therapeutic work with individual patients and their parents, and liaison work with various professional colleagues in a consultative capacity.

Chapters 8 – 11 take us more deeply into the subject, presenting further detailed case studies which afford glimpses into the more primitive and psychotic layers of the mind. In particular, they trace the development of symbolic thought and play from earliest infancy onwards.

The final three chapters are more theoretical. They are for those readers interested in pursuing the conceptual basis of the work, who may themselves be interested in training. Chapter 12 traces the historical development of some of the psychoanalytic ideas presented in this book, from Sigmund Freud to Anna Freud and Melanie Klein, and to still more recent workers. Chapter 13 surveys the present clinical field from the point of view of a psychotherapist at the Hampstead Child Therapy Clinic. Chapter 14 presents the philosophy of training from the Tavistock Clinic viewpoint, and conveys some idea of the kind of receptive mind so necessary to the professional in this work.

# Chapter One

# *The Contribution of the Child Psychotherapist*

## by Mary Boston

This chapter takes a first look at the incidence and causation of emotional disturbance in children. It highlights the importance of the pre-school years and the desirability of increased social and emotional support for parents together with their young infants. The need for social and economic change and for further research into environmental factors is considered, joined with the specific contribution of the child psychotherapist in effecting changes in the inner world of the growing child. The psychotherapist's basic methods are outlined. M.B., D.D.

---

Child psychotherapists are concerned primarily with the treatment of emotional disturbance in children and young people, although they also work in a consultative capacity in a variety of settings which touch the growing individual. The wide range of maladjustment which comes within the psychotherapist's province will be clearly illustrated in the chapters which follow. When carrying out individual treatment the analytic child psychotherapist attempts to help the patient to understand his or her own situation and, in particular, any unconscious factors which may be contributing to current difficulties. The therapist is, in other words, concerned with the patient's 'inner world' – the subjective picture of people and things we all carry around within us, sometimes without even being aware of it, and which may or may not adequately correspond to outward reality.

The last comment is significant. Whatever the part played by unconscious determinants of behaviour, the importance of the outer world is in no way to be discounted or neglected. It is clear that socio-economic factors operate on everyone. They can be a contributory, and sometimes a main cause of the kinds of problems discussed in the next chapter. There we shall find children from a large urban area suffering considerable deprivation in their home backgrounds, where the school classes are too large for teachers to give disturbed children the concerned attention they so badly need.

## Social Disadvantage

There is ample evidence in surveys such as *The National Survey of Health and Development*, a long-term follow-up of four thousand boys and girls born in 1946 (Douglas, 1964), of consistent associations between maladjustment, poor educational progress and social disadvantage. Such associations are also demonstrated in the reports of the National Child Development Study (Pringle, Butler and Davie, 1966; Davie, Butler and Goldstein, 1972). These studies found particular categories of children to be disadvantaged from birth onwards.

Clearly, socio-political change and augmented social and educational services form one of the possible approaches to the problem of maladjustment in children. The elimination of poverty, bad housing, general overcrowding and too large classes in schools would be an important step forward. We are sure of this in general terms. But we still need precise research data on such matters as the effects on development of familiar old-style overcrowding and of new-style high-rise tower blocks.

## Incidence of Maladjustment

Despite the emphasis of the previous paragraph, it is a disappointing and paradoxical fact that an evident increase in national prosperity since the Second World War has led to no reduction in the incidence of maladjustment. On the contrary, delinquency rates have increased, and this despite growth in the social services, the helping agencies and increased educational opportunity. Some of the apparent rise in delinquency may be spurious, a result in fact of society's increasing awareness of the problem and altered methods of ascertainment. Some part of the rise, however, is probably genuine. For its explanation many point to the still evident contrast between the prosperous and the poor (one child in sixteen in Britain is socially disadvantaged [Wedge and Prosser, 1973]) and to the accelerating growth of our dehumanized cities.

It is not at all easy to assess the incidence of maladjustment in the general population. In large-scale surveys, of which there have been in any case few, assessments of disturbance have of necessity had to be made mainly on the basis of teachers' rating scales or parents' reports. The validity and reliability of these is open to some question, although in fact such ratings are likely to underestimate rather than overestimate maladjustment. Professional estimates of the general prevalence of psychiatric disorder have varied considerably, probably as the result of differing methods of assessment (Rutter and Graham, 1970). The Underwood Committee (1955) and the Scottish Education Department Committee on the Ascertainment of Maladjusted Children (1964) were unable to offer an estimate of the prevalence of maladjustment in school children. Much earlier, however, Burt (1933) had judged the incidence of neurotic disturbance among school children to be five to six per cent. Rutter and Graham (1967), employing psychiatric interviews with parents and children after initial screening with parent and teacher questionnaires, reported an incidence rate of 6.8 per cent for clinically important psychiatric disorder in a population of ten- to eleven-year-old children in the Isle of Wight. The same authors later reported a considerably greater incidence in the same population, using the same criteria, when the subjects had reached fourteen to fifteen years. Reviewing studies in infant schools, Chazan and Jackson (1974) reported twelve to fourteen per cent of such children to be either somewhat or very disturbed. Still higher figures are suggested by long-term follow-up studies. Rutter (1973) reports the prevalence of psychiatric disorder in eleven-year-olds in an Inner London borough to be double that in the Isle of Wight – as might perhaps be expected. Richman et al. (1974) in a survey of three-year-olds, again in a London borough, noted seven to fourteen per cent as having significant problems.

## The Pre-School Years

An important fact which emerges from long-term studies is the overriding importance of the pre-school years. Douglas (1968) attributes major differences in educational performance to environmental influences acting during that period. Patterns of adjustment and educational attainment show relatively little change once a child has left infant school.

It is not surprising that it seems to be the pre-school years which are so important. We know that personality begins to form from earliest infancy and that by the time the child reaches school age, or even earlier, he or she is already a well-developed personality. The most important of all environmental influences on the young child are family relationships. In first place for the very young infant is his relationship with his mother and father. The father is especially important in terms of the support he gives, or does not give, the child's mother. The parents together mediate the events and circumstances of the outside world to the infant. Adverse conditions such as bad housing and overcrowding affect the infant primarily through their impact on the parents.

It was Freud who first drew public attention to the fact that personality has its roots in early childhood. Child analysts such as Anna Freud and Melanie Klein have since demonstrated that these roots go back to very earliest infancy. A great deal of recent research, initiated mainly by John Bowlby (1951), has consistently shown the importance of a continuous, loving relationship between mother and baby in the satisfactory development of personality. Although some workers such as Rutter (1972) and the Robertsons (1972) have queried the necessarily devastating effects of early separation from the mother which Bowlby originally postulated, a good deal of current research on child development continues to support the view that an early, continuous and meaningful interaction between mother and baby is crucial for the child's subsequent emotional and intellectual development (Newson, 1974; Foss, 1974). Ainsworth (1974) describes investigations which suggest that babies who have sensitive mothers, who respond adequately to their infants' signals in the first three months of life, cry less and are more 'socially competent' at one year than babies who have not established such primal communication.

## The Vicious Cycle

This fact of the crucial importance for subsequent development of early infantile experience throws some light on what has long been a stumbling block for those attempting to understand the problem of maladjustment in environmental terms alone: the fact that difficulties tend to recur from generation to generation in a family, despite change in external circumstances. Research is suggesting that cyclical processes are at work – for example, in baby battering. Parents who ill-treat their children are found often to be those who were ill-treated themselves. Bentovim (1975) also observed that as many as thirty per cent of battered babies in a hospital series have spent a period in hospital at or soon after birth, so that the vital link between mother and baby seems not to have been satisfactorily established. In this way the problems can be self-perpetuating. Lastly, a good deal of clinical work suggests that mothers who have not experienced in infancy adequate relationships with their own mothers, for whatever reason, themselves find it much more difficult to provide satisfactory mothering for their youngsters. This particular difficulty cuts across social classes, and is found as much amid prosperity as amid poverty.

## Factors Within the Child

The problems, however, do not necessarily reside in the mother or the family alone. There can be a variety of factors in the infant himself which make the mother and father less able to respond to and interact with the child. Here we learn much from detailed observation of infants, which incidentally forms an important part of the psychotherapist's training (see Chapter 14). Recent research (Foss, 1974) suggests that babies already differ considerably at birth. They are not merely 'lumps of clay' on which environmental influences get to work, as has been proposed by many schools of psychological and philosophical thought. Babies differ in general personality, in activity, irritability, 'drive' and many other qualities which are probably innate. In addition babies may be born with specific defects, minor or major, which inevitably affect not only the baby's development, but the mother's interaction with him. This modified interaction itself then affects development. Numerous other physical and psychological handicaps also affect the baby's development and the responses of the parents (Bentovim, 1972). As Rutter (1974) puts it, 'Differences in nature may lead to differences in nurture.' Babies can further differ markedly in their manner of coping with environmental difficulties. Joyce Robertson (1965) has described the different ways in which two infant boys reacted to their respective mothers' temporary withdrawal and depression during a family crisis – a differing response which of course itself may have arisen partly from the mothers' individual ways of interacting with their children.

We draw the conclusion, therefore, that personality development proceeds as the result of a very complex interaction of factors, some of which are innate, some environmental. The infant's very early experience is, however, always a crucial factor in development.

## The Need for Support of the Mother-Infant Couple

The above conclusion, on the importance of early experience, has two major implications for child-care work. The first is that in our attempts to alter the social circumstances which produce maladjustment, we must pay much more attention than in the past to the pre-school period. Here we are thinking not only of the provision of nursery schools and play groups, but of support for mother and infant in the first year of life, as well as for the family as a whole.

There are many pressures in contemporary society which run counter to the findings of research into child development (Menzies, 1975). The devaluing of the mother's (and the father's) role is one example. The pressures on mothers of young babies to go out to work, either from economic necessity or to contribute in a supposedly more important way to society, are another. To the list can be added the enforced separation of mothers and babies in many of our hospitals during the neo-natal period. Such separation is likely to make more difficult the establishment of the vital mother-and-baby link (Richards, 1974; Bentovim, 1975). Not least are the enormous stresses placed on many mothers by financial hardship, poor housing and isolation from the extended family and from other mothers, particularly in new housing developments and high-rise blocks. All these factors together produce a very high rate of depression in mothers of young children. In the already mentioned survey of three-year-old children in a London borough, Richman (1976) established for such mothers rates of ten per cent severely depressed and forty per cent mildly so.

It would seem that social help must be directed particularly towards supporting the mother-infant pair in a wide variety of ways, if we are to make any appreciable attempt to reduce the amount of emotional disturbance currently observed.

## The Inner World of the Child

The second implication of our understanding of the complex aetiology of emotional disturbance, and most notably the importance of the early years of life, is that once disturbance has arisen, further and beneficial change seems not so easy to effect. Some children seem to have constitutional strengths which enable them to overcome environmental deprivation or difficult early circumstances, or subsequently to make use of a variety of kinds of help. In other cases the experience of attempting to solve children's emotional problems through improved environmental provision alone has made it increasingly clear that there are sometimes factors operating within the child himself which make change difficult. Some children, then, seem unable to utilize the help that is offered, perhaps because their view of the world has become significantly distorted in some way. These children cannot respond sufficiently, or even at all, to improvements in the environment or to concerned care. The feelings and attitudes built up from past experience go on resisting change. So the child with a chip on his shoulder who has been badly let down many times, or at any rate feels he has, may continue indefinitely to resist the friendly overtures of well-intentioned people. Most teachers have had this experience of the child who does not respond whatever one does. For such children simple modifications in their 'outside world' are not enough. Some deeper change has to be effected in the structure or style of their 'inner world' – in their feelings and attitudes and ways of looking at life – before they can utilize what the various helping agencies have to offer them.

## The Contribution of the Child Psychotherapist

It is in trying to reach and effect changes in the child's inner world that the specific contribution of the child psychotherapist is made. This is not to say that once a child psychotherapist is involved the effects of external influences are either ignored or underestimated. The therapist usually works as one member of a team, alongside other workers and agencies. In this way an attempt is made on the total problem. Chapter 3 will be specifically concerned with this team work.

The psychotherapist however is *directly* concerned with external factors only from the way in which these affect the child's inner experience. For it is only internal reality that we are able to influence in psychotherapy (Boston, 1967). We cannot undo events that have actually happened in the past, nor is it as a rule helpful to patients to dwell on the past, even though we understand this to be important in the aetiology of the problem. Rather, we try to help the patient to come to terms with past experience, and with his own present personality characteristics, in the hope that changes in his feelings and attitudes will make him more able to benefit by what is offered by his environment.

How exactly does the child psychotherapist set about this difficult task? To answer that question is precisely the aim of this book. The chapters which follow give some detailed accounts of actual procedure in a variety of settings. It needs to be borne in mind, incidentally, that the contributors do not all share the same theoretical views. The question of differences of theoretical orientation among therapists, and the historical background to those differences, is indeed the subject matter of Chapter 12.

There are, however, many aspects of method and technique which all therapists have in common. It is therefore appropriate and useful to outline at this stage, very simply, something of the basic methods of approach in psychoanalytical psychotherapy. This will serve as a guideline to the reader through subsequent chapters. But in any case, this basic methodology is further elaborated and explained in subsequent chapters, wherever an individual presentation differs to any extent from the general position.

## The Methods of the Child Psychotherapist

As a starting point, we may usefully begin by distinguishing psychoanalytical psychotherapy from what is popularly referred to as 'play therapy', or simple play. Although play can have a therapeutic function in itself and although play is also employed in psychotherapy, it will become clear that play is only one of many of the child's ways of conveying his feelings and thoughts to the therapist. It is the understanding of the communication rather than the opportunity for free play which is therapeutically important.

### *Establishing the setting*

Once a child has been brought into individual psychotherapy – by any of the routes described in Chapter 3 – the first task of the therapist is to establish a suitable setting in which the child can communicate, as we hope, his innermost feelings and anxieties. The provision always of the same room, the same toys, the same hour and so on facilitates observations and offers a certain predictability and consistency to the patient. A further very important ingredient of the total setting is the therapist's receptive and unprejudiced frame of mind, open to whatever the child has to communicate. The therapist seeks to maintain a neutral, non-directive attitude, which will permit and encourage the patient to express himself freely. The child can allow hostile as well as friendly feelings to emerge within the firm limits of the treatment room and setting.

### *Observing, understanding and containing*

Within this setting, then, the patient's behaviour can be observed in close and continuous detail. An active attempt is of course also made to *understand* his communications, not only the verbal but still more the non-verbal. Quite tiny details of the child's behaviour and manner may in fact be very important to the therapist's attempt to establish contact with non-verbalized feelings, phantasies and unconscious conflicts. Children very often do not communicate in words, but reveal what is passing through their minds in their actions and play. Chapter 8 shows us what happens, for example, when a child does not initially talk at all, but does play. Chapters 9 and 11 describe children who have difficulties both in talking *and* playing, where the importance of other details of non-verbal communication becomes very clear.

Having a therapist's exclusive attention for the period of a whole session, someone who provides a space in her mind, or an 'internal mental space' as Shirley Hoxter puts it in Chapter 10, is often a unique experience for the child patient, who sometimes makes immediate gains just from such attention and understanding. The child experiences the treatment situation as one in which anxieties are held or *contained*, to use the technical term, in much the same way as they normally would be by the mother's responding appropriately to her infant's anxieties and uncertainties. The process of containment helps modify the fears and make them more bearable (Bion, 1962; Winnicott, 1965). As a rule, the patient soon develops a relationship with the therapist, an essential part of the treatment process about which more will be said later.

### *Interpretation*

Interpreting, as we call it, means putting into simple words, appropriate to the patient, the therapist's understanding of what is taking place in the developing relationship between the two of them. The aim of the interpretive statements is to help the patient himself gain insight into his behaviour and feelings as they arise in this relationship; and into any unconscious phantasies which, without his conscious knowing, may be colouring his perception of reality. The hope is that gradually he may be able to contain his anxieties for himself and have progressively less need for the therapist (or others) to do this for him. The kinds of evidence on which the therapist bases his interpretations have already been briefly indicated. These will be discussed in much more detail.

### *Transference*

Merely explaining to the patient what causes or motivations might be producing his difficulties and symptoms is never in itself sufficient. Intellectual explanations do not produce change. For change to occur an experience at the emotional level is necessary. That is precisely why the relationship between patient and therapist is so important. It provides the opportunity for the patient to *re-experience*, in relation to the therapist, some of the anxieties and conflicts that originated in the crucial early interactions (or perhaps lack of them) between the parent and himself. Freud termed this therapist-patient relationship 'transference', because the patient transfers to the therapist his habitual ways of relating, ways which have their origins in his past, reaching right back to infancy. Chapter 10 shows in detail how a characteristic of an infant's behaviour may appear and reappear in ever new editions as personality development proceeds. The function of transference is crucial to an understanding of this book. As Dora Lush says in Chapter 3, it is the psychotherapist's main tool.

## A Case Study

How can a psychotherapist know what is going on in the patient's mind? How can observations of the play and behaviour of a child give us clues to his innermost thoughts and feelings, of which even he himself may not be aware? This case study of a five-year-old boy, from the early days of psychotherapy, illustrates the kind of information which the child's play can give the psychotherapist and the way in which this information is then used.

Clive was referred to a psychiatrist at the age of five because his parents were worried about his interest in feminine things and his liking for dressing up as a girl. The psychiatrist and psychotherapist who saw him, together with his parents at the initial interview, thought further exploration of the child's problem in individual sessions with the psychotherapist might be helpful.

Following Melanie Klein's play technique (see Chapters 3 and 10), Clive was given a box of toys, containing small dolls representing parents and children, a tea set, some little cars and a selection of animals, bricks, plasticine, drawing equipment and so on, for his exclusive use.

Clive explored this material and looked under the skirts of all the female dolls. He was especially interested in the mother doll's ear-rings, the granny's lace and the little girl's bow. He then asked if he could paint. He painted a picture of a boy and a girl, with the girl looking much more colourful and attractive than the boy. She had long golden hair and a blue dress while the boy had black hair (like Clive) and black trousers. Clive said he liked the girl best.

The therapist was meanwhile making comments intended to encourage Clive to talk to her about what he was doing. Later in the session she shared with him her tentative thoughts about what he was showing her. (The therapist's comments are not presented here, as this is not intended to be a detailed record of a session with a child – examples of detailed sessions are presented in later chapters. The aim here is to give examples of Clive's play and communication-through-behaviour, to discuss what can be understood from them).

Clive then found a pair of scissors in the box, called them 'funny scissors' and snipped the air with them. He then playfully snipped them in the therapist's direction. Then he quickly made a snip in the granny doll's dress and then cut the man doll's trousers right off. Here, in response to a comment from the therapist about his anxiety in relation to the differences between boys and girls, Clive said, 'When I'm in bed my wiggy gets big and I have to keep calling Mummy for my blanket [a cuddly piece he took to bed with him] and for an apple, 'cos I can't get to sleep.'

Clive then put the baby doll into the arms of the mother as if it were being fed. The boy doll came along and knocked over the mother and baby, as then did the girl and father dolls. Clive expressed a wish to take the boy and girl dolls home with him. (This was not allowed.)

In the third session two weeks later, Clive was initially a bit reluctant to come into the room. He then played at 'weddings', saying the father and mother were getting married. But he put a little girl doll by the father, asking, 'Is she as big as Daddy?' Then he tucked the children dolls between his legs and said, 'They are not born yet.' He could not find the scissors this time, although they were in the box. He was worried about the wind blowing in the window, and frightening things were made to happen to the father and grandfather dolls, such as falling into a river or being attacked by crocodiles, so that they had to call out 'Help!' He also took the therapist unawares by quickly looking under her skirt.

In the fifth session Clive asked about the labels on the door, wanted to switch the light on and questioned the function of a socket in the room. He then made the doll family have a party, but granny got caught by a monster. This made 'granny's boy' scream and his screams made a storm which knocked the house down and also the parents off the couch where the game was being played. Then all the family got into the teapot to keep safe from the storm, except father who was going to set fire to the teapot. When asked why, Clive only said, 'He's going to burn the picnic.' At the picnic everyone had a cake, but the baby had special food.

In this material we see how the child will express his phantasies through play. Yet how do we understand them, and what light do they throw on his emotional problems? With Clive we have evidence of his preoccupation with sexual differences (looking under skirts, for example), of his interest in and envy of feminine things. And further, of his wish to be able to have the 'not born yet' children inside himself (that is, between his legs). He also tells us of his anxieties about masturbation and the act of falling asleep. In his wedding game, which incidentally he played repeatedly, we see his preoccupations with parental relationships, as well as the child's wish to take the parental role (for example, the little girl doll was going to marry Daddy). We see his jealousy of the mother-baby couple (the mother feeding the baby is knocked over). We hear of omnipotent screams which can knock the house down, and there is also a fear of a very punitive father, who will burn up the picnic.

These phantasies are already illuminating, but in order to use the child's communications in a way which will be *therapeutically* helpful, we must direct our attention to those which seem to be most emotionally immediate for the child. We must, in other words, get in touch with what the child is actually feeling in the session. Evidence of real here-and-now anxiety is seen in Clive's reluctance to come into the room at the third session, his worry over the wind, his snipping with the scissors plus his later 'losing' them, and his suspicions about the socket, the labels on the door and anxiety about who might come in. All these clues suggest to us that, in spite of Clive's appearing to play so freely, he is actually pretty anxious about coming to the therapist altogether, and about the purpose of the treatment. The most important interpretations to make at this stage would be in connection with these here-and-now anxieties and about what the therapist might be going to do to him. For any child's suspicion of a strange person is inevitable and will be there even if covered up by apparent friendliness and trust. Is the snipping with the scissors, for example, an indication that Clive is afraid, knowing as he does that his parents want him made into a proper boy, that the therapist is going to perform some (cutting) operation? But it's better to be the one who does the snipping than be snipped! Clive thus simultaneously communicates the anxiety and defends himself against it. One could take this interpretation as a tentative hypothesis, for confirmation or refutation of which one would look to the patient's responses.

It might seem puzzling that a little boy could be frightened of an operation to make him into a boy – an unusual version, almost a reversal, of the more expected castration fear. It was indeed puzzling. The psychotherapist needs to be able to tolerate this feeling of puzzlement, to bear a feeling of uncertainty for a time, until the material can gradually be elucidated. It was some sessions later that Clive volunteered, 'If I lose my bosoms [patting his bottom], I'll be a boy'! This remark not only confirmed the therapist's suggestion that he might be frightened of what she was going to do to him, but also revealed the mainspring of his femininity. He did not merely wish to be a girl, but felt, in some aspect of himself, that he actually *was* the mother with the bosoms. This seemed to be his way of dealing, as an infant, with the loss of a close feeding relation with his mother at the time of weaning. Instead of being the baby who had to learn to be independent, to give up sucking, he became, in unconscious phantasy, the mother who had the bosoms (confused in his mind with his bottom) – a never-ending source of supply.

Of course there were other factors in Clive's psychopathology which threw additional light on his femininity and on the reasons why he had come to use this particular way of dealing with anxieties experienced by all developing infants. Parental attitudes and the fact that he was an only child were very relevant. It is not our purpose here, however, to give a complete account of the long period of regular psychotherapy needed to help Clive to sort out some of his confused feelings and to come to terms with them.

To come back to the early sessions: the scissor-snipping play also provides an example of transference, as it bears on what is actually taking place in the relationship with the therapist. One might look at the picnic situation in this way, which can also represent an aspect of his relationship (his 'picnics') with the therapist. The picnic, then, would represent the nice time he was having with the therapist, playing these games and so on – but coupled with the fear that some other jealous figure might intrude or attack (the father who sets fire to the teapot). When *he*, Clive, is the baby with the mother, so to speak, 'someone else' may interfere.

## Projection

In trying to understand a patient's session material, we also have to keep in mind the psychological mechanism of projection. Projection means attributing one's own feelings or other aspects of oneself to others, and is a further very important concept to the child psychotherapist. We shall be examining examples of this process in the behaviour of children attending small groups in primary schools. The child patient employs projection in his play, making the toys express aspects of himself. For example, it was *granny*, not Clive, who was caught by the monster; *granny's boy*, not Clive, whose screams brought the house down; the *girl* wanted to marry father; the *others* attacked mother and baby; *father* set the teapot on fire. As these are all Clive's own ideas, they can be considered principally as projected aspects of Clive himself. Yet he is not ready at this early stage to have these projections interpreted for him. They have to be accepted and 'held' by the therapist until they become appropriately meaningful in the developing transference relationship. This 'holding' often allows further material to unfold.

We must also always bear in mind that children do not necessarily use play material in the ways that might seem obvious to *us*. The family dolls can be put to quite different uses by different children and by the same child at different times. Roles can be readily reversed; or the figures may represent only parts of people; or the same toy may represent a succession of different people. These fluctuations and fleeting changes have to be observed in their kaleidoscopic detail and their sequence noted if we are properly to understand the play. The manner of the play itself, the tidiness or messiness, the destructiveness or carefulness, the use of the very room – all these aspects, too, have to be noted if we are to grasp what the play, or indeed the lack of play, signifies for the individual child. As we shall see, some patients cannot play or use material symbolically at all.

## Summary

From this discussion it can perhaps be seen that there is no mystique about interpretations. The interpretations arise from detailed observation and assessment of the evidence as it actually unfolds before us. Naturally, interpretation also requires a skill and an ability to get in touch with the patient's feelings, an intuitive sense for the appropriate comment and the appropriate moment – which makes child psychotherapy an art as well as a science.

# Chapter Two

# *Working with Small Groups of Children in Primary Schools*

## by Susan Reid, Eva Fry and Maria Rhode

This chapter takes a closer look at emotional disturbance as faced by teachers. Some children experience their emotional and developmental difficulties principally in the school situation. Here we show one of the ways in which they may be helped in the school setting itself.

The Tavistock students who worked with the small groups described were already professionally qualified either as psychologists or teachers. They undertook this group work during the pre-clinical part of their further training in child psychotherapy. The techniques used are not the same as those of the individual psychotherapy session, which are described elsewhere. The purpose of this chapter is not to particularize the differences and resemblances in the two situations, but to give further examples of the kinds of behaviour which the psychotherapist tries to illuminate. M.B., D.D.

---

**The Background to the Work**

Tavistock students began taking small groups of children in primary schools in 1966, when a trainee employed as a remedial teacher realized that the children were using her classes to work on their personal emotional problems. This realization led to the establishment of groups specifically for that purpose. Knowledge of these groups spread by word of mouth among heads of schools. Many felt that there was a real need which the groups might help to meet. When the Tavistock Clinic became involved in this work, it was found that almost all teaching staff agreed that they had more disturbed children in their classes than they could hope to deal with while conscientiously pursuing their job as teachers. Some staff were more hopeful or more despondent than we were ourselves about the amount of improvement that might be expected as the result of forming these small groups.

The schools in which we worked were mainly within one Inner London borough. This was a 'difficult' borough, in which there were far more disturbed and deprived children than its child guidance clinics could accommodate. In any case, in our work we could see many children who would either not have been suitable for psychotherapy, or who for a variety of reasons could not have kept regular appointments as out-patients at a psychiatric clinic.

In the event, the groups proved to be of benefit both to the psychotherapy students and to the teachers in the schools. For the students there was a valuable opportunity of experiencing a variety of disturbed children, as well as the chance to discover the workings of a primary school. The kinds of difficulties teachers encounter and first-hand experience of the lives of the children and their social conditions are valuable background data for any therapist. On the teachers' side our contribution began by relieving them of the most disturbing children for some part of the day. Our usefulness developed as we became seen as people who had time and interest to listen to the teachers' problems, and who could suggest new ways of looking at persistent difficulties.

## The Groups

The following is a general summary of the work we carried out in the different schools. There were, of course, variations of detail from school to school: for example, some of us saw each of our groups twice a week, while others saw them three times a week. Boxall and workers at the Institute of Group Analysis have discussed approaches similar to ours in principle, though differing in their emphasis and various points of technique (see References).

Children were selected to attend our groups because their behaviour in the classroom was creating various difficulties.

In all cases it was the teacher who made the referral. We found the staff were well aware that a withdrawn child could be at least as disturbed as a child who threw chairs about. The teachers' personal bias did probably have a certain influence on their selection of children - one, for example, referred three children, all of whom were withdrawn.

In one school, nineteen children (fifteen boys and four girls) attended the groups. Some of these dropped out for a variety of reasons during the course of the year and others joined. The largest group in that school comprised six children; the smallest group comprised three children, though in actual practice a 'group' might consist of one child on his own, if the others were absent. We now feel with hindsight that there should be no more than four children in a group and perhaps only three. Each group attended two or three times a week for the duration of a double school-period. We habitually collected the children from their classrooms, though some soon began to come to the group room on their own. We tried to keep the initial composition of the groups as stable as possible; however, it proved necessary on occasion to make changes in order to achieve a better balance, or to break up a particularly disruptive alliance. In every case the reasons for such a change were made quite explicit to the children concerned. One of our firm rules was that each child came only with his own group at the proper time, and that if anyone were absent he could not be replaced by someone else. The children were therefore in no way regarded as interchangeable.

To serve as example, the setting of one group is described now in detail. (The settings varied from school to school: some of the issues dealt with below might or might not arise, or be replaced by others.)

The group room in this case was at the top of the school, with windows facing the street and others giving on to the roof. It became necessary for these to be nailed shut, since the worker found herself spending too much time looking after the physical safety of children who were testing what kind of limits she might set them and who could not be trusted to protect themselves. Other significant details were the locks on the door of the room and on the cupboards where the toys, paints and other equipment were kept. It was felt to be extremely important to provide a setting in which stealing was physically difficult and in which the door represented a firm boundary for the children, as well as a bar to incursions from without – such incursions had occasionally proved chaotic. These general arrangements helped to give the children the feeling of being securely contained within the room. They relieved the worker from having to spend all her time and energy attempting to prevent verbally what could be better prevented physically.

The room further contained two main work tables, two desks, two stock cupboards, a cleaner's cupboard and a sink. A very important additional feature was a number of pipes along the ceiling. These soon became a testing ground. Children would swing on the pipes for a variety of reasons, such as attracting the worker's attention, defying her, forcing her to lift them down, proving how unreasonable she was, expressing anger and so on. The worker's policy became to suggest, for example, that she could see that they were annoyed with her, but that it might be more satisfactory to express this in a way that was not dangerous and at the same time would make it possible to discuss matters and possibly put them right.

Working equipment comprised drawing, painting and modelling materials, jigsaw puzzles, toy cars and lorries, toy soldiers, a doll family, some plastic animals, clothes for dressing up, basket-weaving kits, a compendium of games, and a few other items. Some children would bring along sewing they had begun in their classrooms, while others asked for knitting materials. A punch-bag was provided, with the suggestion it was better to hit that than another child. Each of the children had a folder of his or her own, on which he wrote his name and in which anything he worked at in the group, or anything finished he did not yet want to take home, could be kept. Everything a child completed was his to take away, but one of the rules was that nothing unfinished was to leave the room. The exception was work brought along from the classroom, if the teacher had agreed to it.

Rules about what was permitted in the group were kept as few and as related to commonsense as possible. Children were not to injure themselves, one another, or the worker; not to damage the room or one another's things; not to interfere with another child's work; not to dash in and out of the room. This last point was negotiable, since frequently the children felt they must show their teachers at once if they had succeeded in making something, and school policy on this matter was very lenient. In general principle however, the worker felt that a child should be either in his class, or with her, and not oscillating between the two - although such a rule might sometimes have to be further modified, as in the case of one genuinely claustrophobic boy. It was always made clear to any child who chose to return to his class to stay that he was welcome to rejoin the group at his next scheduled time.

Sanctions when the rules were broken - as of course they constantly were - varied according to the specific situation involved. Sometimes the simple intervention of the worker might be enough to set a discussion going. At other times she had to be more firm - to take away a toy that was being misused, for instance, after announcing her intention of doing so if the misuse did not stop. In the very favourable circumstances of this particular school, it was made clear that the headmaster would support the worker in enforcing necessary rules. However, he could also be invoked as a benevolent father figure who would wish to be shown the children's work. As the year progressed, the worker needed to invoke outside authority less and less frequently. Very occasionally she might have to ask the children to leave before the end of the scheduled time, but she would try to convey that this step was not intended as a punishment. For instance, in a situation in which they were deliberately creating mess faster than she could clear it up, they could choose to help (or at least refrain from hindering) or leave while she used the remaining time to set the room in order. As ever, it was then emphasized that they would be welcome to return at their next session.

Depending on whether the worker spent preliminary time assisting with classroom teaching, she might or might not have foreknowledge of the individual children which would help her in assigning them to groups. When such knowledge was lacking, she fell back on more general principles in seeking helpful combinations. Thus, she would try to have in any one group both children who were violent and children who were withdrawn. She would also consider the composition of the groups with regard to age, so that the members might be all of one age or else more like a family group. They would not, for instance, be all of the same age with the exception of a single, isolated child. Time-table considerations were important here, since the children could not be taken out of their classes during games or swimming. As already mentioned, it occasionally also proved necessary to rearrange a particular group.

## The Children

The children, many of them immigrants, came from deprived backgrounds in which broken marriages, unemployment, violence at home, and adult and teenage delinquency were familiar occurrences. The parents frequently had a poor relationship with the school. Even when full child guidance treatment was available, it was usually unacceptable to them: they might feel it to be a label of madness, as did Anna's parents in the case discussed below (page 48), or they might be genuinely unable – because of pressures of work, say, or illiteracy – to keep regular appointments. These difficulties did not arise in respect of work groups that formed part of the normal school day.

The children referred to the groups came with a great variety of problems. Those whose withdrawal showed their disturbance and those whose violence disrupted work in the classroom represented only two among many patterns. Others might have learning difficulties not accounted for by poor intelligence or lack of application. Many were referred for stealing. Bed-wetting was another widespread complaint and quite a number of the children suffered more or less severely from illnesses having a strong psychosomatic component, such as asthma and eczema. Some of the children displayed bizarre behaviour patterns in the classroom that could not obviously be related to any events in the school day and so were particularly puzzling and worrying for teachers, whose role did not permit them to explore such behaviour further. Within the setting of the groups, however, where limits were both less narrow and more predictable than in the classroom, such puzzling patterns could eventually be seen to be transference manifestations. One little girl, for instance, behaved in a variety of incongruous ways, so much so that the worker felt her own sanity threatened by them. Once it became clear, however, that the worker *was* managing to keep her own balance, without having to get rid of the little girl, it emerged that the child's mother was in fact mad. Her daughter had had to accompany her during her trips to the hospital where she had electric shock treatment.

Now let us follow three more detailed studies of children referred to groups and the kinds of behaviour changes that were observed in them.

**John**

John was nine-and-a-half years old and in his third year at Junior School. He was extremely small, and his babyish face made it difficult for one to remember his real age. He was not a severe problem in the classroom, though he distracted the other children by giggling and whispering. He also refused to do any work at all and was almost completely unable to read. He had no friends among his classmates, but had formed a destructive alliance with the next most troublesome boy, Daniel, from whom he was inseparable. He spent much time getting piggy-backs from Daniel, with whom he usually stood apart giggling, instead of joining in the class games. He appeared to be using Daniel to misbehave on his behalf, since he took every opportunity of getting Daniel into trouble. This he achieved by reporting him (usually inaccurately) for having misbehaved in ways John often chose himself.

Apart from his inability to learn in class, John was doing a great deal of exceptionally furtive stealing, sometimes of considerable sums. He was often found flooding the boy's lavatory, either by turning on the taps or by urinating on the floor. Coats were found stuffed down the lavatories after he had been there, though it was never actually established that he was responsible. He was a confirmed bed-wetter, but frequently expressed contempt for children who wet the bed, saying that this happened only to babies.

John was placed in a group with two girls: Sarah, eight years old, and Anne, nine years. During the first five or six weeks his behaviour was exemplary. He often said that he did not like girls like Sarah who swore and messed up the room; also that Sarah was very greedy in the way she tried to take all the toys for herself. Instead he formed an alliance with Anne, with whom he retired to giggle behind a cupboard, clearly with the aim of making Sarah feel the one left out of a romance.

Meanwhile he was very carefully observing the worker's reactions to Sarah's behaviour. He tested the worker himself repeatedly, by reporting misdeeds that his friend Daniel was supposed to have committed. During this initial period his chief problem in the group was his inability to persist with anything long enough to finish it. He seemed to feel very keenly the disappointment of having nothing to show for his time – as was true in the classroom also – whenever the girls took something they had made to show to their teachers.

John did a few times attempt to make things, but always gave up. He would say that his attempts were no good as soon as the worker had to stop helping him to attend to the others. His difficulty in persevering therefore seemed related to his inability to let the surrogate mother go. If the slightest thing were wrong with his work, he would throw it away. He agreed with the worker's suggestion that perhaps he expected her to throw him out in this way if everything he did were not perfect. His demand for perfection was at this time still projected on to others.

Gradually he began to talk about his feelings of being persecuted. His class teacher always picked on him. The headmaster did not trust him and only liked girls anyway. (John had a younger sister.) His father had no time for him because all his free time was spend with girlfriends. John would savagely thrust nails up the taps on the sink while saying this about his father. He gave expression also to phantasies of flooding the room and setting his parents' house on fire.

Besides becoming more open in his enjoyment of extremely babyish behaviour, which he had come to realize would be tolerated, John began to elaborate on a preoccupation with spiders. These were vengeful spiders, sometimes fathers and sometimes mothers, but always pursuing him because he had robbed them. He spent much time directing the worker to make such spiders out of paper and to arrange them on webs of knitting wool, in which she had to pretend to be caught. She would then be imprisoned and sometimes devoured. So she was made to suffer the fate he feared for himself.

At this time John did not yet acknowledge his feelings as

his own. For instance, he would inform the worker suddenly, 'Miss, my Mum doesn't like you.'

'Why not?'

'Because you said I was dirty.'

'Really? I don't remember saying that. Do you think you're dirty?'

After many such exchanges, John began to grin whenever he reported what people supposedly thought, as though expecting the ruse to be seen through. However, he never made the implied suggestion explicit.

Soon enough John's reputed stealing began to come more into the open within the group. At first he tried to take things away before he had finished them, calling the worker a pickpocket when she intervened. He attributed to her his own wish to steal as he had previously attributed it to his friends. With the repeated experience that these attempts to steal were usually unsuccessful, but equally that they did not bring on retribution, a second stage followed. The stealing was now no longer furtive. John made sure it was impossible to overlook. His stealing and the worker's intervention became a recognizable game. A long period of preoccupation with the question of what was rightfully his, during which he developed his ability to share the worker's attention, led up to his learning to complete things and to make presents. Some actual illustration may help to make these developments clearer.

On one occasion John made a joking attempt to 'steal' a basket he had not yet completed. The worker took it away from him, but a moment later he pointed out to her that it was no longer on the table. However, he lifted up the front of his jersey to show that he did not have it on him. It seemed plain that he must have the basket somewhere, but he left at the end of the session without her having been able to discover it. A few minutes later he returned, saying the basket had been hidden under the back of his jersey, and he would leave it until the next time.

Then, however, he left behind things he could legitimately have taken – an item he had actually completed, and an empty cigarette tin the worker had given him to replace one he had himself brought to the group, but which another child had taken from him and spoilt. This pattern of not being able to keep what was rightfully his because of his involvement in stealing, or because of the feeling of having stolen, was an important determinant in his learning difficulties. His ability and willingness to take in knowledge in the classroom improved greatly at the time he began to feel able to return to the worker things he had stolen, and even to give her presents of things he had made.

The need to steal itself had to do with John's feelings of 'not getting enough' without it. This meant, in the group situation, not getting the worker's exclusive attention. The underlying motivation and need were evident in John's inability to persist in a task if the worker were elsewhere. When he had become more confident of being able to get enough attention without stealing, and of the good relationship with her still being there even when she frustrated him, he was able to make and give her presents.

At this time, John suddenly told the worker one day that she was an apple tree full of apples. He was going to eat all the apples himself and not leave any for the other children. Or, on second thoughts, he might in fact let them have some. The apples sometimes had worms in them, but the last one he had eaten had been all right. The worker simply accepted this without attempting to comment. In the group setting one is often unable to discover, as one may in psychotherapy, what event in the outside life of the child has triggered a given remark. John's statement was, however, an extremely telling account of the way in which his experience of maintaining a good relationship, in spite of its limitations, made him able to be more generous towards the worker and, most important, towards other children.

In another instance of the same type of communication, John informed the worker virtuously that he had been given 15p but had lost 5p. She asked him why he had lost it – had he not felt he deserved it? He agreed he had not felt good about the money, but would not say why. A few days later he told her suddenly that the 5p had turned up again.

Guilt of this kind – the feeling of not deserving something – became particularly evident just before Christmas, when John's intelligence was assessed as low enough to justify a special school placement, although in fact he finally only went to remedial classes. He interpreted the suggestion of a special school placement as a rejection by the Junior School in retaliation for the damage he had done or felt he had done. He was very upset by the situation. Just before the Christmas holidays he told the worker that he felt ill, that he did not want his dinner, and that he was doubtful whether she would return in January, because he felt he had worn her out. She told him that she would like him to eat his dinner and that she did intend to be back in January. The floor was very wet at this point, as the worker was mopping up after another group. John commented, 'It's like a swimming bath,' (or a flooded toilet, perhaps) and went off saying to himself that everyone would be back in January 'right here in all this muck'.

When the groups did begin after the holidays, and it also became less likely that he would be sent to another school, John began to experience the worker as someone who would not be devastated by his bad behaviour. He used the group meetings very efficiently as a containing setting for his problems and brought his negative self to the sessions – while his teacher therefore reported him as having become co-operative and eager to learn in the classroom. In fact he carried his capacity for such useful splitting to the extent of treating the worker in a perfectly reasonable ten-year-old manner if they chanced to meet anywhere else in the school, but producing his difficult side in full the moment he came through the door of the group room.

This difficult side consisted largely of playing the fool very ostentatiously, all the while complaining that his teacher paid no attention to him. At length he announced that indeed he was a fool. When the worker asked him who called him this, he replied, 'I call my dad that at home, and then he chases me. I like being chased.' This led to a discussion of whether he could not get the attention he wanted in a more positive way, by making things, for instance, instead of by disturbing others.

It was at this point that the worker made it explicit that her failures to attend to him right away did not come from any ill will, but from her own limitations and from the fact that there were other children to be seen to also. She suggested that his class teacher might face similar problems. John appeared to accept this interpretation with regard to both the adults mentioned, though he still insisted (while half-smiling, however) that they would both rather tell him off for misbehaving than praise him for doing well. At the same time he became less preoccupied with stuffing nails up the taps, his plans for dealing with the worker after catching her in the spider's web became more benign, and he was more able to complete items of work and to save them for himself as well as give them as presents.

John began his remedial classes without the worker having been warned, so that he missed a group; in the next session he produced greater chaos in ten minutes than in the whole year. It seemed he was deliberately setting out to create as much mess as he could to punish the worker for what he took as an attempt on her part and that of his teacher to get rid of him. After discussing this possibility with him, the worker re-arranged the time of his group, suggesting explicitly that he could be on good terms with his class teacher, his remedial teacher and her, all at the same time. This helped somewhat to deal with his anger at being sent out of the school, and also with the tendency to relapse if progress meant separation from people he was attached to. The worker hoped also that it might mitigate to a very slight extent his tendency to play adults off against one another.

When he was re-tested at the end of the year, John's intelligence was found to be thirty per cent higher than previous assessments – which, however, his worker still felt to be an underestimate. His behaviour in class was then said to be satisfactory. When his worker left the school at this time John was able to express both his anger and his sorrow, but did not react by reverting to his former patterns – as he might have done in order to attract attention. Instead, though he could clearly have benefited greatly from more help, he continued to make progress in his class, probably at least partly with the idea of giving pleasure to the adults he was fond of.

## Leonard and Tony – a Group of Two

This group consisted of just two boys with remarkable interlocking personalities. Tony presented himself as a tough guy and bully. Leonard ended up forever the intimidated weakling and follower. In the threesome formed with the worker, the processes of first projecting and then gradually taking back into the self the more unwanted aspects of personality were very strikingly illustrated.

Leonard wanted no part of being the leader or aggressor. He habitually looked to others to take the blame for his often messy and occasionally quite destructive activities in the groups. In despair, or placatingly, he would complain, 'Miss, they make me do these things.' Tony, on the other hand, found any show of weakness or dependence on adult parental care very threatening, indeed hardly bearable. He projected the more helpless and vulnerable parts of himself into Leonard and the worker. In the material presented below, she had to carry this part of him as well as to bear the scorn and contempt he then heaped on her, backed up by Leonard as his 'accomplice'.

Leonard was nine years old and Tony was ten when the worker formed the new group with them. She had known both for a year and had worked with them in other, larger groups. Tony had been passed on from a yet earlier group with the comment that he was 'a frightened and insecure boy who tended constantly to assert his independence and toughness through physical fighting and competition, and by often taking the role of ring-leader'. He had shown no substantial change of behaviour during his first two years in small groups at his school. The present worker first had him in a group of older boys, where he still found it difficult to express any feelings of tenderness or the need to be cared for.

Leonard was proposed for a small group by the headmistress of the Infant School, with the observation that he was 'a boy who had never been allowed to grow up as a boy, and who still behaved like a baby'. When he came up to the Juniors, he became destructive of other children's work and generally disruptive in class. He was an isolate without friends who tended to cling to his woman teacher. In his first group with the worker he spent a lot of time playing very messily with sand, water and paints and his consequent efforts to clean up the mess were compulsive and pitifully ineffective. He was generally ingratiating with the worker and isolated from the two other first-year boys in his group. These two formed a permanent alliance and usually played with Leonard only if one or the other was away from school.

Leonard, like Tony, showed little change in his first year with the present worker. Their relationship in the new group to each other and to the worker seems to have gone through two phases, the first roughly up to Christmas and the second from the New Year onwards. The first of these periods provoked a great deal of worry and doubt in the worker about the usefulness to the boys of the change and of the group as such.

Until about a month before the Christmas break Leonard showed an alarming willingness to be bullied by Tony into deriding the worker and her ability to help them. In his previous group Leonard had developed some trust in her and had regularly appealed to her for protection from the other children's roughness, besides co-operating with her in preserving some semblance of order in his group. Now he seemed to merge with Tony completely and to lack any self or a will of his own. Even during the first group year he had accused the other children of causing chaos, being silly or mad. Now it was as if in Tony he had found the perfect embodiment of this projected behaviour. Tony did indeed cause havoc and also made Leonard 'do things', apparently through intimidation – Leonard acted out Tony's 'madness'. Afterwards he designated Tony as the author and perpetrator of the chaos the two together created. He divorced himself completely from all responsibility. Tony's participation in the group did away with any necessity for Leonard to face the part of himself which willingly contributed and thoroughly enjoyed rendering helpless an adult parental figure (the worker) by means of the complete chaos the two of them often created. Leonard protested his innocence and tried to maintain in the worker's eyes his old image of an obliging, basically good boy, occasionally bullied into excesses of mischief by bad boys such as Tony.

Some of the situations Leonard and Tony set up caused the worker to feel particularly uncomfortable and helpless. For example, during a session in November, midway through the first term, Leonard and Tony started a barrage of verbal abuse towards the worker. Tony whispered sexual terms and words for contraceptives into Leonard's ear which Leonard was then to shout at the worker. Leonard looked at times confused, as though he did not understand or know half the words. Nevertheless, he shouted them over and over in unison with Tony, with a satanic smile on his face. The two of them together completely drowned the worker's voice and made her feel quite ineffectual. She felt useless and helpless and had no idea how to break up their verbal assault. None of the exchanges could be taken as a sign of genuine worry or interest in the matter of adult sexuality or the reproductive functions. The whole situation continued to deteriorate as the two boys got more and more out of control and more and more excited by their own shouting. Tony expressed contempt at the idea that the worker and her husband could have any fruitful exchange or a constructive relationship in their life outside the school and away from the children. Tony had Leonard. Together they made a pair, whilst the worker was left out, alone and helpless – a mere contemptible woman.

The session finally ended with Leonard getting hurt and crying, becoming once again the helpless little boy who looked to the worker for protection. This conclusion was the outcome of a rather wild game purporting to be a 'circus performance' and devised by Tony. In it the two boys acted out quite literally the complementary roles of 'master' and 'underdog', as Tony insisted and Leonard complied in the following 'acrobatic' act. Leonard bent over and crouched with his hands on the floor and Tony then repeatedly jumped over his head, occasionally hitting or kicking Leonard's head 'accidentally' with his 'bovver boots'. The atmosphere of tension thus generated was really very difficult to bear, and the worker felt obliged to keep a constant close watch on the pair to prevent a serious mishap. She began to wonder where Leonard would draw the line and ask for her support in resisting being bullied into such deliberately painful, spoiling and unconstructive ways of passing the time. Despite his humiliation, however, Leonard seemed to participate willingly, caught up in the defiant spirit and excitement of Tony's game. It was difficult for the worker to withstand the mounting tension and not to interfere actively to stop the game.

In retrospect, the worker realized that from early on there had been indications of Leonard's hidden strength, but he took his time about showing this more openly. At this time, near Christmas, Tony had grown quite fond of his class teacher, who was now teaching him for the second year. In class he started to produce some regular and adequate work for her. He also got involved in the class Christmas preparations and frequently stayed away from the group for rehearsals of a show in which he was appearing.

Leonard used this opportunity to develop a one-to-one relationship with the worker. In particular he involved her in play-acting stories which he made up. These revolved around the mother-baby relationship and his desire to make quantities of plasticine food with which to feed her. He also evolved a war game in the sand tray using a large number of plastic soldiers and he showed great ingenuity in his strategy and tactics of defence. He accepted a set of rules and did not try to cheat but made other efforts to win. His self-confidence grew. More and more he began to stand up for himself and to defend his own constructive games from Tony's interference. Finally, he even showed Tony he could beat him at his own game: in one of Tony's tests of physical strength and endurance, balancing a light wire cage on his head, Leonard could now hold out longer than Tony. Leonard's aim also proved the better when they competed in throwing bits of plasticine at a bull's eye the worker had drawn on the wall, in an attempt to channel a more indiscriminate and dangerous throwing of objects around the room. Both these games had been devised by Tony, a year Leonard's senior and looking the bigger and sturdier of the two. Tony now seemed a rather pathetic figure trying to maintain his tough, he-man image under the circumstances.

Not to be outdone, however, Tony then started to bring a school chess set to the group, in order to show off his superior ability in a mental skill. This seemed at least a step forward from his previously exclusive preoccupation with tests of physical strength. On occasion now he could express his worries when in the group. He made up stories and games of cops and robbers in which Leonard and the worker also had their roles. In these, too, he expressed a great deal of worry lest the characters be allowed to commit crimes of theft and physical violence and get away undetected. Indirectly, he seemed to be asking if the worker could stand up to his more violent feelings and receive the phantasied murderous attacks he and Leonard visited on her, without buckling under or taking revenge or rejecting the two boys. Tony's growing ability to communicate these worries culminated in his seeking out the worker and consulting her about a very real problem. At the beginning of the summer term he had been so disruptive in class that his teacher threatened to exclude him from an approaching outing to the zoo. Tony was genuinely upset as much by his teacher's disapproval as by the impending punishment. He needed to mull all this over away from his class. Then, on his own initiative, but asking the support of the worker, he sought out his teacher to discuss his feelings about the situation and to apologize, with the promise of some extra hard work in class. He was so eager to put his plan into action that he left the group early that day.

Though Tony still had to be watched, because he was a poor loser and tended to lash out when he lost, he could now begin to allow himself to be miserable and subdued. Often he spent a quiet time in the group's comfortably furnished 'cupboard-cum-camp'. He frequently used a physical complaint like a sore throat or cold to elicit sympathy and a bit of extra fussing, while he would lie there in the cupboard among some cushions and dressing-up clothes. He clearly enjoyed the extra care and attention he thus received.

What emerged was a two-fold use of the worker's time. Both Leonard and Tony now brought out their more private worries whenever they had a bit of time alone with her; while in between these private consultations, both showed a growing tolerance of each other's differing interests and temperament. When together, they were each willing to co-operate in games the other had thought up, such as Leonard's war game and Tony's chess. They worked out and accepted a set of rules for the shared games, which the worker then had to referee. When an argument arose and she had not for some reason witnessed the incident in question, she was told off in no uncertain terms for failing in her policing functions.

By the end of the school year Tony was able to stop his remedial classes outside school, where hitherto he had spent two half-days a week. Despite the remaining problems with his quick temper, he had become acceptable as one of the class. Leonard, for his part, coped with a shattering personal crisis when his father deserted the family just before the end of the school year and just before the worker left the school herself. He was able to confide his feelings about these events to her and to ask for support from a number of persons at the school who mattered to him, including his class teacher and the headmaster.

Although Leonard was a boy whom the group experience had made more receptive to individual psychotherapy, it is doubtful whether his mother could have supported this. He made good use of his two years of small group experience and was able as a result to develop his character and emerge from social isolation.

For Tony it seemed vital to witness both the worker's attitude to the weakness and helplessness shown by Leonard – when she helped him rather than deriding his dependence on her – as well as her own ability to bear and survive such similar states of helplessness, when reduced to it by the boys' combined attacks. In a smaller group and with a younger boy Tony no doubt felt less threatened and so was eventually able to show his more vulnerable side, the tender aspects of his nature. The time and setting were then ripe for him to take these aspects back into his conscious personality. The process was mediated by his experiencing these aspects of his personality second-hand as projections, carried temporarily for him by Leonard and the worker.

**Anna**

Anna was five years old and had been attending the nursery for a year. She had Italian parents but could speak neither Italian nor English. The headmistress described her as 'a very peculiar little girl'.

Anna's first year in the nursery had apparently been a tempestuous one. When she was distressed she would take off her shoes and socks, bang her head against the wall and tear out her hair by the handful. In this distressed state she would sweep all the toys from the tables, throwing some around the room. At other times, however, she was completely withdrawn. She had an excessive fear of the toilets and refused to use them. Yet she would sometimes crawl behind the lavatory bowl and lie there curled up, refusing to come out.

The child had been referred to a guidance clinic but her attendance there was rare, because her parents refused to take her – as the worker later discovered, they felt the clinic was 'for mad children'.

Since Anna was terrified of leaving the familiar confines of the nursery, the worker was faced with the practical problem of how actually to get Anna to the group room. She decided to spend some time in the nursery to give Anna a chance to get used to her. Up until the first half-term the worker made regular visits to the nursery, where she also had the opportunity to discuss Anna with the new nursery teacher. The latter was to prove an extremely kind and perceptive person, with whom the worker could co-operate closely.

The worker's first impression of Anna was of an attractive little girl, her red hair severely pulled back from her freckled face and secured at either side in big corkscrew curls. She was almost clinically clean and smelled strongly of soap. Nevertheless, an overwhelming impression of Anna's social isolation is conveyed by the notes from these early visits.

The first occasion Anna was observed in the nursery, she was playing by herself. She was walking round and round a group of tables, her arms held out in front of her, shaking her hands.

Occasionally she would break into a run, at which point she smiled. Suddenly she came up to the worker, put her hands on her shoulders and slowly and deliberately smelled the worker's hair. Then she said 'Mmm' and smiled at her. The worker returned the smile and asked the little girl's name. The child mumbled 'Anna' and continued on her journey round and round the tables, pausing from time to time to smell one or other of the children's hair in the same way. At length, the worker decided to put Anna into a group with three other children.

Wayne was a lanky six-year-old boy who had considerable problems in relating to other people; he seemed to live in a phantasy world. He had very strong feelings of his own inadequacy, and was referred to the group because he was forever in trouble. He caused chaos in the classroom, was always demanding attention and had no friends.

William was a seven-year-old West Indian boy, one of a family of six, who was a problem both at home and at school. In school he was very aggressive, always in fights or stirring up trouble in the classroom. He frequently became uncontrollable, and in these moods it was impossible to reach him either by a gentle approach or by threats. It became clear that William was his family's scapegoat and that they had rejected him completely. He arrived at school in ragged and dirty clothing, frequently smelling strongly. His mother had appealed to the headmistress to have William taken into care.

The third child, Neville, was a small ten-year-old. His father was West Indian, his mother Irish. Neville was referred to a group because of his excessively aggressive behaviour. He was responsible for running a protection racket in the school, and was given to uncontrollable attacks on both children and teachers. He had actually thrown chairs at teachers, kicked them and so on. Although Neville formed attachments to people and tried to buy their affection with presents, he could not sustain relationships. His home background was extremely insecure, with his father in prison for running a brothel and his mother a prostitute.

As for Anna, the worker went to the nursery to collect her, quite prepared for the first session never to take place. However Anna appeared to recognize her and walked slowly towards her. The nursery teacher then said to Anna, 'You are going with Mrs Reid.' Anna seemed not to have understood. However, the worker put out her hand and said, 'Come on, Anna.' To her surprise Anna took the offered hand and followed the worker out of the nursery. They went to the nearest classroom to collect William. William said, 'I know Anna, she comes into our class.' With this he bent down and said very gently, 'Hello, Anna.' They then collected Wayne. The worker told Anna that this was Wayne, and Anna repeated 'Wayne'. Wayne was delighted and beamed. Upstairs in the Junior department they collected Neville. After the worker had introduced them, Anna repeated 'Newille'. Neville chuckled with glee. 'She said "Newille",' he said. William remarked defensively, 'That's 'cos she's Italian.'

The party had to climb two more floors before they reached the group room. Anna clung tightly to the worker's hand and gave a little skip. She began chattering but the only words that could be understood were 'Newille', 'William' and 'Wayne'.

During the first session it became clear that the three boys were delighted with Anna. They were extremely gentle with her and fascinated by everything she did. Anna seemed to be the princess to whom the three boys could play Prince Charming. Part of her attraction seemed to rest in the fact that as far as they were concerned (in the words of Wayne), 'Anna can't do nothing.' She therefore presented no threat. Even Wayne had now found somebody who could do less than himself. 'She can't even talk, Miss,' he said. It also seemed reassuring to the three boys to find that they could be gentle and loving. Neville and William were specially protective towards her and would fight for her attention. Being able to express this gentle, loving side of his personality towards Anna made it in turn easier for Neville in particular to recognize these needs in himself and so for an adult to work with them.

The one aspect of Anna which the boys found most difficult to cope with was that she could not tolerate being touched. For the first month or so she would not even let them hold her hand walking to and from the group room. They persisted in trying to hug and cuddle her but she continued to refuse to allow this. The children in the group nevertheless immediately became very important to Anna. The nursery teacher reported that she heard her muttering the boys' names to herself as she wandered around the nursery.

Anna, in fact, played a very important part in getting her group to behave as a group. The three boys, who previously had had nothing to do with each other, would join up at playtime to come to the nursery wall which separated the two playgrounds to call for Anna. The three would spend playtime after playtime leaning on the wall chatting to Anna who, always delighted to see them, would run to them calling their names.

Within the group the worker allowed Anna to explore and do much as she pleased. The boys, although they fought amongst themselves, were very tolerant of her. Anna took refuge in the familiar, and session after session she would play with the paints, arranging them in order and protesting loudly when one of the boys replaced a paint pot in the wrong order. Each session she would ask the worker to draw her, naming the parts of the body as they went along. Anna became obsessed by names, her most frequent question being 'What's 'is?' (What's this?) 'This' was applied indiscriminately to people and things alike. Soon she knew the names of all the children in the different groups. Towards the end of the first term she surprised the nursery teacher by telling her the name of every child in the nursery. Previously the teacher had believed that Anna was not even aware that the children in the afternoon nursery differed from those in the morning.

Some time after the first month Anna began to allow the boys to hold her hand. They would squabble endlessly over this treat. No one else was allowed to touch her and that was a source of immense pride to the boys. The children in the nursery itself, however, were still wary of Anna and referred to her as 'that funny girl'. Anna did begin to approach the other children in the nursery, but these overtures were not always successful. The nursery children were not able to show her the same tolerance she found in the group.

In spite of her father's strictures about not returning home dirty, Anna took courage and painted her first picture. Her curiosity and growing confidence overcame her remaining fears and she became fascinated by paint, clay, glue and so on. She delighted in making mixtures in pots, tipping the colours into each other and squeezing glue through her fingers. Her greatest joy was to refill the paint pots. An obsession with the colour blue could be observed. Around this time she would only draw, paint or crayon in blue.

There were set-backs of course. At the end of the first term she spilt paint on to her dress and tights. She became very upset and wandered distractedly around the room putting her hands in the paints. Then she covered her head with her hands crying 'No, no'. She finally came and sat quietly on the worker's lap but could not relax. Then she hopped down suddenly and, leaning on the worker's shoulder, smelled her hair. It was the first time she had done this in the group.

It seemed that Anna experienced the worker as an adult who could understand her feelings and needs, and as someone who provided a setting in which she could be safe along with other children. In the nursery when she became frightened or upset she would call for the worker and keep repeating her name.

From time to time during the week Anna would ask the nursery teacher if it was time for her group, saying, 'Come now Newille and William.' The sessions seemed to become increasingly important to her. Anna now also made efforts to be part of the group activities. In one December session of the first term, Wayne and William lay on the floor drawing. Anna turned to the worker and said, 'Paper.' She was given some and lay down on the floor beside the boys. She looked and saw that they were drawing figures. She now did the same. Having finished her drawing, she said, 'Anna.' William said, 'She wants you to write it, Miss, like before.' He went over to Anna and holding her hand with the pencil in it, he asked for the letters. He now guided her hand and wrote 'Anna'. Anna rewarded William with a smile and he said delightedly, 'Anna, William.'

William in fact showed himself to be particularly perceptive towards Anna. Anna took great pleasure in turning on the lights as soon as she entered the group room. On one occasion entering the room, she seemed disappointed to notice that the lights were already on. William quickly switched them off, swung Anna round and lifted her up to the switch. Anna flicked them on and off, each time giving a throaty chuckle and saying, 'Oh, lovely lights.'

At the end of the first term Anna's father came to see the worker. He told her that Anna was 'a bit better' and could now say a few words. But she cried at weekends and kept repeating 'William'. During their long talk, the father told the worker a lot about the family – about his wife who refused to speak English, who had been shocked after Anna's birth to find 'babies so dirty' – Anna was in fact toilet-trained by six months. How, also, he was left to look after Anna during most of the day and how it had been necessary for him to find shift work in order to do that. Quite at a loss to know how to cope, he had left Anna uncomplaining for hours on end in her cot. When he was at work the mother in her desperation would lock Anna in the toilet. During their talk, the worker tried to persuade the father of the importance of Anna going to the child guidance clinic. But he said that his wife would not take her, because the clinic was for 'mad children', and he himself could not, because he was working.

Over the next two terms Anna continued to make progress. She began to draw and make things. The worker began setting definite limits for her and expected her to wait for attention. During one session Anna as usual asked the worker to draw her. She collected her book and selected a sharp blue pencil and brought them over. 'Mrs Reid – Anna's hair,' said Anna, pointing to the paper. The worker was occupied with Wayne and so suggested that she asked William to draw her. She refused this idea and, looking worried, repeated 'Mrs Reid' more urgently. 'In a minute, Anna,' the worker told her, 'I will draw you in a minute.' Anna seemed to accept this promise. She sat on the floor holding her crayons, repeating to herself, 'In a minute, Anna.' From this time on, whenever Anna could not have the worker's attention or could not have something because someone else was using it, she would say 'In a minute, Anna,' as though to reassure herself. In upsetting moments for her, the worker also comforted Anna with the phrase 'Never mind, Anna,' and this, too, Anna in turn used to comfort herself. The nursery teacher reported that she often heard Anna mumbling to herself, 'Oh dear, never mind, in a minute,' in moments of stress.

Anna nowadays tried to join in the activities of the other children in the group far more and to copy the things they made. She demanded the worker's attention less and would turn to Neville and William for help.

Outside the group Anna had made great progress. She now joined the rest of the school for special assemblies, harvest festivals and the like, although her behaviour there was not always appropriate. She would move around and sit somewhere else if she felt like it, and also saw no reason not to ask her teacher or her worker loud questions in the middle of the proceedings. In her usual desire to know everyone's name, it took the form of pointing to somebody and asking loudly, 'Who's this one?'

In the nursery Anna made a friend, a little West Indian girl, kind and motherly to her. As Anna extended her relationships it was always to the West Indian children she reached out. She loved to be allowed to give out the milks, but was adamant in her refusal to give a milk to any of the white children until all the West Indian children had been served.

Anna could also be seen sitting down with other children at story time, clapping her hands and trying to join in the songs. She became most distressed when the music stopped.

School holidays were a problem. Anna fretted and cried and her parents became exasperated. She expressed her feelings about a weekend break when the worker collected her for her Monday session: 'Yesterday was Sunday, Anna not coming to Mrs Reid, put Sunday in the dustbin.'

In the summer term of the last year of the group, Anna joined the reception class during the afternoons. In the morning she remained in the nursery. Her afternoon teacher showed great patience, as Anna was still not at a stage when she would do what was asked of her. When her teacher said, 'Come on, Anna, do this like the other children,' Anna became angry. 'Anna no [is not] like the other children.' She refused to do physical education or dancing because these activities involved getting undressed.

In Anna's second year in the group, the Christmas term was a very exciting and rewarding one. Her greatest efforts had been in learning to speak. She asked endless questions and was able to make complete English sentences, although she was still far from being fluent.

At the beginning of the Christmas term Anna made a very important breakthrough. Her teacher had asked the worker to help Anna to take part in physical education and dancing. When the worker joined the class for their lesson, Anna was sitting on a bench, wistfully watching the other children dancing with her hands clasped together, just as the teacher had described her. After a little time and persuasion, Anna took off her shoes and joined in the dancing. But she found it difficult to move safely on the slippery floor. The worker told Anna how much easier it would be if she took off her socks. Anna hesitated, then quickly tore them off. She looked worried and stood staring at her toes for a while before joining in again. Soon, however, she was dancing rapturously – she called out, 'Oh, lovely dancing, Mrs Reid.' Suddenly she stopped dancing and rushed over to the worker. She pulled excitedly at her dress, then rapidly discarded her top clothes and various petticoats, announcing, 'Now Anna like other children.' From now on Anna could not stop talking about the movement lessons and pestered continually for 'the time for the taking off the clothes'.

Her teacher reported many other changes in that same week. Anna now *insisted* on doing exactly the same as the other children. She wrote a sentence: 'Anna is a girl.'

During this term she took part when her class led the school assembly and in fact had the main role. Wayne had now left the school but Neville and William were there, very proud of her. On the way to the group room that same day Neville said, 'Did you see our Anna this morning? Wasn't she great?'

Anna also took part with the rest of her class in the Christmas play. After the play the worker saw Anna standing with her mother and father. The worker was struck by how happy they looked together and was very surprised when Anna's mother said, 'Such a lovely play, very good Anna,' in English. During the following term Anna's mother began taking her to the child guidance clinic.

In the group Anna became steadily more adventurous. Her drawings were quite recognizable and she made such objects as clay pots. She could accept the limits the worker set her and displayed a strong sense of humour. By the last term of the worker's two years in the school Anna could read and write. She no longer stood out in her class as she had done, although her behaviour was at times unpredictable and still a little odd.

Very strong bonds had been established with William and Neville, but she no longer relied on them outside the groups. In the playground Anna could be seen playing with her peers the current favourite game, 'The Big Ship Sails through the Alley, Alley, Oh!'

**Workers and Parents**

The amount of direct contact the workers had with the parents of children coming to their groups varied from case to case. Depending on the judgment of the head teacher, the parents might or might not be informed that it was felt their child could benefit from this opportunity for special help. Whether the parents were informed in this particular way or not, all tended to see the workers as teachers who happened to be taking small groups. They therefore felt much less threatened by the group than by the idea of attending a child guidance clinic. We have seen, in the case of Anna for instance, how clinic attendance would have been impossible because her father was at work all day and because her mother feared that her child would be labelled 'mad'. The pattern of events in that case, in which improvement in the child relieved the parents sufficiently of guilt or worry for them to be able to talk about the problem, was common in the experience of many workers. The parents' experience that someone trying to help the child was also interested in their difficulties and sympathetic towards them could be very productive in helping them feel less frightened of subsequent contact with a clinic.

From the children's point of view, it was important that the workers should be able to have a good relationship with their parents if and when the occasion arose. As in the relationship between workers and teachers, a good rapport helped to lessen the tendency of many of the children to play adults off against one another. However, it was often necessary for considerable time to elapse before the children felt they could trust the worker not to join with their parents against them or otherwise betray their confidence.

The issue of confidentiality was altogether an important one. Inevitably the children began talking in the groups of their feelings towards their teachers and parents. These feelings were of course often negative ones. The worker tried to let the children feel that she could accept and allow their point of view, without therefore turning against the other party. She might, for instance, ask how they felt they themselves might have reacted when faced with their own behaviour, had they been in the position of the adult they were complaining about.

Although workers felt that contact with parents could be valuable in the ways mentioned, they saw their primary task to be understanding the children's behaviour and dealing with it in the group situation. Contact with parents could not substitute for this. Such contact, however, could be useful in forming a more realistic picture of the pressures the parents, as well as the children, were under. It could be helpful, too, in counteracting any tendency for the worker to feel that she alone knew what was best for a child.

## Workers and Teachers

Much of what has been said about the worker's relationship with parents applies equally to her relations with teachers. As already indicated, the basic worker-teacher relationship was one of mutual help. From the teacher's point of view it began with the worker relieving him or her for a while of the most troublesome children. The worker was further useful to the teacher as a sympathetic listener and a source of new ideas. By discussing the child with the teacher, though without betraying the child's confidence, the worker gained useful information. It was helpful to know why a child had been referred and later how he was behaving in the classroom. The frequent discovery that a child was splitting his 'good' and 'bad' behaviour between teacher and worker helped both adults to put the behaviour in perspective, to take it less personally and so cope with it better. As indicated, the fact that adults were clearly able to co-operate in dealing with him, despite his determined attemps to play one off against the other, proved extremely important to the child. This was particularly the case with those who came from broken homes.

Some specific instances of the use teachers could make of workers now follow. And it should not be forgotten that the willing ear of the worker also relieved some of the pressure usually carried by the head.

One teacher discussed with the worker how her own childhood experiences were recalled by a boy who wanted a special relationship with her. She commented that thinking aloud about the situation, with someone she knew to be interested, helped her to see the role of her own past feelings more clearly. These had made it difficult for her to deal appropriately with the child's demands. In other cases a teacher might say how exasperated she was by a piece of behaviour. The worker could then go on to speculate what this behaviour might mean for the teacher personally, besides being simply disruptive. Mary, for example, was a child incapable of maintaining the good relationship with her teacher that she urgently wished for, a problem rooted in her many experiences of loss. Mary's extremely provoking behaviour in the group seemed designed to test whether she really drove people away. In the course of this testing in the classroom, she did in fact reduce a new teacher to tears, with devastating effect on both of them. They were subsequently able to discuss their feelings about the situation with the worker, at first separately and then together. The outcome was that Mary was able to continue in that teacher's class.

A similar incident concerned James, whose younger brother had attended a group. The brother had met with a fatal accident during the school holiday, and although James returned to school apparently little affected, the worker involved was uneasy. She knew that the dead boy had been severely bullied by James, who had played the role of the 'good' child in an extremely disintegrated family. She felt he must now be feeling extremely guilty about the death, at the same time being unable to share his preoccupations with anyone. The worker therefore made a point of discussing James with his teacher. The teacher reported that James was now unrecognizable, provoking her past all endurance until she punished him. She was helped by the idea that his actions might be a measure of his trust in her. The worker specifically suggested that James was using the classroom to get rid of feelings of guilt that he could not show at home.

The usefulness of attempting to understand the meaning of a child's behaviour in such ways became clearer as time passed. Teachers then began to refer more withdrawn children, even if these were not an immediate management problem. Even pupils not attending groups seemed to have an intuitive grasp of their purpose and would often ask to come in at playtime to discuss situations that were troubling them.

## Containment Within the Group

A useful function of the groups lay in providing a regular and stable opportunity for a child to have a sustained relationship with an adult and with other children. In that relationship problematic aspects of a child's character could be worked through. For the enterprise to succeed it was necessary for the physical setting, as well as the other individuals involved, to be able to survive attack. Each worker had to discover her own limits of tolerance and learn to deal with chaotic behaviour within these limits. A failure in this area would have been a failure to provide security.

It was largely to increase the sense of security that most of the rules and practices described earlier were gradually evolved. To re-iterate some examples, the existence of a locked door established the group room as a place apart. Unacceptable behaviour could be brought here instead of being broadcast through the school. We saw in the case of John how important this detachment of the group room could be. The regularity of the meetings and the stability of group membership were also an essential demonstration that something reliable could survive attacks. On this basis 'family feeling' developed among the children in a group long before group themes emerged.

A further very important aspect of containment was the acceptance by the worker of repudiated aspects of the child. These, by the mechanism of projection, were ascribed either to another child or to the worker herself. Projection, already described in Chapter 1, has been seen in action in all the detailed case descriptions given in this chapter. It is a mechanism often used to make a worker feel rejected. Feelings of rejection were among the feelings least tolerable to the children themselves: projections of this kind could occur even without the child being physically present in the group.

Charles, a latchkey child with no friends, was terrified of the possible effects of anger and slipped out of his group at the remotest chance of any confrontation. He then spent half a year refusing at each session to come to his group, but later attended regularly another group with another worker. He was also eager to see the first worker again when she paid a visit to the school; he seemed to have been helped by being allowed to reject an adult, who nevertheless remained friendly. The feelings of uselessness projected on to her had proved not impossible for her to bear. However, a worker might not *always* fall in with the wish to cast her consistently as a bad figure – to make her play the witch in a game, for instance – but might instead comment on how the child seemed always to want someone other than himself to be the bad one.

A withdrawn child might project his own violent impulses on to another child, and then feel at his mercy. Such children would be more able to show these violent feelings themselves after testing and observing the worker's response to the more overt disrupters. When frightening impulses proved containable and not annihilating to the recipient, they could then be acknowledged as part of the child himself. The need to ascribe them to someone else, and then submit to him, consequently disappeared. Bullies also could begin to show more tender feelings when they saw that the worker looked after the more vulnerable children, instead of ridiculing them.

## Nurture Within the Group

The model the group leaders hoped to provide for the children was that of an adult with the time and desire to respond to their communications – further, that of an adult working together with other adults to this end. This model closely resembles that of the sensitive, caring parent they had failed to find in their own home lives. We hoped – and often observed – that this experience of being 'nurtured' could be carried over into other settings. For example, working through emotional difficulties arising over parting from a group worker could make the otherwise difficult yearly change of teacher easier.

The behaviour of the children sometimes involved very primitive phantasy material of the kind described in later chapters of this book. It was often very difficult for students to interpret this material accurately, particularly in the non-clinical setting of this kind of group. Even when a worker thought she could understand some of the deeper unconscious phantasies, she did not make them explicit in the group situation, if the child were not to some extent already conscious of them. That would be persecuting to the individual, and would also create expectations that could not be fulfilled in a school setting. However, one might well put into words a phantasy that the child was patently conscious of, or otherwise verbalize feelings the children seemed to have towards workers or one another – in particular we put into words the hostile feelings that the children had towards workers. This verbalizing helped both to contain the feelings and to clarify the distinction between forbidding destructive actions, and condemning destructive impulses.

Sarah, persistently throwing clay out of the window, could not be stopped by requests or warnings of exclusion. However she responded to the suggestion that she should keep the mess inside the room where it could be dealt with. The more therapeutic interpretation – 'you want to put all the mess outside for fear it cannot be dealt with' – was sometimes taken by groups as an incitement to further action. In general, therefore, we found it more helpful to supply a positive, practical suggestion in which the understanding was implicit. Sarah probably responded also because at this point the worker was not angry nor attempting to use insight as a weapon or a means of control.

A further illustration shows how some very deep material – here, the envious wish to steal the babies of a mother felt to be keeping all sexual creativity for herself, at the same time neglecting the child – can be handled without being explicitly verbalized in that precise form. During the last group before the Easter holidays, Christine repeatedly stole a plastic kangaroo with a baby in its pouch, forcing the worker into the role of a depriving authority figure. Christine withdrew into a corner. Then another girl began moving the handle of a mop back and forth between her legs in a very provocative way, looking at the worker with a challenging expression, obviously deliberately depicting intercourse. She agreed with the worker's suggestion that she was imitating what mummies and daddies did, whereupon Christine chimed in, 'That's what Miss is going to do one day.' The worker replied that it was also what Christine was going to do one day, and asked how many children she hoped to have. Christine responded by giving back the plastic kangaroo and making a copy of her own out of plasticine, which she asked the worker to look after until the end of the session. When the worker's comment made her feel she was now allowed to think of herself as a future mother, she could allow the worker to fulfil a mothering function for her, in spite of the gap imposed by the coming holidays.

**Conclusions**

This chapter has tried to show some of the behaviour disturbed children can present and to illustrate the ways in which attendance at small groups may help to contain and deal with it. Groups offer many possibilities, especially for children for whom attendance at a clinic is not feasible, for whatever reason. The integration of the groups into the school day obviates the emotional and practical difficulties of leaving the school for aid. It also avoids the issue of 'labelling' in the eyes of the children and their parents. Clearly, many of the children might well have turned out to be more disturbed than was apparent, and many could, in fact, have benefited from individual therapy. Indeed, in the absence of a therapeutic setting such as that described in subsequent chapters, it would actually be very difficult, if not impossible, to understand accurately all the details of a phantasy or to assess changes in the children's deeper character-structure, as distinct from their overt behaviour. Some of the striking results obtained, therefore, could be ascribed to the fact that 'nurture' had often been an experience missing from the child's previous life.

In summary, work – especially when co-ordinated with the efforts of class teachers, remedial teachers and others – does appear to have sufficient flexibility and significance to meet various needs of disturbed children.

# Chapter Three

# *The Child Guidance Clinic*

## by Dora Lush, B.A., PH.D.

In the previous chapter we were given a glimpse of some of the kinds of children who have difficulty adjusting at school. We saw how some of them can be helped in small groups. These disturbed children are often those who have been deprived of adequate opportunity for an understanding relationship with concerned adults, either because of problems in the home background or because of too large classes in schools. Such children are able to make good use of the extra opportunity which is offered by the groups. There are other children, however, for whom the small groups do not seem enough – and in any case many schools at present do not have such facilities.

Some disturbed children may therefore need to attend a psychiatric clinic. In this chapter a typical setting where child psychotherapists work and where children may receive psychotherapy is described and the details are set out of what happens when children are referred by their schools, or by their parents, or by a doctor. We are introduced to the child guidance team, their methods of assessment and to a sample of the problems the children present. The classified symptoms and backgrounds of one hundred children who were considered suitable for individual psychotherapy are included in the review. Some of these are examined in detail. M.B., D.D.

**Stephen: a Boy with Multiple Symptoms**

Stephen was first referred at seven by his doctor, who thought him to be mentally retarded. He was described as very inhibited, living in a world of his own. He also had asthma and eczema. His father had died when he was three years old. Unfortunately, due to our lack of staff, Stephen could not start psychotherapy for two years. His problems meanwhile persisted: he was making no progress at school, could not read or write at all and could hardly count. However, the educational psychologist found him to be of average intelligence. Every report described Stephen as slow and dull, and I believed it would take a long time in therapy to break through defences which had existed in him for years. This was not at all the case. The first session was rich - Stephen talking freely, revealing conscious problems probably never previously verbalized and indicating his unconscious phantasies. It was as though he had always been waiting for a chance like this. His 'living in a world of his own' seemed to have been a defence against feelings of total confusion.

Stephen revealed much of his very confused thought processes during the first few therapy sessions. A few examples will suffice. He displayed a mix-up of reality, imagination and fiction. For example, he said I resembled a human-type robot on a television programme. When he could not remember the robot's name, he confused the robot, me and his own thought processes, saying to me, 'Your trouble is that you can never remember your name.'

Stephen's thinking often seemed inconsequential, simply because he omitted several linking steps. For example, he would say, 'The trouble is that I'm the sort of person that likes cars.' We had to find the missing links. They proved to be, that his sister did not like cars, she broke his cars accidentally and then he was upset as he liked cars. Stephen considered that cars were more alive than people, and this view instanced a further aspect of his confusions, that between living and non-living matter. For example, he thought body parts such as hands were replaceable. He often made puns and used words inappropriately. He could be totally lost, even in a district he often visited, and seemed to have no sense of time. Past, present and future were all mixed together. He said that he had a very good memory for the future. He also had an imaginary companion, an invisible figure he called Goss, probably connected with his dead father. Sometimes he confused himself with Goss, blaming him for his own actions.

In spite of all this confusion, a good prognostic sign was Stephen's involvement in the therapy from the start. He co-operated well, spoke freely and continued the dialogue with me internally between sessions. Thus he frequently thought he had told me things which he had in fact not mentioned. It is worth reporting Stephen's first session in detail as so much emerged. Necessarily the account has been edited slightly, as verbatim material is so unwieldy.

*The first session*

Stephen came along with me readily after his mother left, but complained the stairs to my room were hard to climb. I said that as children did not usually find the stairs hard to climb, he was possibly suggesting that something else was hard – coming to see me at the clinic and what that might mean. Stephen agreed thoughtfully, as if he meant it, and indeed listened carefully to everything I said throughout the session, adding his own opinions. After the usual preliminary explanations about the times and lengths of sessions and the toys, Stephen looked through the box of toys, commenting and asking questions about them. I interpreted this behaviour as a wish to ask questions about the therapy situation and me as well. He agreed, but then talked about the plasticine and his wish to be an inventor. He gave a long, confused description of his invention to stop burglars shooting and hurting people in banks, which involved sheets of plastic and glass. In his account he seemed to identify himself with the people who might be shot. I said here that he was communicating his feeling of having to protect himself to stop himself being hurt. (I remembered, too, the description of him living in a world of his own.) Stephen agreed about his own fear of being hurt and this led him to talk of his father, whom he was said not to remember. He abruptly said, 'My father died,' and told me his father had worked for the railways and had been killed in a train crash (which was not actually true). He said he felt his father was still alive inside him, but also talked sadly about his being dead. Although this was our first session, I sensed already that Stephen felt close to me. I suggested that he was worried about people dying when they were important to him. I said perhaps he was worried I would die before we really got to know each other, just as his father had died before Stephen really got to know him. Stephen nodded, and then described how his father once changed his nappy when he was a baby and accidentally dropped him on his head. I felt he was communicating his fear that, even if I did not die as his father had done, I might let him down – in particular, perhaps, if I saw he was dirty or messy. His father had let him down (dropped him) while changing his nappy. It was not important whether this story of his father dropping him was a real memory, a phantasy or something Stephen had been told; what was important was that he was communicating it to me at this moment in our relationship.

Stephen then complained that his mother and sister always asked what he had been doing. I therefore emphasized that I would regard whatever he said as secret. He then told me he did have a secret and described the imaginary ghost companion. He became confused at this point, and rather poignantly said he had a mixed-up mind. I acknowledged his awareness of his need for help, and he readily agreed he wanted help to understand why he felt mixed-up.

While talking, Stephen had been playing idly with the plasticine, and now he talked again of his wish to be an inventor, saying sadly his father would have helped him if he had been alive. Confusion arose again, when he said he wanted his father to have helped him to invent a special train which would have prevented his father being killed in the crash. Stephen was confusing past, present and future. He enacted his phantasy of the fatal train crash. I was later told this was the first time he had talked about it. Again I was conscious of his fears of being hurt or of hurting others he loved, such as his father. Underneath was his fear that he had had something to do with his father's death. I began to try to sort out the reality from the phantasy. Stephen seemed relieved and now played calmly with the cars, expressing his pleasure at having them just for himself, and agreeing with my comment that he was pleased to have me just for himself too. Stephen then once again talked about his favourite robot television programme, but still kept to the theme of life and death, describing robots as people who had died and only looked alive. Here we have confusion of the interwoven themes of life and death, phantasy and reality. I discussed these confusions with Stephen. Once again he became calmer. It was time to stop the session. Stephen was happy at the prospect of coming twice weekly in future.

This first session suggested Stephen had been consciously or unconsciously hoping for help and realized at once that here was a suitable setting for it. He thus immediately felt able to verbalize some of his anxieties about his father's death and the confusion he felt himself to be in.

In spite of the severity of Stephen's disturbance, I felt the outlook was favourable because of the various indications that emerged in the first few weeks of therapy. These included the strong, meaningful transference relationship between Stephen and myself. A further favourable sign was his intuitive awareness of the meaning and purpose of the therapy. He persisted in his wish to understand his inner world, even when faced with painful thoughts and feelings. He listened to what I said and often responded by saying something like, 'Here's another aspect to what you were saying.' Yet another feature of his positive attitude to psychotherapy was that he rarely missed a session, even when physically quite ill.

At the time of writing Stephen has been in therapy for a total of four years and has made excellent progress. He started to learn to read a year after psychotherapy began, and is now average for his age in all school subjects, except mathematics, where he still experiences confusion. His thought processes seem normal. He is no longer enuretic. He no longer has asthma and eczema and no longer gets lost in time or place. He has the normal interests of his age group and a few friends. There is every hope that he will grow up to be a happy, normal member of our society.

## The Staff of the Clinic

The typical child guidance clinic is multi-disciplinary – that is, staffed by members of several different professions. As a rule, the members of the team are the child psychiatrist, the educational psychologist, the child psychotherapist and the psychiatric social worker.

The task of the child psychiatrist is to conduct diagnostic work and possibly also the treatment. He is medically qualified and has undergone further training in child psychiatry, perhaps especially in the psychoanalysis of children. Often he will carry out the first interviews with the child and family. Psychiatrists differ individually in the way they work, but they usually give the team an initial account of the severity of the child's disturbance and the state of the family dynamics, including both overt and hidden aspects of relationships. The psychiatrist tries to assess the nature of the child's feelings, his degree of anxiety and aggression, and so forth. The child's relationships within and outside the family are considered. The psychiatrist can often judge whether the child will respond to psychotherapy or whether other methods of help are indicated. He tries to obtain an overall view of all aspects of the child's endowment and environment and judges whether the current situation is likely to deteriorate, improve or stay the same.

When he interviews the parents, as well as trying to understand how they see their child and their own roles in the family, the psychiatrist attempts to assess their motivation for treatment, for without parental co-operation little can be done. Sometimes a good deal of initial work is needed before parents accept psychotherapy for their children.

Some psychiatrists like to see all the members of a family together. Others favour individual interviews. If the patient is adolescent, the psychiatrist may not see the parents at all, in case this should adversely affect his relationship with the patient. The psychiatrist's diagnostic interviews may prove to be sufficiently therapeutic for further treatment to be unnecessary.

The educational psychologist plays his part in the diagnostic process by formally testing the child. Intelligence tests are commonly given, especially when there is an educational problem involved. Projective tests are also used to explore the child's personality and emotional functioning. In such tests a child may be asked to make up stories about pictures shown to him or to say what he sees in deliberately vague patterns or inkblots, or may be asked to complete unfinished stories and sentences. His answers give the psychologist clues to his phantasies and so help to provide a picture of how he views the world and the people around him. Special tests on attainment in specific school subjects may be given when necessary.

On the basis of his test results and his general contact with the child, the educational psychologist can himself also form a judgment about a patient's likely reaction to psychotherapy. He is also in a position to provide the team with much factual information about how the child functions intellectually and emotionally. A change of school might be indicated or special remedial education. The educational psychologist is the liaison officer between the schools and the clinic. He may himself also undertake remedial teaching with children who are slow or blocked in their educational progress.

The training of an educational psychologist consists of an honours degree in psychology, followed by training in teaching, actual teaching experience and further training in educational psychology. This team member can therefore be of great specialized assistance to teachers in helping them to understand and aid the children in their classes. Not all children with difficulties can or need attend the clinic. The educational psychologist also helps and advises the staff of special schools and remedial classes.

The psychiatric social worker, or P.S.W., is again involved in the diagnostic process. He usually obtains a general history of the family from the parents and listens to their account of the child, his problems and background. This procedure may take several interviews. He will then often continue to see one or both parents regularly, perhaps in conjunction with the psychotherapist treating the child, or even if the child is not being seen regularly. The academic background of the P.S.W. is a training in social work, often leading to a degree, and then further specialized training in psychiatric social work.

The child psychotherapist may likewise be involved in the initial diagnostic procedures, but his main concern is with the subsequent therapy, if that is decided upon. The child psychotherapy training is described in detail elsewhere in this book. Briefly, it consists of an honours degree in psychology or an allied subject, appropriate experience with children and a four-year specialist postgraduate training in child psychotherapy.

In most clinics a case will initially be discussed at a case conference, where collective decisions on psychotherapy, parental support, remedial help, change of school and the like are taken. After the case conference the parents will be seen and the recommendation discussed with them. No action is taken, however, without parental agreement, except in occasional cases, for example where cruelty or extreme neglect has occurred. If it is mutually agreed that the child should have psychotherapy, the psychotherapist will usually see the parents once by themselves before treatment starts. This not only enables him to form a first-hand impression of them and their account, but also gives them the chance to meet the person who will be treating their child.

A typical case might concern a Mr and Mrs Smith, who are worried about their son Johnny. He is seven years old and has extreme temper tantrums which disrupt the whole family. The parents now get in touch with the child guidance clinic, either direct, or through the recommendation of their general practitioner, or John's school. They are given two appointments at the clinic. During the first appointment the educational psychologist gives Johnny an intelligence test and some personality tests, possibly also tests to ascertain whether there is any brain damage. During this same time the psychiatric social worker interviews the parents about Johnny's early history, the history of the temper tantrums, about the family generally and how Johnny gets on at school and with other children. At the second of the two interviews the psychiatrist sees Johnny, talks to him, watches him play with toys, possibly asks him to do some drawings or make some plasticine models. In this way he forms some idea of what Johnny is like and already, perhaps, reaches some understanding of the temper tantrums.

With the parents' permission the clinic obtains further reports about Johnny from his school and from his doctor. The psychiatrist has probably seen Mr and Mrs Smith after seeing Johnny, especially if he feels he wants more information. All the workers involved then meet at a case conference, discuss their findings and collate them with the reports from outside the clinic. The child psychotherapist is probably also at the conference, although he has not as yet seen Johnny. After discussion and evaluation of all findings, it is decided that it would be appropriate for Johnny to have psychotherapy. It is also decided that the parents should be seen. The psychiatrist and the P.S.W. therefore see the parents again to acquaint them of the decision. Both parents are pleased Johnny is to have psychotherapy, after an explanation of what this involves. Mrs Smith also seems rather pleased that she will have an opportunity to discuss her problems with someone. Mr Smith is less sure and says he cannot spare the time from work. It is agreed, after some discussion, that Johnny and Mrs Smith will come weekly to the clinic, after both parents have met the psychotherapist, and Mr Smith will come occasionally to talk about how he views what is happening.

This is a brief example of the procedure that often occurs; however, every case is unique and is of course treated as such.

## The Children

Children are referred to child guidance clinics for a wide variety of reasons. As any one child may present several symptoms, no easy classification of children by symptoms is possible. A recent analysis, however, was made of the data concerning one thousand children referred for full psychiatric investigation during the last five years to a busy urban clinic, where the author of this chapter worked. Economic backgrounds vary considerably in the district where the clinic is situated. The results of the analysis can therefore claim to give a general view of the situation in clinics throughout the country in so far as age, sex, problems, backgrounds and other factors are concerned. It deserves mention that as this clinic was under the authority of the local Education Department there was probably more emphasis on children presenting school problems than would be noted in clinics run by hospitals or other bodies. Two-thirds of the referrals of children to the clinic in question arose purely out of educational difficulties. These children were seen only by the educational psychologist. Their data is not included in the following results.

### *Source of referral*

About a third of the children given full psychiatric investigation were referred by school medical officers, or by doctors working in general practice and hospitals.

Another third were referred by the schools themselves. A further small number came through the social services or the courts.

Approximately a quarter were brought on the initiative of parents who had recognized that their children had problems.

Although this initiative does not necessarily lead to a successful outcome, it makes a hopeful beginning.

*Age at referral*

The age of the children referred ranged from under five years to over fourteen years, with the greatest number falling between eight and eleven. It is usually found that most older children (adolescents) seeking help prefer to attend centres that specifically set out to meet the needs of their age group.

*Sex of the children*

As is generally found, approximately twice as many boys as girls were referred. Many conjectures have been made on the reasons for this habitual bias. It is possible, but unlikely, that boys are subject to greater stress. It is more probably that boys tend to react to internal and external pressure in more overt and aggressive ways than do girls. A boy who reacts with violence or anti-social behaviour is more likely to be brought to a clinic than a girl whose disturbance reveals itself in a quieter way.

*Reasons for referral*

The main symptoms for which children are referred can be grouped in the following broad categories. Any given child may of course present more than one symptom.

1 Nervous disorders, including fears, anxieties and inhibited behaviour.
2 Habit disorders, such as enuresis, sleep or speech disturbances.
3 Behaviour disorders, principally meaning aggressive behaviour.
4 Psychosomatic complaints, such as asthma or eczema.
5 Anti-social behaviour, such as stealing or truancy.
6 Psychotic behaviour.
7 Educational difficulties.

These broad classifications give only a rough idea of why children come to clinics. However, the data was assembled on the basis of these categories. About two-thirds of all children, then, were referred for behaviour disorders or anti-social behaviour. Their behaviour seemed broadly directed against other people. The greater part of the remaining third was equally distributed among nervous disorders, habit disorders and educational difficulties.

Using a different classification system, I myself have re-classified the symptoms of the one hundred children most recently considered suitable for psychotherapy at this same clinic. The ratio of boys to girls of this smaller sample was again about two to one. The age distribution was also similar to that of the larger group. The intelligence distribution was normal. It must be emphasized, incidentally, that cases considered suitable for psychotherapy are not necessarily the most ill or disturbed children coming to the clinic. A prerequisite for therapy is regular attendance. Unless there is also parental co-operation, it is better not to begin at all.

*Home backgrounds*

The backgrounds of children considered suitable for psychotherapy do not, on examination, support the idea sometimes put forward that therapy is the prerogative of middle-class children. The backgrounds were often materially poor. Bad housing was mentioned in twelve per cent of cases. Here home circumstances were so desperate that many aspects of the children's lives were affected.

An important finding was that one-third of the children were living with only one natural parent. The loss of a parent by death, divorce or desertion is itself a traumatic event, leading often to disturbance. A further fact of great interest was that over half the children of the sample were the eldest in their family. That statistic did not include the few only children. Mothers are probably more anxious with a first child, and the children themselves may be more subject to stress. Other important background factors noted were marital discord and parental disturbances, including deep depression and violence, and intolerance and rigidity to a psychotic degree. Further relevant factors that each concerned a few children were physical trauma arising from accidents, several hospitalizations when young, hospitalization of a parent, and traumatic events in the family, such as death or accident to a brother or sister.

*Symptoms presented*

These hundred children we are considering came to the clinic for a variety of overt reasons. It was rare for a child to have only one symptom and it was not always easy to isolate the main reason for referral. Sometimes a particular symptom seemed predominant, but as the investigation proceeded it became clear that the child had other significant difficulties. I therefore tried not to classify the children according to one symptom in each case, but included all and any that emerged. The total percentages given therefore add up to more than one hundred.

As might have been predicted, disturbed relationships with parents or brothers and sisters were mentioned in about half the cases. Difficulties with children outside the family were described in about a third. A wide variety of difficulties connected with school were mentioned. Thus 14 per cent of the children had a phobia about school and were unable to attend at all, and a similar number disliked school intensely although they continued to attend. Approximately 20 per cent of the children behaved so badly at school that the teachers formally complained – mainly about stealing and aggression. About 25 per cent of the children presented learning difficulties, such as inability to read or day-dreaming and lack of concentration.

Personality traits were often given as the reason for concern. About 18 per cent of the children were described as having temper tantrums or being 'uncontrollable'. A few young children were excessively restless and sometimes an investigation for organic damage was indicated. One-third of the children were described as anxious. Many anxieties or phobias were specifically noted about school, that is, about certain lessons, especially physical education and swimming. Further phobias included fear of the dark, separation from parents and hypochondria. About one-fifth of the sample were described as timid, solitary or withdrawn. Occasionally such isolation was felt to be serious. Eight children in fact showed signs suggestive of early schizophrenia and in two others an autistic pattern was evident. Some 15 per cent of the children were thought to be depressed, while others were subsequently found to be suffering from underlying depression. Obsessional acts and compulsive thoughts were noted occasionally.

Psychosomatc manifestations were fairly frequent. Some 10 per cent of children had asthma. Other physical symptoms occasionally encountered were eczema, stomach pains, loss of appetite, vomiting, migraine, temporary deafness, loss of voice, frequency of urination and assorted aches. Speech defects were noted in 8 per cent. Nightmares or night terrors were mentioned in 10 per cent of cases; sleepwalking and night-time hallucinations occurred occasionally, and insomnia rather more often.

Many disturbing habits were mentioned. Some 15 per cent of the children were bed-wetters and 5 per cent soilers. Other less frequently noted habits were compulsive masturbation, violent rocking, picking and eating rugs, pulling out and eating own hair, nail-biting and compulsive eating. Several children had suicidal thoughts and one had made a serious attempt to kill himself. Rare reasons for referral included elective mutism and regression to babyhood.

This wide variety of symptoms occurred in a sample of only one hundred cases and such variety would probably prove to be typical of most clinics.

## The Aims and Methods of the Psychotherapist

Children are brought to child guidance clinics for many different reasons. The task of the child psychotherapist is to help the children with their problems. The theoretical basis of treatment is a model founded on psychodynamic concepts and insights of the kind pioneered by Freud, Adler, Jung and others. Not all clinics necessarily use entirely the same set of concepts.

In child psychotherapy, as in the psychoanalysis of adults, the aim is to free patients from what is believed to be the domination of unconscious phantasies deriving in the first place from babyhood. The hope is that reactions to current situations will become progressively less influenced by these phantasies. The child psychotherapist has to understand in detail how early emotional experiences, mostly now no longer in consciousness, seem to have shaped the child's present difficulties and disturbances. The therapist allows the child to re-experience, and then helps him to understand, his infantile feelings. Understanding is the first step to overcoming.

The most suitable setting for psychotherapy is a room

where the child can play among some simple toys, with materials for drawing, painting and modelling. These will be employed by him in the course of his play. The play, in this setting, is not an end in itself but a means of identifying unconscious processes. I myself was trained in the theory and techniques established by Melanie Klein. Following her prescribed practice, each child has a box of toys which are kept for him alone. These include small dolls and animals and, as stated, painting, writing and modelling materials. Water is also to hand. The same room should be available for each of the child's sessions, and the furniture be changed as little as possible.

Broadly speaking, the play of small children in psychotherapy serves the same purpose as the free association of adults in psychoanalysis. Older children, of course, may prefer to draw, paint or talk. By observing the child's behaviour, understanding can be gained of what the child is really, or unconsciously, doing, saying and feeling. One also observes how he relates to the neutral – as far as possible – figure of the therapist, who represents people who were the objects of love, hate and other emotions in his early life. A neutral attitude on the part of the therapist in all that occurs allows the expression of all sorts of feelings by the child and notably the emergence of unconscious material. The therapist's interpretation of these behaviours and expressions is conveyed to the child in words he can understand: this interpretation is the psychotherapist's main working tool.

## Some Case Studies

Although a classified list of symptoms is interesting and of some value, the child psychotherapist nevertheless looks at each child as a whole and unique person – and since each child is considered as such, the work of the child psychotherapist can never be dull or repetitive. Every child psychotherapist will have a wide variety of cases, unless he particularly wishes to specialize. He will as a rule have patients of both sexes, varying ages and contrasting symptoms and personality types. Reactions to psychotherapy also vary. Some patients will seem very disturbed, their thought processes confused, their emotions inappropriate and their hold on reality slight – yet respond well to therapy. Other children may seem on the whole normal, apart from one symptom such as bed-wetting or nightmares – yet be difficult to treat. I have come to feel that motivation on the part of the patient is centrally important: by motivation, I mean the *wish* to understand oneself. Necessarily, the fulfilment of the wish will involve some mental pain, as it means facing up to parts of oneself that were not only previously unconscious but may be very unpleasant. It means accepting mental responsibility for one's feelings and actions. The ability to face mental pain seems to bear little relation to age, intelligence or severity of symptom. All children have a certain amount of resistance to understanding themselves, but the degree of resistance varies greatly.

Once the child realizes that therapy provides an opportunity for serious consideration of his problems, this realization alone occasionally leads to a swift amelioration of symptoms. Such relief will often encourage further participation in the therapy. An instance was the case of Barry, an intelligent boy of six, seemingly normal except for nightmares, night terrors and hallucinations, which had persisted for some years. He would wake up terrified of things he appeared to see coming at him from the door or window. He was said not to remember these events during the day – a claim in fact disproved in his first session with me. I will not describe his play in detail, but it soon seemed to be connected with his anxieties about going to bed. I talked about the fears I felt he was showing, but without actual reference to his nightmares and hallucinations. Barry then said, 'Last night I had a bad dream. There were monsters coming through the window at me and I was frightened and had to run to the other side of the room.' I linked this statement with his aggressive feelings, shown in his play, towards his parents who then in his imagination seemed to turn into monsters and chase him in retaliation. Barry continued enacting the nightmares but seemed more relaxed, and was pleased at the idea of returning the following week. Therapy provided a setting in which it was possible for Barry to acknowledge the nightmares and hallucinations. From then on constructive therapeutic work was possible.

The function of the psychotherapist is not to provide the child with a substitute parent. The possibility of this misunderstanding has to be kept in mind, especially when treating deprived or bereaved children. Usually the sex of the therapist does not affect the treatment – at different times the therapist can stand for male or female figures in the child's phantasies. A case in point was Tim, who was seven years old and lived only with his mother. He was brought to the clinic because of depression, including attempts at suicide by running into a busy road. From the start of therapy, Tim was clearly searching for the father he had never known. His parents had separated before his birth. He constantly asked me to play boyish games with him. It was therefore important from the start to talk about his wish for me to be a father to him. It was of course useless to attempt to be a substitute father for fifty minutes a week. To help Tim, I had first to help him to understand his self-punitive feelings which led to the suicide attempts. These were related to his largely unconscious feelings of responsibility for his father's departure, although of course it had nothing directly to do with him. Also to his own conflicting feelings – his sadness at not having a father, but at the same time his pleasure at having his mother to himself. Psychotherapy eventually helped Tim to make more satisfactory relationships in the world outside his home and to find father-figures in teachers and youth club leaders.

Sometimes psychotherapy cases begin with a referral for the wrong or inappropriate reasons. An example was Richard, brought to the clinic by his mother when he was twelve. She found him difficult at home and he still had nightly enuresis. She gave a picture of a lonely, depressed boy who was always tired. She wanted Richard sent to boarding-school so that she could concentrate on her complicated relationship with her husband. The clinic staff was firm, however: we told the mother that Richard was obviously not ready for boarding-school and suggested twice-weekly psychotherapy. Therapy lasted only eight months, but was most successful as Richard entered into it fully from the first. He talked freely about the family situation. Soon he came to appreciate his feelings of being left out of an exciting relationship between his parents, and his consequently conflicting feelings of love and hate towards them. He came to understand that his constant tiredness and excessive need for sleep was an effort to escape internal as well as external conflict. As Richard verbalized and faced up to his feelings and the part he played, overtly and in his phantasy, in family dramas, he became much more able to cope with the real world.

Although Richard would have benefited from further therapy, his mother, delighted with his improvement, still pressed for boarding-school. The clinic staff now felt Richard had improved sufficiently to be able to cope with boarding-school life. He was less dominated by sexual phantasies about his parents, he no longer wet the bed, he no longer needed excessive sleep, and he was generally happier and able to make friends. It was also clear that a reasonably pleasant school would be a more satisfactory environment for him. In the event, Richard settled well at boarding-school and was happy there.

## Henry: a Case of School Phobia

Sometimes a child's potential response to therapy is difficult to assess during preliminary diagnosis. Henry, for example, was eight-and-a-half years old when first referred to the clinic for his pathological fear of attending school. He was quiet and sullen with both the psychiatrist and the educational psychologist, but his school attendance improved somewhat and his mother was seen a few times at the clinic. She then stopped coming. However, a year later she was back, bringing Henry with her. He was now refusing to go to school at all.

Henry's mother at this point described many additional symptoms displayed by her son. He was very hypochondriacal about injuries and illnesses, both real and imaginary. He had a fear of ghosts and said he was frightened of going mad. He was scared of swimming and going on boats or ships. He was terrified of the dark and had had disturbed sleep since first starting school. His disturbed sleep was accompanied by enuresis, recurrent nightmares and sleepwalking. Perhaps not surprisingly, he insisted on sleeping with his parents. Though of average intelligence, he could not read at all. At the remedial reading class he had attended for a while he had spent his time drawing monsters who said, 'Go away.'

There were several possible immediate causes of Henry's school refusal. His regular teacher had left and he knew that the substitute teacher, whom he also liked, was only temporary. His two older brothers were for the moment out of work and of these his favourite was planning to join the navy. Henry feared the brother would be drowned. Recently he had been upset when his father had a slight accident. Also recently, he had killed his hamster by hugging it. In treatment all these incidents and situations soon emerged as relevant to the school refusal.

The first therapy session was not at all promising, as Henry seemed to experience the clinic and myself as an extension of the somewhat unsympathetic school he was supposed to attend. The head teacher there, in no way understanding of Henry's school phobia, had told his mother to spank him and send him back to school – in the first session Henry clearly expected me to do just this. He was on the verge of tears and would not look at me while I explained about the toys being for him and about the frequency of sessions. I verbalized his fear that I would punish him and force him to return to school. I explained I was interested in him very much as a person, rather than just interested in returning him to school. Henry then made his first comment, a scornful, 'My foot!' Then, however, he talked a little about school and a teacher called Miss Cross. I suggested he felt I was the cross Miss, so acknowledging his latent anger and fear of me. He nodded curtly in agreement. I sensed a slight relaxation in him at the end of the session, but wondered how long it would be before he could participate fully in therapy.

There was a dramatic difference in Henry in the very next session, three days later. He ran up to my room eagerly, looked through the box of toys previously ignored, and proceeded to model a house happily in plasticine, talking easily about it. Occasionally he looked at me trustingly. During the interval between the two sessions I had somehow stopped being a completely threatening person for him.

From then on the twice-weekly therapy progressed well. Henry now showed a continual wish for insights, even when acting wildly during the session. He talked readily about the things that worried him. At first the main themes were his strong feelings of persecution by the school and his own terrible fear of imminent disintegration. He revealed his persecuted feelings in drawings of horrific monsters capturing tiny children. After much discussion about the way he felt he was being captured by the terrifying school, and how this related to feelings he had had as a helpless baby, the monsters in his drawings became less horrific. Now he began to draw himself as a strong man – indicating a growing ability to cope with his fears.

Henry often acted out his terror of disintegration in the sessions. He had periods of confusion which no one else seemed to have noticed – probably, therefore, he only felt free to show them in therapy. As if illustrating his fear of disintegration, he would act as if he were literally coming apart, continually pulling up his trousers and always wearing two belts. His behaviour during the session sometimes seemed very mad. He would behave as if he and everything else were being fragmented into tiny bits that were then all over the place. So he ran about wildly, would not speak in sentences, and tried to stop me doing so. He said 'Eh? eh?' to almost everything I said. I tried repeating things until we were both in fact quite muddled. He contradicted everything I said, and then denied his own contradiction. He seemed to need to project his confusion on to me. For example, when I once talked of the muddle he was making of my words, he responded with, 'Muddle, puddle, you dirty girl.' I sensed one of the meanings behind this confusion of speech and action, namely his wish to get rid of his own frightening muddle inside and take in my more normal thinking processes in its place.

In spite of his frequent hyperactivity, Henry seemed to listen to me and to want to get something from me in the sessions. He appeared to be re-experiencing very early feelings from babyhood, of not being held or contained enough, both literally and metaphorically. After much interpretive work on these matters, his confusion and hyperactivity lessened considerably.

Within a year Henry had improved greatly in many areas. The most striking advance was probably in the quality of communication between us. Many of his symptoms had disappeared. He had by now gone back to a different, more sympathetic school, which gained also by never having been the focus of his earlier pathological fears. Henry still found it difficult to return to school after any break or holiday, but even that hesitation gradually vanished. As his confusion lessened, he quickly began to learn to read, and soon read fluently. His bed-wetting ceased, his sleepwalking recurred only occasionally. He also now managed to sleep in his own bedroom, again showing how much more secure he felt: he could now allow his parents to live their own lives.

At the time of writing, after two years of psychotherapy, Henry still has some phobias. He is still frightened of swimming, although he goes happily on ships and boats. He is apprehensive about going to secondary school and he still finds it difficult to go to school at all if his mother is ill. Generally speaking, however, therapy has helped him a great deal: he is warm and loving, and he can now face sadness and depression without being overwhelmed by it, or having to deny it completely, as he used to do.

## Co-operating with the Psychiatric Social Worker

The child psychotherapist works, of course, in close collaboration with all his colleagues. When a child is in therapy, however, collaboration is often closest with the psychiatric social worker. The usual arrangement is that the psychotherapist sees the child and the psychiatric social worker sees the parents. The two appointments may be simultaneous, for the convenience of the mother. If the patient is adolescent, however, it is often better for the appointments to be at different times. In this way the adolescent can feel more responsibility for his own treatment and, most important, the arrangement increases his sense of privacy.

Psychiatric social workers differ in their individual approach. Usually they like to work with both parents, but depending on the situation may see them separately or together. In practice often only the mother attends the clinic, as the father either genuinely cannot spare the time or prefers to hand over the whole problem to his wife.

The main emphasis of the work will be on the mother's own feelings and her view of the family situation. The mother's early history is, of course, relevant to her present attitudes and feelings and so has to be gradually evaluated and understood. The hope is that by carefully working through her own feelings with the P.S.W., the mother may achieve insight, together with altered possibilities for action. Change in the mother's attitudes may be fairly essential, to match up with changes in the child – otherwise she may find it difficult to cope with a previously submissive child who has become more openly rebellious, for example. Obviously, adult behaviour is no more solely ruled by common sense or conscious wishes than is child behaviour. Unconscious wishes and feelings have equally to be understood by adults before behaviour, thoughts and conscious emotions can be modified. Helping the adult to achieve insight, then, is the basic task of the psychiatric social worker. He will use the relationship built up between himself and his client as a basis for understanding his client's other relationships.

Here is a brief account of collaboration between child psychotherapist and psychiatric social worker on the two sides of an actual case.

Laurie was eleven when he began psychotherapy at the clinic. The immediately precipitating factors were his anxiety and nightmares following a minor car accident, but subsequently other problems emerged. Laurie himself was of superior intelligence, did well at school work, but was otherwise very immature. He was content to let his mother make decisions for him and he had no friends of his own. Laurie was the next to youngest in a large family, most of whom were already grown up. His mother, partly consciously and partly unconsciously, was attempting to keep Laurie and his younger sister as babies.

In therapy, Laurie was at first unable to express any aggression or even to admit having any wishes at all of his own. This position changed under therapy, but still he could not express anger when his mother refused to allow him to do something he wanted to do – for example, to take part in a school journey. However, Laurie did at least now realize that he felt thwarted.

Our work had to be two-fold. Laurie had to be helped to understand that his perfectly normal desires connected with growing up and natural independence were not automatically equivalent to attacks on his parents. At the same time his mother had to be helped to see that her over-protectiveness arose not only from genuine love, but also from her wish to keep the two youngsters as babies. As Laurie succeeded in expressing more independent wishes, his mother also began to change. She could begin to allow him to use his new powers of judgment, to travel alone, to choose some of his own clothes and spare-time activities. Probably little could have been achieved without a simultaneous and complementary change in son and mother. Without increased understanding on both sides, pathological aspects of the relationship would have persisted.

## Other Ways of Helping Disturbed Children

Individual psychotherapy lasting months or years cannot, for the foreseeable future, be available for all children who actually need it. Even if training facilities were increased, there would still not be enough child psychotherapists to meet the considerable demand. Other ways, therefore, have to be found of helping children with problems. Sometimes, indeed, these supplementary methods of helping may be not just expedients, but in fact the best way of working; in other cases, however, they must unfortunately be seen as only second-best to the unavailable child psychotherapy. In these circumstances of large demand and small supply, cases for individual psychotherapy must be carefully chosen.

Sometimes very short-term psychotherapy, possibly lasting only a few sessions, can be of great help. This holds true when the child is aware of the problem, the difficulty is actually near conscious level and there is good co-operation. If a child or adolescent is seen at a time of crisis, when he very much wishes to focus and work on his problem, it can be that long-term psychotherapy is unnecessary.

A further approach is through family therapy, where all or some members of the family are seen together as a group, either for just a few sessions, or sometimes for extended periods. The family group will include the actual 'patient' referred: it can help him as well as the others when inter-relationships between all of them are untangled and examined.

Group psychotherapy with children or young people not related to each other is another possibility. Such groups may not be as economical with regard to professional time as is sometimes assumed, but they can be helpful, especially with more superficial problems.

A child may be helped indirectly when only the parents are helped, if they come to understand themselves and change their ways – this holds good even if the child has specific problems in his own right. Ideally, however, skilled help should be available to both child and parents.

All these various methods are psycho-dynamically based,

but sometimes we must think, too, about changes in the environment. Occasionally a change of school to one more suited to a particular child's needs is sufficient. When we are faced with a very disturbed family situation, sometimes the only answer is fostering or placement in a boarding-school, a hostel or other residential centre. In these cases supportive therapy may well be needed to help the child with his feelings about the change, with his phantasies about the family, why he is leaving them and so on. Again, sometimes a deprived family is helped by being given better housing. Apart from helping materially, the change may relieve the mother's depression or loneliness, for example, although some casework is likely to be also necessary.

Yet other methods of help can concern and deal with a specific symptom a child is suffering, for example, speech therapy, remedial reading or writing.

## Conclusion

This account is my view of my own work in a child guidance clinic. I must stress my conviction that individual psychotherapy is often the only real answer when seeking to help a disturbed child. Psychotherapists do differ among themselves, but all have a great deal in common, namely their orientation towards the unconscious meaning of behaviour, thoughts and feelings as the crux of any solution. Apart from his own treating of individual children, the child psychotherapist's knowledge of child development and unconscious processes enables him to make a valuable advisory contribution to the work of a clinic generally, and to many other institutions and settings concerned with the education and welfare of young people.

# Chapter Four

# *Child Psychotherapy in a Day Unit*

## by Dilys Daws

Chapter 3 described how the child guidance clinic is organized and how the child psychotherapist functions in that setting. This chapter describes the practice of psychotherapy in a day unit, where children spend the whole day in the building in which they receive therapy. The effects of the setting on the children are discussed, and something of the meaning of the framework in which therapy takes place emerges. M.B., D.D.

---

I work as a child psychotherapist in a day unit connected with a child guidance clinic. As in the clinic itself, the therapeutic staff of the Unit is a team comprising a psychiatrist, a psychiatric social worker, an educational psychologist and a child psychotherapist. In my Unit they all work part-time, and the staff also consists of three teachers, employed by the I.L.E.A., together with three assistants who are employed by the Health Service. Finally, there is a full-time secretary, a caretaker and a cook, all of whom are also employees of the Health Service.

The Unit is situated in a large, old house. It is a comfortable and attractive setting for the work, very much like a small school – technically, the Day Unit is in fact a hospital-school. The school, then, is made up of three groups of children, each taken by a teacher and an assistant together. The groups are small, averaging six children at any one point. The pupils may be full- or only part-time. Groups are arranged roughly according to age, the ranges being from around 4 – 7 years, 7 – 10 years and 10 – 14 years.

Children are originally referred by an outside psychiatrist. They are then seen by the psychiatrist at the Day Unit for further diagnosis. In particular, an assessment of their suitability for the Day Unit is made, a procedure very similar to that of the Child Guidance Clinic. As in that setting, parents are seen by the psychiatrist and the psychiatric social worker. The parents are able to discuss their child's problems, and the way in which the Day Unit might help him is explained. Again as in the clinic, the child is tested by the psychologist to discover where his strengths and weaknesses lie in cognitive ability. Psychotherapy may be recommended at this stage, or the decision may be deferred until after the child has spent some time in the Day Unit.

The Day Unit is a short-term placement intended for children who have broken down in the normal school setting. These may be relatively normal children, who can be helped over their difficulties and so return fairly rapidly to normal schooling; or they may be children who will need special education and care of one kind or another until they are ready to be placed permanently in an appropriate type of special school or other institution. The more normal children are often admitted at a point of crisis where they are not only vulnerable, but at the same time particularly accessible to help. They and their parents can often be reached quickly and effectively and the child returned to normal school within a short time. Children who are more disturbed and, perhaps, come from a disturbed home setting, will need a longer period before the organized and containing framework of the Day Unit can begin to help them.

Some of our children are school-refusers. These children are often given a time limit of stay at the Unit, but in practice they are able to return to their own schools surprisingly quickly, taking into account the lengthy time they may have been refusing or truanting. Others are children behaving unmanageably in their own schools, who perhaps only attend the Unit part-time; these go back to their own schools for the rest of the week, so that the link with a more normal environment may not be lost. The balance of normal school attendance is gradually increased, until they are finally back full-time at their neighbourhood school.

Although the method of attending two schools does have the advantage of maintaining contact with a normal environment, we also find that it creates special problems. Some children find that the relief of spending part of the week in the understanding and sheltered atmosphere of the Day Unit is so great that it more than compensates for these additional problems; others find the strain of maintaining relationships in two places too great. Nevertheless, on balance, not only does the contained setting of the Unit help these acting-out children to control their own violent impulses, but their own school can more easily find the resources to cope with them for only part of a week. So the child usually finds himself more welcome at his own school than when it was bearing the full brunt of his disruptive behaviour.

Some children undergo a prolonged diagnostic and observation spell at the Unit. Diagnosis is not always easy with, say, a non-communicating child – the difficulty is in establishing exactly what the non-communication represents. Is the child severely subnormal, or psychotic? Is the disturbance primarily an emotional one? Or is there a combination of these and perhaps still other factors? Some very confused 'infants' settle down rather rapidly in the nurturing atmosphere of the youngest group and their potential for communication and learning quickly appears. Other very deprived children blossom emotionally and make intellectual strides in our special atmosphere. Even after improvement is manifest, such children may be kept for a consolidation period, before moving them on to suitable permanent placement.

Much supportive and interpretive work is demanded of the psychiatric social worker with the parents of all our children, to help them to come to terms with the nature of their child's illness and to support them through the process of realization. Work with parents, as well as helping them in their own right, can of course directly benefit the children. Many subnormal children behave in a very disturbed way, partly because of the additional confusion of unrealistic demands on them by parents and others; these children also react to the parents' distress in the face of the deficiencies of their child. Parents have to be helped to look at their child's capacities realistically and then taught to provide the sort of care and understanding the child needs. As the child's confusion and disturbance lessens, he in fact becomes able to make fuller use of his limited abilities. The improvement is then both rewarding and comforting to the parents.

One sad aspect of working in a setting so geared to the individual difficulties of chaotic children is that there is often no place really suitable to send them on to permanently. This is not merely a reflection of the difficulty of parting with children with whom so much has been done, it is part of the reality of how few long-term facilities we have – for example, for autistic or psychotic children.

Other children worked with successfully at the Unit are those of apparently normal intelligence, who have been quite unable to learn. In a small non-threatening environment, learning becomes possible. The child's particular learning problems are isolated by psychological testing, and appropriate remedial teaching can then be given in a way he can utilize. The child who has, as it were, been unable to find a place for himself in the large classes of a normal school, who has been unable to make contact either with the teacher or with the work offered, can find his anxieties diminished in our simplified setting. He is then able to master the symbolic structures of numbers or letters.

## The Psychotherapy

Against this background of the regular day-to-day working of the Unit we can consider the practice of psychotherapy. I work in ways basically similar to those described in Chapters 1 and 3, in that I see children individually and privately in my therapy room. I see them at agreed times, usually once or twice weekly, at a set time and for a fixed length of time, just as in a child guidance clinic. The difference is this: the child who is my patient and I myself each know that the other is there, in the same building, at other times of the week. We see, hear and know about each other. In various ways we make use of this extra knowledge.

In some ways the process of transference could be upset by the situation. It must confuse and disturb a child to meet his therapist in the corridor and so have to confront the feelings that he currently associates with her in his treatment. Conversely, one could argue that treatment is enhanced by this being together under the same roof. The general, diffuse therapeutic environment perhaps supports the intense and otherwise isolated experience of individual psychotherapy.

In an environment that is therapeutic in its totality I have to ask myself what my *specific* therapeutic role is. I formulate this as making the patient's unconscious processes conscious, and as helping him to take responsibility for his own emotions. By recognizing the role he is playing in his relationships with others he can understand the contribution he makes to his own external reality. I feel these tasks can best be accomplished in a private and confidential setting, one that is protected as far as possible from all intrusions. Personal psychotherapy involves the transference of often painful feelings to the therapist and the projection of fearful anxieties. These best and properly belong with her in the setting of her room. For this reason I try to have no contact with my patients outside their sessions other than through a smile of recognition or greeting as we pass each other. Only exceptionally do I enter the classrooms during school time. Even such fleeting contacts can make it more difficult for the child to use me purely as a neutral reflection of his own emotional states.

One child, Robert, finds beginnings and endings difficult. It is painful for him both to come to his session and to leave again at the end. For him therefore it is very hard if I suddenly turn up and intrude myself on his thoughts. He will often retaliate later by rushing down the corridor to my room and knocking on the door while I am with another patient.

Some children feel doubly disappointed by the fact that they know I am in the building and yet do not come to special festivities. All children in treatment explore to what extent their therapist remains only as someone who reacts and interprets within a closely defined setting. Many children regret in a general sense that their therapist does not come, loaded with gifts, to their birthday party. In the Day Unit, however, they may specifically feel that I reject an important part of them, by choosing to stay away from the birthday or Christmas parties within the Unit. I agree this holding-back could be both interpreted and felt as a rejection of the communal friendship offered me as part of the network of relationships within the school, but I feel too that I belong as a therapist separately and privately to several of the children. By going to one child's party (or to a general party) I would in a sense betray the private relationship with the others.

The situation I describe arises in institutions where most of the children have individual therapy available to them, either with me or with other outside therapists. It is perhaps more appropriate in schools for maladjusted children to work, as many therapists there do, through a therapeutic, less intense relationship with many or all the children in the school – as well as in the more structured psychotherapeutic relationship with specially chosen children. I believe that my keeping to an 'isolationist' and precisely defined way of working accords with requiring of my patients that they come and go at set times, and do not intrude on other patients' time with me.

However, it remains obvious to the children that I do function as a regular part of the Unit and that I have a continuous relationship with their teachers and the other staff. I believe, though, that the children usually trust me to keep the content of the therapy sessions confidential. I always make a point of telling the child that I do, although emphasizing that I do discuss with the teachers 'how he is getting on'. I also use this phrase at times in connection with my contact with parents. Where I do not obtain trust, I feel this to be part of the psychopathology of the child that currently requires working on. Curiously enough, my experience is that although children frequently see me talking to their teachers, there is less fear of my betrayal of confidences to them than to the parents with whom I have little direct contact. I think this shows that even though psychotherapy takes place in a setting alongside other adults of great importance to the child, the psychoanalytic aspect of the setting is nevertheless felt to be quite separate. So the therapy room is maintained as the place where the child is able to transfer and project feelings deriving from early primitive relationships, and not from the immediate feelings that are generated in and by the school. This finding should also be of comfort to parents of children in treatment, who themselves often feel very vulnerable about the material their child is presenting to his therapist.

That treatment takes place within a co-existence of therapist and teachers is nevertheless a situation which produces much useful material. Some children easily accept the position of different workers having a common aim; others need to split the staff and assign them different psychological roles. We can sometimes see a parallel in the roles assigned to us with those the parents have adopted in their marriage. Or sometimes we feel that the child is more consciously trying to play us off one against the other, as perhaps he is doing at home. Given good co-operation between therapist and teacher, we adults can observe what is happening without being damaged by it and our mutual involvement can increase the child's feeling of support.

The feelings that patients have about the building in which the Unit is housed are also worth noting. Only the therapy room, not the building as a whole, can be used as a container of the intense feelings about therapy; but remaining in the same building, as the therapist does, probably supports and extends the therapy.

While most children in time learn to cope adequately with literally bumping into me at odd times in the Unit, I have found that many are quite unable to tolerate seeing me getting into my car and driving away. Now I always try to avoid leaving the premises at times when my patients may be outside the building. Separations are very much a part of the basic material that properly belongs inside the sessions. There is great need to work on the material of ending a session and on the longer holiday breaks, where primitive feelings of abandonment must be dealt with. Gratuitously to arouse those deep feelings about separation outside treatment, feelings that of course have been transferred to the therapist, is quite unfair to the patient.

The relationships between those children who are in therapy with the same therapist are of great interest. In clinics, waiting-room relationships are often formed – the special recognition of fellow patients. In the Day Unit, however, fellow patients may have to sit side by side all day in the classroom. Rivalry with the other child or children involved can be expressed quite specifically. Two of my patients come to mind as rivals, and also somehow as comrades-in-arms: each has once invaded the other's session to give me an urgent message about whether he could or could not come to his own session later. Particular difficulties arise when children know that other children have more, or fewer, sessions than they. Roger, in the youngest group, was aware when he began twice-weekly therapy with me that other children in his group only came once a week. At first he repeatedly looked through the toys in his drawer and anxiously asked, 'How much do the other children have?' I said I thought that it was how much *time* they had with me that was worrying him. When his question nevertheless persisted, I said that perhaps he felt his greed for more of my time than anyone else was so great that I had not been strong enough to resist it. He was visibly relieved by this comment and was able to begin playing with the toys.

Harold, on the other hand, was full of delight at the sight of his drawerful of toys and asked me who the other drawers belonged to. I did not tell him. To be on the safe side, he bombarded the outside of all of them with his toy cars.

Robert, a boy of ten, is bitter that I see another boy from his group immediately after one of his own sessions. He threatened to bring a penknife to kill him. The problem of sharing is not just one of sharing a professional worker. It is one which evokes all the early intense feelings of anger or despair at having to share the mother, which, incidentally, even an only child can experience. These infantile feelings are experienced more strongly in the day unit situation than in the child guidance clinic, where they may well remain solely as fantasy* material in the child's mind, and not be something the child is actually faced with daily in a real situation.

Although most children in the Unit do have individual therapy, the few who do not must presumably have fantasies about what therapy is and why they have not been chosen. I think also that as a known and daily visible therapist, I must figure in the fantasies of children in therapy outside. In our own rather intense atmosphere where nearly everyone is in therapy, there is ample opportunity for expression of feelings about me, by my patients, to other children. One girl, who was in therapy elsewhere, asked my name. When I told her, she exclaimed, 'Oh, you're the one that Martin *hates*!'

Knowing that I saw other children from his class group, Roger, aged five years, virtually referred himself: he asked his teacher if he could come to see me. It was, in fact, some time before I felt it was possible to start treatment, as it was likely that he would leave the Unit at any moment if his family decided to move from the area. When it was finally established that we had a year in which to work, we started

*The spelling 'fantasy' is used to denote conscious fantasy and 'phantasy' to denote unconscious phantasy.

therapy. Roger and I were both confirmed in our hope that he was a child who could use this form of help. However, he and I have had to work within the limits of knowing there is only one year to use; for any real chance of sorting out the profound confusion and despair underlying the outward impression of a charming and verbal little boy, several years of treatment would be needed.

Difficult or disruptive behaviour before or after a therapy session can be thought of as 'acting-out' in relation to the therapy and is often disturbing to the classroom situation. However, it can be picked up as a heightened experience of what the child's disturbances are about. Jane, whose impulses were often uncontrollable, needed actually to walk down the corridor to my room to make sure it was not her day for treatment. Martin dramatized his difficulty in coming for treatment in scenes in the classroom beforehand. With both these children, the teachers were understandingly involved and able to help them.

It is of course unfortunate if feelings that only belong in therapy spill out and disturb the classroom and other children. Robert, who often feels trapped in the therapy room with his own destructiveness, calls outside the door for help from his teacher. I interpret these fears, and also suggest he keeps all this upheaval contained within the therapy room. He then threatens he will scream when he gets back to the classroom. He is aware of my feelings of helplessness that my interpretations cannot follow him to the classroom, that I have been able to give him so little in the session that it will not last after he leaves my room. In therapy, one does hope to keep the expression of violent feelings contained exclusively within the session. One hopes, too, that the child may become easier and happier at home; if the child's behaviour at home is for a time *more* disturbed as a result of therapy, the therapist is grateful for parents' forbearance and understanding. When a child in treatment at the unit behaves in these ways, it comes over to the therapist as a very tantalizing and intangible form of communication. The behaviour may also be, and in fact may be intended to be, destructive of the relation between therapist and teacher (or therapist and parent, and so on), and even more so of the reputation of psychotherapy itself. It can be the means for a child to denigrate his treatment (so that perhaps it stops or cannot touch him); it can be the way for a child, who feels hopeless of ever having his destructive impulses sufficiently contained, to demonstrate how apparently impossible this is.

There is a particular need to try to leave the patient at the end of the session feeling that his anxieties have been relieved and dealt with appropriately by the treatment. To this end, some children may need a preparation time before therapy and a cooling-off period, a time for reflection, afterwards. The time it takes to walk from the therapy room back to the classroom is not sufficient for this. I feel that to be one of the greatest drawbacks in practising psychotherapy in the place where the child spends his day. There is, so to speak, no space round the therapy. Time spent in preparation for a session, and in quiet reflection afterwards, can be thought of as a vital part of the analytic process. Just as the time spent in sleepily digesting his milk, before actually falling asleep, can be an important part of the feeding experience for a baby.

Another limitation that I feel in working in a day unit is the lack of involvement with parents. Although in a child guidance clinic the therapist may have little or no direct contact with parents, as long as a child is actually brought to treatment by a parent the glimpse one has in the waiting-room can be very revealing. One can form some idea of the state of health of the parent and of his or her relationship with the child. Furthermore, the administrative route into therapy for children who enter the Unit before starting treatment is a less direct one, and may involve the parents less. They may not have specifically sought treatment at all – they may not have known it even exists. It comes as part of the package deal offered by the Unit. The contacts parents initiate with the Unit, and enquiries about their child's progress, may centre only on the teachers and the classroom. One could however speculate whether lack of specific support and interest at home in the therapy is a real drawback for the child, or whether the supportive Unit entirely replaces this need.

There is also a temptation in the Unit setting to by-pass hostile parents – that is, to treat children whose parents have grudgingly agreed to allow therapy, but whom one knows would never actually make a weekly journey with a child to a clinic. In our recent experience of the case of Rochelle, a girl with school phobia, the treatment was broken off very soon after she returned to normal school, although we felt she still very much needed to continue in therapy. Her family would not tolerate the idea of treatment when it was separated from the Day Unit.

Sometimes, of course, it can be an advantage that it is not the parents who have the responsibility of bringing a difficult child to treatment. Parents who are contending with their own resistances, or who cannot contain their child's resistance to coming, are spared this ordeal. However, the onus of getting the child to the therapy room in the Unit is then put on teachers. Sometimes this arrangement can bring up issues damaging or at least irrelevant to the current relationship between the teacher and the pupil; furthermore, a child with intense resistance to treatment may deal with it by refusing to come to the Day Unit at all.

I mentioned earlier that not all our children are in therapy. The ones who are not are mainly in the youngest group, which is in many ways a nurturing group. It seems necessary for some of the children in this group to go through an almost primary nurturing experience, with the opportunity for considerable regression, before they reach a point where psychotherapy becomes appropriate. Only then can the conscious and unconscious processes be linked together and worked through. The healing work of integration here begins through an initial experience of the containing environment, before the raw wounds of early deprivation and anxieties are uncovered.

The difficulty in differentiating between psychotherapy and the therapeutic environment as a whole is a stumbling block, both in theory and practice. Teachers and therapist may as people be happy to know that a child is getting better through their combined efforts, but it is nevertheless important in allocating the therapist's time to know which children have been helped and in what way by individual therapy. The Day Unit as a whole provides an enabling environment which helps the child towards the next stage in life: psychotherapy hopefully accelerates a process of integration begun by the Unit. It should also help the patient to take inside himself a better conscious understanding and insight into his own feelings. And by a process similar to that of weaning a baby, the treatment should work towards its own termination, leaving a sense of enrichment inside the patient.

Some patients have particular difficulty in admitting to themselves that they are having therapy, even when they are to some extent participating and benefiting from it. Being in a day unit can paradoxically help them to hide the fact of therapy from themselves. Asking the patient to come for treatment at half-term when the Unit is officially closed is one way of sharply separating treatment from school. To some children the Day Unit when closed is a frighteningly dead place, while others are thrilled (perhaps too much so) to be selected to share the Unit with me in the holidays. Some older ones are able to concentrate on the work of treatment and are grateful not to have an interruption, but Martin, the boy who can only grudgingly bring himself to therapy, still maintains that I owe him the tube fare for the one time I did ask him to come at half-term.

The difficulty for the patient is in his own formation of a concept of what has led to his cure. This concept may be important in determining in later life what sort of help he seeks if he is in need.

A related problem is the matter of continuing treatment after a child officially leaves the Day Unit. One often feels that a child is at the stage where he can cope well externally with a normal or special school, but still needs to continue in treatment to progress psychologically. When Oscar left the Unit to go to an Educationally Subnormal school, excellent arrangements were made to bring him once a week to me for therapy. Yet for this child the effect seemed devastating: coming into the building only to see *me* seemed to underline for him his exclusion from the Unit and his beloved teachers. He was barely able to make use of therapy for some time. Oscar is the eldest of five children. His 'exclusion' from the Unit seemed to him to link very closely with his feelings of disillusionment as his mother replaced him with other babies. From one point of view, the circumstances of the case proved to be the way to get to the heart of this central problem. My feeling grows, however, that when therapy has been so intertwined with a therapeutic environment, it cannot be easily disentangled.

With some children, then, it seems better to terminate therapy when they leave the Day Unit, although in other circumstances one would prefer to continue. In this way they can at least make a fresh start, leaving their problems behind them, so to speak, in the building of the Day Unit.

The termination of Day Unit attendance can be difficult

also for parents. When we told Martin's parents that we felt the time had come for him to leave the Unit and end treatment, they agreed and were appreciative of the changes in Martin. He had been excluded from three different schools before coming to the Unit; now he was being welcomed back full-time to his primary school. His mother was, nevertheless, worried about losing the support of knowing that the Unit shared her concern about Martin. She said, 'I thought the Day Unit would always be there.' She also felt bereaved of her relationship with the psychiatric social worker. In fact, she and the social worker do keep some telephone and written contact, and this has helped the parents support Martin in his full-time return to normal school. Where parents need continued help and support themselves, they are usually transferred back to the local clinic which originally referred the family.

In Martin's case, we terminated his treatment in a way new to me. Through many of the stages of his treatment, Martin had had difficulty in acknowledging either his need for it or the help it undoubtedly gave him. By reason of the second circumstance, he was unable to face the feelings connected with the end of treatment and missed several sessions. I then arranged a meeting which included Martin and his parents, the social worker, Martin's class teacher and myself. At this meeting we traced Martin's progress over the years he had been in the Day Unit and weighed up his achievements. The family, as a whole, were able to look at the work that had been done and perhaps in a way take back the responsibility of him to themselves. This is not how I would normally choose to end treatment; but for a child who seemed unable to do the work of termination internally, a public acknowledgment that treatment had taken place seemed to be a possible alternative. The week after this meeting, Martin was able to come to my room for a short part of his final session and made plasticine letters forming the words GOODBYE DAWS.

When the continuation of therapy seems desirable, and is possible, I now transfer patients to the parent clinic and am fortunate to have this facility. It means that I can separate off what the child has gained and achieved in the therapeutic environment of the Unit from the work on the continuing internal problems in the child. Some children manage this transfer very easily and resume therapy in another building and a new room, focussing on the continuity of therapist and their familiar toys. For others the change of place seems to be too much, and for a time at least the containing function of the treatment disintegrates. To some autistic children, places and objects sometimes appear more important than people. To the autistic part of many of us, our security may be symbolized by a place or an object. I am reminded of Esther Bick's observation that some babies can travel the world as long as their mother is with them, while others disintegrate if they cannot sleep in their own familiar cot.

One of the satisfying aspects of the Day Unit is working alongside teachers who are with the children all day. It can be supportive for teachers and therapist alike to share the burden of working with disturbed children. In many ways teachers have the more difficult role in containing several disturbed children throughout a whole day – and without what I feel is not only the tool but the protection of psychoanalytic interpretation. It can be easier for the therapist to cope with bizarre or violent behaviour by confronting it directly for what it is and encapsulating it within the therapy. The teacher's job is perhaps to manage the disturbed behaviour in such a way that the child feels himself and his sickness accepted, but then additionally to help the child relate to his group in the most normal way the child is capable of.

I consider my role in the Day Unit to include discussing with other staff the unconscious processes underlying how the child is behaving at any one time. This can be done without infringing the confidentiality of the children. The teachers with whom I work of course do not need advice from me on handling a child as such, but I hope that their own intuition is enhanced by a shared insight into the unconscious processes at work within their pupils. Furthermore, I think people working with disturbed children find it helpful to be able to describe the impact that the children have on them, and the ways in which the child's behaviour resounds within themselves. When a teacher appreciates objectively how a child is aiming for his own personal vulnerable spot, he is already armed against the attack.

In working together, teachers and therapists are not only aiming at forming a solid framework to support and contain disturbed children, who try to divide adults and make them separate containers for the irreconcilable parts of their own personalities, but they also enjoy the spirit of co-operation in the endeavour of helping these young people grow and develop.

My problem is really that of how much information to share. In the area of what comes from me, I have perhaps solved the problem. I think I am able to communicate an idea of the progress and psychic health of the child without betraying the secrets of the consulting room. It is, in fact, incumbent on me to relay my frequent opinion of the state of integration and inner strength a child has reached, as part of the information on which decisions about new schools or placements are made.

The greater difficulty for me is in deciding how much information to take in; and this problem is itself two-fold. First, there is information which comes from the teachers of the groups and, via the social worker, information which parents like me to have about what is happening at home. Part of the fascination in practising psychoanalytic therapy is the wanting to know all about a person. In my view it is also necessary to know the major reality framework in which the child lives out his life. At times, however, too much awareness of details of what is actually happening outside in the objective world can blur and distort the therapist's perception of what the patient is actually communicating or projecting at any particular moment. The vital material to be worked on is often not the dramatic events actually taking place now, but the forgotten conflicts of many years ago.

The second source of information from outside comes directly from the child himself. I have already described situations where I feel that parts of the child's behaviour in the Day Unit relate to me as well as to his teachers and the group he is in. I am made much more aware of all his difficulties in his school group than I would be if he were in a distant school. Often I think I am meant to take note of these. Sometimes, in any case, I take classroom difficulties as my failure to contain the relevant feelings within treatment. Sometimes I think the child specifically *intends* the failure to be seen as mine. At yet other times, of course, a child overwhelmed by passionate unconscious feelings is unable to distinguish where he can appropriately unload these. In the early stages, the whole of the Unit often has to be used as the container for the devastation inside him.

In conclusion, I hope to have presented a picture of the week-to-week experience of practising psychotherapy in a day unit, one which might both encourage and at the same time caution anyone considering providing therapy in such a setting. I have dwelt at length on the technical details of how I organize the setting for psychotherapy because I feel the administrative framework to be an important basis of therapy. It at least partly determines the quality of the therapeutic work which can take place within it. In the same way I feel that mothering is experienced by a baby not only in the sense of being physically fed and emotionally loved, but also in being offered an organized framework in which to feel secure.

My thanks go to Dr Margaret Collins, until her retirement Medical Director of the Day Unit, and the other colleagues with whom I have worked in the Day Unit.

# Chapter Five
# *The Child Psychotherapist in a Day Centre for Young Children and Parents*
## by Mary Boston

This chapter describes the work of a psychotherapist in another kind of day unit. We have seen suggestions in previous chapters that our attention in the future may need to be directed much more towards support for parent-and-child, in particular for the mother vulnerable to isolation and depression – such support may be vital to the promotion of healthy emotional development. At the day centre for pre-school children described here, an attempt is made to offer help to parents in the company of their children. M.B., D.D.

---

First we will look at some of the problems of children attending the Day Centre.

**Anxious Children**

Some children are excessively anxious and literally cling to their mothers, perhaps making nursery school attendance impossible.

Tessa, a pretty, wide-eyed, soft-spoken little girl of two-and-a-half, was so clinging that her mother was unable to go anywhere without her, even to the toilet. She would not sleep alone and also had temper tantrums. Six-year-old Nita was similarly clinging and rather slow in her speech development. She had a feeding problem which seemed to date back to a traumatic weaning from the breast, when she refused to take a bottle. Sally, at two, had become phobic about dolls and about her own feet. Angela was another child inseparable from her mother, but she was aggressive towards her, scratching and attacking her in a way which her mother felt unable to cope with – Angela, in fact, partly belongs to the next category.

## Children Difficult to Manage

Peter, in addition to being excessively clinging to his mother, appeared to have an insufficient sense of danger. This led to frequent falls. He would also climb up on to furniture and fling himself off into space, calling his mother's name and apparently expecting her to catch him. Her anxiety was such that she always had to be there, ready. Leonard, at four, was brought because of his aggression and temper tantrums, in which he provoked his mother into loss of control. Andrew was overactive, always on the go, never still, wandering off and never seeming able to concentrate on anything. He would even get up in the night and wreak havoc downstairs while his parents were asleep. His mother was quite worn out and at the end of her tether. Darren's mother, on the other hand, complained that her son was not active enough – he tended to sit around and was slow in talking, as well as clinging compulsively to her.

Sometimes the main difficulty is presented in toilet training. Children may be referred for functional diarrhoea or soiling and for other physical symptoms.

## Children Retarded in Development

Another fairly large group of children referred to the Day Centre are those with delayed development, particularly youngsters with slow or absent speech. These are children who may be slow in reaching all the various milestones of development – by the age of three or four they are still not talking. They are frequently referred to us for investigation. Attendance at the Day Centre can provide a period of extended observation so that the situation may be assessed.

Joseph was a very handsome little boy of two-and-a-half, whose movements were well co-ordinated and who looked intelligent, yet was not speaking at all. He also had some peculiar mannerisms. He would be preoccupied for long periods with small things such as a drip of water. He tended to avoid looking at people. He was admitted to the Day Centre for extended observation, so that the range and manner of his retardation could be assessed. Some children referred with this type of retarded development have proved to be autistic.

Other children have a more specifically linguistic problem. For example, Doris, not quite four, had hardly any words, yet in other respects her development was normal. The psychologist assessed her intelligence as dull, but by no means subnormal. She responded adequately to adults and children and did not show autistic features. Interestingly, Doris could call her little sister by name but had no name for herself.

Derek, on the other hand, had normal speech development, but refused to speak at all at school. He was also quite mute at the Day Centre for a long period. A small percentage of children referred have been complete 'elective mutes'. A case from another hospital is described later in the book (Chapter 8).

## Emotionally Deprived Children

We have had a small number of very deprived children who have lacked consistent emotional care and adequate relationships.

Billy was one such. He lived in a children's home and attended the Day Centre by reason of his very unresponsive and difficult behaviour. He was intellectually retarded and showed autistic features.

## Problem Infants

Some under-twos have attended the Day Centre with their mothers, sometimes while still in-patients at the main hospital. Problems usually centred on severe feeding difficulties, resulting in failure to thrive. Sometimes there was the danger of battering.

Melissa was referred at the age of four months, because her mother could not stand her crying and was frightened of her own aggression towards the baby. Helen's mother was worried both about her feelings towards her baby and because at one year the baby showed no signs of attempting to crawl. She would only sit and not attempt to move forward to grasp objects. She did not seem backward in other respects, however.

We see, then, that a cross-section of children present a wide cross-section of problems. As regards their families some rough groupings are possible. There are those where the child's illness or handicap has had widespread repercussions on family relationships. The parents or the siblings are under stress and the situation produces marital problems and depression in the parents. In other cases it is really the parent or parents who are the ill ones in the first place, while the child seems relatively normal. Most families come into a potentially normal group but there may be particular problems in inter-relationships or specific difficulties in defined areas. In families where there is an actual failure of love and care, the task of getting to the Day Centre often proves, by definition, impossible.

## The Organization of the Day Centre

Psychotherapy with individual children, as described in previous chapters, is work which is painstaking and very time-consuming. Only a comparatively small proportion of children can receive such individual help. Attention is therefore increasingly directed to a consideration of how the psychotherapist's skills might be used to benefit a wider number of children. Can the child psychotherapist, in particular, make any contribution to the prevention of mental disturbance in children?

We have already seen that much of the disturbed behaviour of school-age children has its roots in very early childhood. Basic personality is shaped in the early years by a complex interaction of constitutional and environmental factors, the most important of the second being family relationships. As we saw, disturbances in those all-important early relationships can arise from many sources – illness or difficult temperament in the baby, illness or depression in the parents, temporary domestic upheavals and crises at critical points of development. Sometimes personality difficulties stemming from the parents' childhood influence the kind of relationships they form with their own children. Early disturbances in family relationships, of whatever origin, may build up as the years go by into persisting unfavourable patterns of interaction. These especially can lead to more enduring difficulties.

By the time therapists see children, vicious cycles have often already been established and long-term help already is essential. If we turn our sights towards the prevention of mental ill health, it is logical to consider the situation of the pre-school child and his parents, to see whether some intervention at an earlier stage of development could be helpful. This kind of consideration, urged by the paucity of existing facilities for disturbed young children, has led to the experimental establishment, in London and other parts of the country, of centres where children can attend for several hours daily (Bentovim and Boston, 1973).

I shall now describe such a day centre for disturbed young children and their parents and discuss in particular the contribution which the child psychotherapist makes to its work. My grateful acknowledgements are due here to Dr A. Bentovim and the staff at Great Ormond Street Hospital for permission to describe the early years of what is very much a collective venture. However, owing to organizational changes in the course of time, this account does not necessarily portray the current situation.

The Day Centre in question came to be established at a paediatric hospital, where a large proportion of the referrals were under six years old. Apart from those referred directly for psychiatric assessment, many of the patients who presented physical problems were found also to be emotionally disturbed. These families were therefore also referred for psychiatric help. The Day Centre, an extension of the Psychiatric Department within the hospital grounds, provides a setting where observation of problems can be made over a period of time and the most appropriate form of help carefully assessed. It also attempts to provide a therapeutic environment which will give emotional support to children and parents in difficulty.

The Centre is run very much as a nursery group, with the usual kinds of nursery school equipment. But there is a very important difference: parents are encouraged to stay with the children, and the staff work with both children and parents. This arrangement obviously has repercussions on the pattern of attendance at the Centre. For example, it proved impractical for most mothers of these very young children to come all day every day, particularly where long journeys were involved. The majority of families therefore attend one or two days a week, from 10.00 a.m. to 3.30 p.m.

There is also a higher staff-child ratio here than in the usual nursery. Each family is assigned to a particular worker, who is responsible for two, or at the most three, families on any one day. Every day about eight to ten patients attend together with a parent. Usually this is the mother, though fathers are invited to come where possible. Pre-school brothers and sisters also come in many instances, and during school holidays older siblings sometimes come too.

The group present on any particular day contains children of a variety of ages and diagnoses. Where, earlier, children had been grouped according to the kind of problem they presented (autistic, aggressive, infant and so on), the too great homogeneity in the group had appeared to lead to strain on both workers and parents. That was especially true when the group consisted entirely of autistic or aggressive children. On the other hand, there *are* other difficulties with heterogeneous grouping: it is sometimes not easy to fit some children into particular groups.

Although the parents are invited to remain at the Centre, the programme for the day is organized so that parents do have some time apart from their children. Equally, of course, mothers are encouraged to spend time playing and interacting with their children. Parents, children and workers all take meals together, but there is a parents' room where mothers can go for breaks. In this way the over-clinging child can gradually get used to short separations. The mothers can relax and talk to each other in this special room and the daily parents' group also meets here. This group is led by a social worker or psychotherapist; shared problems are discussed and parents are helped to face their feelings about their own and about other children's handicaps and difficulties.

The group sessions supplement the case work of the psychiatric social workers with most of the individual mothers and some fathers. Individual case work is of particular importance, as without it many parents would be unable to tolerate the stresses and anxieties of attending the unit together with their children and attendance might not be maintained. The sessions with the psychiatric social worker usually occur weekly or fortnightly. The Day Centre social workers, on the other hand, relate to the parents as well as the children during the whole of the day. These workers are people with a wide variety of backgrounds in nursing or social work wishing to have further experience with disturbed families. The main therapeutic task is carried by these workers, in turn supported by the consultant psychiatrist and other members of the psychiatric team, who work in a consultative capacity to the unit.

A psychiatric team from within the hospital department is also responsible for the diagnostic assessment of the children referred to the centre. Psychiatrists may additionally undertake regular treatment of families or children attending the unit.

The psychologist's role is an important one. She not only assesses the children's intellectual capacities and carries out a developmental assessment, but may advise on nursery teaching techniques or devise specific behaviour modification programmes or teaching for some individual children. In this, again, she co-operates closely with the Day Centre workers.

### The Psychotherapist

How and where does the child psychotherapist fit into the team? Psychotherapists may undertake the treatment of individual children or families. They also act in a consultative capacity to the Day Centre staff generally, helping them to observe children and parents, and to develop insight into the processes observed. Psychotherapists may also work with the parents themselves, either individually or in groups.

### Individual Psychotherapy

Undertaking individual psychotherapy with children found to need help, in addition to that provided by the Centre itself, is an obvious task for the psychotherapist, as well as for the psychiatrist. The previous chapter has already described in some detail the child psychotherapist's role in treating individual children attending a day unit. In this chapter I intend to focus mainly on some other aspects of the psychotherapist's work in a day unit where less individual psychotherapy is available.

In a unit for pre-school children, such as ours, where parents are being worked with fairly intensively, there is the hope that individual therapy for children, always very expensive to provide, may not be necessary in all cases. The global intervention of the Centre at this early stage may be enough to obviate that need. In fact, a proportion of the children would not be suitable for psychotherapy in any case, for a variety of reasons - it is well known in clinics, for example, that it is not easy for parents with very young children to attend for regular interviews.

Where individual therapy for these young children is nevertheless indicated, Day Centre attendance does have the advantage that a preparatory period at the Centre serves to allow an assessment of suitability for therapy and also helps to build up the kind of relationship with parents in which treatment is likely to be supported. When Day Centre attendance takes place concurrently with individual psychotherapy, clearly the mother's needs can be more adequately met.

Richard came into individual psychotherapy after an initial period of attendance at the Centre, where his aggression towards other children was difficult to manage. He seemed out of touch with reality and his confused, anxiety-provoking communications suggested that more help was needed than our group situation alone could provide. His mother had been very rejecting of him: it is unlikely that at the start of attendance she would have been willing to bring him regularly for treatment. However, when she had established a relationship not only with her psychiatric social worker, from whom she had individual case work, but also with Day Centre workers and other mothers, she was able to bring him up from the Day Centre to the psychotherapist for regular sessions.

In the case of Desmond, individual psychotherapy was begun when his period at the Day Centre was coming to an end, with a view to helping him with his deep-seated problems over separation and loss. Leonard, whose aggression at home has already been mentioned (page 103), had individual psychotherapy with a psychiatrist from the very start of his Day Centre attendance, in order to relieve the home situation as quickly as possible.

**A Family Case**

Sometimes the child psychotherapist, possibly together with another staff member, may see a child with his parents. This kind of help may be indicated when family interactions are felt to be especially relevant to the case, and where insufficient help can be given with such interactions in the general nursery setting.

Ronald was a little boy of three-and-a-half who was brought to the Day Centre because of being completely unmanageable at home. He had always been a difficult baby, rejecting his mother's ministrations (so she felt) even at a few months old. He had screamed incessantly during his first year. By the age of two his mother found him quite uncontrollable and could not even prevent him running into the street. With other people, however, he tended to behave quite well, so that the parents felt no one believed how awful he was at home – instead, they felt everyone blamed them for bad management. In the Day Centre the workers observed that although Ronald's mother appeared outwardly to handle him in a reasonable way, she in fact gave him 'mixed messages' by, for example, forbidding him to do things, but in inviting or challenging tones. Nevertheless, Ronald behaved pretty well in the Day Centre, as his parents had predicted. They said, however, that he was getting worse and worse at home and en route to the hospital. The culmination was an occasion when his mother was asked to take him off the train because of his behaviour. The parents were desperate and so it was decided to see whether family interviews might be helpful.

Mother and father, who expected Ronald to be well behaved in an interview situation, were amazed that he showed himself almost immediately in his true colours. Defiantly he did everything that was forbidden – spitting, attacking, wreaking havoc with the room. Ronald's contra-suggestibility and intolerance of frustration were at once apparent, but so was the parents' lack of responsiveness to Ronald's cues. Their competitiveness and 'controllingness' in relation to the play material was obvious. For example, during this first session, the parents were talking to the therapist, demanding her attention and quite oblivious of the fact that Ronald was trying to show them the little toys he had just unwrapped. When he now started to shout, they instanced the shouting as an example of his impossible behaviour, apparently not having registered that he was trying to show them the toys. He just throws tantrums 'out of the blue', they said. Much of Ronald's behaviour was indeed impossible and he demonstrated this forcibly in the sessions. Yet numerous indicators in the first and subsequent meetings showed how much this child felt his needs and demands were being ignored or misunderstood. This non-reception seemed to him like an actual exclusion or rejection, sometimes even an attack. He retaliated as best he could with violent behaviour and language – intended, it seemed, to get himself across at all costs to his parents, as well as to revenge himself on them.

In one session he was holding his tummy as if it hurt and the therapist asked if he had a pain. 'No,' said his mother, 'he's always doing that.' 'I *have*, you bitch,' screamed Ronald. He seemed to feel that his mother did not appreciate his pain. The therapist wondered if this feeling could have its roots in similar situations in the past, reaching right back to infancy. Ronald had apparently sucked well at first but later tended to turn away from the breast and scream. More frequent feeds were recommended, then transfer to a bottle, but the baby's screaming did not abate. At ten weeks he was said to be overweight, although he had been fairly small at birth.

One cannot know exactly what went on in those early months, but the evidence of the excessive weight suggests that more frequent feeds were not the right response to Ronald's early screaming. Possibly the mother, or her advisers, were not able to distinguish between cries of pain or anxiety and cries of hunger, a problem all too familiar to mothers of colicky babies. Maybe Ronald was a particularly difficult baby, whose needs were difficult to meet. His screams and lack of response might then have undermined his mother's confidence in her ability to provide for him, so making her gradually less able to respond intuitively to his cues. A vicious circle seemed in this way to have been established, one which became progressively worse as time went on. In its course the child took vengeance on his parents for misunderstandings felt as pains or attacks.

The parents' own life histories no doubt contributed to their difficulties in coping with Ronald. The mother had had a very competitive and jealous relationship with a younger brother. It is possible that Ronald's unplanned arrival, interrupting her career, revived some of the feelings she had experienced as a little girl, when the arrival of her brother had interrupted her exclusive relationship with her mother. These parents, only just out of their own teens, were immature and not yet ready for parental responsibility. And they were especially not ready to accept and cope with a young child's anxieties.

This much was illustrated in that first family session, for when their attention was drawn to the toys which Ronald was showing them, they tried to take the toys over, in competition with the child. Father went on drawing pictures on the board, even though Ronald had now turned to something else. When Ronald made a plasticine gun and 'shot' it at his father, the father bent the barrel of the gun back towards the child. While this of course was 'only' a game, it probably represented unconscious processes at work in the family. We could say that Ronald was continually 'shooting' his anxieties at his parents. Their fending off these anxieties, in their inability to respond adequately to them, no doubt felt to the child as if the anxieties were being shot back at him. We had some additional evidence that the mother was projecting certain feelings of her own into the child by her mixed messages. While overtly demanding obedience, she seemed unconsciously to be inviting rebellion. Ronald was perhaps the recipient, by projection, of a rebellious part of herself.

In this family interview - and in five subsequent ones which only the mother and Ronald attended, the father being unable to come - the therapist began to understand a little how very frightened Ronald was. She could see how much of his defiant, provocative behaviour was in fact a kind of bravado against very deep-seated anxieties, particularly of being rejected and literally thrown away. He experienced his mother's continual complaints about his naughtiness as a wish to get rid of him. He acted this feeling out by getting right into the rubbish bin. He also attempted to make the therapist feel shut out and unwanted in a variety of ways, such as by saying, 'I don't like you,' and having to be forced to come into and to stay in the room. It was as if he felt he could get rid of the feeling of being unwanted by making the therapist experience it instead of him. He also felt very shut out from what he felt were the good 'mummy things' – represented by the contents of his mother's bag, which he was continually fighting to get at. 'If I were a girl, I'd be a mummy,' he screamed. Although outwardly not wanting to come to the interviews, he was obviously very much upset by the breaks between sessions. He then felt shut out of the therapist's room.

When the therapist shared with him and his mother her understanding of his anxieties, and also of his intense frustration at the beginnings and ends of sessions, he began to settle to more constructive play during the sessions. He expressed his need by making the little boy doll call 'Help!' In the fifth interview he was able to express his despair by falling off the table and saying he was 'dead' and that he did not like being alive – his mother found this interview extremely disturbing. Although the joint sessions had been very illuminating and notably helpful to Ronald, it was now felt that they were too difficult for the mother to tolerate. It was decided to arrange separate therapists for the child and the parents. It was evident that Ronald was a very disturbed little boy who could benefit from more prolonged individual therapy.

However, understanding Ronald's despair seemed to lead to a change in his behaviour. He became more overtly depressed but very much more manageable. His mother felt she could now cope on her own and no longer wished to undertake the long journey to the Centre. A very limited amount had been achieved, but it is possible that some benign intervention in the vicious cycle of events had taken place, which might make continuing development possible. Six months later, the mother reported that Ronald was 'all right'. A year afterwards, he had settled well at school.

## The Group Experience

Only some of the children at the Centre will have individual psychotherapy or family therapy at any one time. Others may have different kinds of individual help, such as speech therapy, or special teaching and behaviour modification programmes with the psychologist and Day Centre workers. For many children, however, it is the group experience itself which seems most helpful – the opportunity to begin to relate to other children, and for parents and children to interact with one another in a supportive environment.

Let us look at what happened to Sally, the two-year-old who became phobic of dolls. Her terror of dolls developed after the birth of her sister, when Sally was seventeen months old. She attended the Day Centre with her mother and little sister one day a week for a period of fifteen months.

At first Sally was very timid, clinging to mother, frightened of other children and of touching any dolls. She was also afraid that dolls would fall. At the same time she seemed attracted by the Wendy house. Her worker supported her in this interest and encouraged her and her mother to play in this area and with the dolls, although not forcing her in any way. The psychotherapist observed that the mother tended to treat the dolls in a very realistic way, almost as if they were babies. For example, saying, 'Shh, don't wake her, she's asleep,' with great conviction. To this Sally reacted with appropriate awe. When mother picked up the doll, Sally looked alarmed – 'Put her back in the cot, she's asleep,' she said. It was noticeable that Sally tended to ignore her little sister completely.

The psychotherapist compared her own observations of Sally's and her mother's behaviour with those of their worker and the other Day Centre staff, at the weekly seminar. (These seminars are held by the psychotherapist for the Day Centre workers. At these meetings insight and understanding of the children's and parents' behaviour and relationships are developed.) It was felt in the seminar that Sally's terror of dolls probably sprang from her hostile feelings towards her baby sister. Further, the mother might be reinforcing Sally's confusion between dolls and babies by her too realistic attitude to dolls. It seemed important that Sally's jealousy be accepted by the mother, so work was directed towards helping her understand and tolerate this. Sally also experienced with her worker a relationship in which aggression and jealousy could be expressed and accepted. Sally's mother at first tended to deny all aggression and jealousy in her child, emphasizing how 'good' Sally was.

Sally made quite an attachment to her worker, expressed paradoxically as anger and aggression towards her when she returned from holiday. She began to play with children of her own age and occasionally with smaller children. For a period however, she was hostile to her little sister. After a few months she no longer seemed frightened of dolls. Her mother seemed more at ease with her and no longer demanded such 'good' behaviour. Gradually Sally became more relaxed and began to enjoy participating in the Day Centre, playing well with others, her sister now included. She could stand up for herself and at the same time be protective to her sister. She was talking more and was able to start nursery school before she left.

In the Day Centre, the child finds himself in a new setting where an attempt is made to understand his problems and his communications, where responses to him are likely to be very different from those he has habitually experienced. Sally found herself in an atmosphere where dolls were treated as dolls rather than as babies. She saw other children drop or throw them without dire consequences. Her worker was able to help both Sally and her mother to differentiate fact from phantasy, and to play with the dolls in a less confusing make-believe way, rather than as real babies.

In the case of Peter, the boy with the inadequate sense of danger, everyone did not rush anxiously to catch him, as his mother did, whenever he climbed on anything. In the less fraught atmosphere he was helped to differentiate between what was really dangerous and what was not. He experienced with his worker a relationship with someone more able to respond with containing firmness to his incessant demands. Although his mother was at times critical and resentful of this relationship, she also was gradually helped in the group and in individual case work to manage Peter better.

The most important therapeutic factor in the group experience seems to be the understanding and acceptance of anxieties and feelings. This acceptance is engendered by the whole Day Centre ambience, mediated certainly by the individual workers in relation to their cases, but also by the total group of workers, mothers and children. It is especially important that the aggressive and hostile aspects of relationships between parents and children, usually least tolerated by parents, be recognized and understood. This is not to say that they should necessarily be allowed uncontrolled expression.

The excessively clinging children described earlier were helped to tolerate short separations from their mothers through their workers' support and understanding, during the planned brief partings which occur routinely in the course of the day. In the case of inhibited children like Sally, where hostility and jealousy are denied and unacceptable to the mother, the recognition of such feelings and the tolerance of some expression of them diminishes the child's need to project her hostility into phobia-producing objects. The mother on her side is helped to recognize the jealousy. Where children are overtly aggressive and controlling, the setting of firm limits and the establishment of a secure framework within which the aggression can be expressed, helps the parents to cope with the aggression. It helps also to diminish the omnipotence of the phantasies of both mother and child. Thus Desmond, whose brothers had died, was able to experience a live 'family' where his aggression did not prove lethal, as he had feared in phantasy. The general tolerance of a variety of feelings and anxieties in the Day Centre is found to produce greater communication at all levels. It seems even to help actual speech development in the many non-communicating children.

'A child finds it worth his while to learn to talk to express his wishes and thoughts, when he has the hope of having them understood.' (Harris, 1969)

## Psychotherapist and Staff

We have seen that it is the Day Centre workers, who spend the whole day with the parents and children, on whom the main responsibility for providing a total therapeutic environment falls. The child psychotherapist makes only an indirect contribution to this difficult work of the staff. The therapist's contribution relates to three main areas:

1 Observation.
2 Developing insight, understanding and techniques of working.
3 Helping the workers to understand and to bear their own inevitable anxieties.

The psychotherapist may make her own direct observations of children, as she did with Sally. This helps her to discuss and contrast the worker's observations, and to draw attention to the kinds of details of behaviour which may be relevant in a particular case. In this way the workers are helped to observe more acutely. Sometimes she observes a child for the purpose of assisting in initial diagnosis or of assessing his suitability for psychotherapy.

Day Centre workers discuss aspects of their work with the psychotherapist in the weekly seminars already mentioned. In these seminars insight into the processes at work in the group and in the relationships between workers and patients is developed. Gradually we hope to understand those elements that seem to be therapeutic and those that seem unhelpful. From such understanding it is further hoped that appropriate responses to patients will follow and acceptable techniques of working be developed. The Day Centre workers do not make verbal interpretations of unconscious infantile feelings in a group setting, as would occur in psychotherapy. Their understanding is transmitted through their behaviour and responsiveness, in much the same way as the 'ordinary good mother' communicates with her infant (Winnicott, 1965).

In work with parents, it is important for staff to refrain from giving too much direct advice but instead to 'encourage parents to follow their perceptions and to use their latent resources, without increasing their feelings of helplessness, dependence and failure' (Harris, 1966). The worker needs to support, not take over, the mother's role. She needs to help the mother to relate to her child, while sharing with her the burden of his care (Folkart, 1967). Her function is a holding one for the family, in Winnicott's sense (Weddell, 1961).

As many of the parents are also extremely disturbed, this task can place considerable strain on the workers. Staff discussions with the psychiatric team, including the psychotherapist, in which support can be given to workers in bearing anxieties, are an essential part of the therapeutic work of the Centre. Obviously, feelings of anger, despair and inadequacy can frequently arise when one works all day with such disturbed families. Discussion can help sort out how far the anxieties stem from the projections of children and parents, and discussion also increases the capacity to bear the fact that there are no ready-made, easy solutions. All can share the experience of 'not knowing' and of trying to reflect and learn.

## Parents in the Day Centre

The all-day attendance of parents along with the children

makes this day centre different from some others and also from most nursery groups. The arrangement has the advantage that attempts can be made to work directly on family relationships. It further makes available much needed support to parents, thereby helping them to be more able to give the concerned care which is essential for the healthy emotional development of their young children. Nevertheless, such attendance also creates considerable problems, both for workers and for the parents themselves. They may find the group setting extremely stressful. As we have seen, individual support by the psychiatric social worker is necessary with most parents.

Parents have to come to terms with their disappointment that the workers do not take over their lives and responsibilities, but expect their active participation. They must weather the initial stress of attending the Centre. If they can clear these hurdles, parents do seem to derive considerable help, in much the same ways as the children, from the understanding atmosphere of the Day Centre. Here anxieties and hostile feelings can be expressed and tolerated, without leading to rejection. The Day Centre group, comprising workers, other mothers and children, seems to function as an understanding 'mother' for the mothers, so meeting the parents' own infantile needs until individual case work can help them to differentiate their own needs from those of their children. The Day Centre's mothering role is especially important for mothers whose nurturing capacities have been impaired by poor relationships with their own parents. They can gain support and confidence from the receptive and non-condemning attitude of the workers, who are then able to help them sort out the many confusions in their management of their children. Distinguishing between a child's real needs and demanding, controlling behaviour may well alleviate the child's separation and feeding problems. When firmness is disentangled from punitiveness, fluctuations from over-indulgence to unnecessary restrictiveness are less likely to occur.

The worker's sharing of the difficulties, even when sometimes no solution is found, can of itself help the mother to be more tolerant. John, a very whiney, hyperactive, aggressive, post-encephalitic child, was a great burden to his mother and family because of his destructive behaviour. Here there was only a limited amount which could be done for the child, but his mother gained some relief from sharing the burden. In many cases shared experience promotes increased tolerance all round.

The parents' group, which meets for forty-five minutes every day, is a further means by which parents can support each other. They discuss common problems and anxieties, and learn that their own difficulties are not unique. The group provides a forum for the voicing of complaints and a place where strong feelings can both be ventilated and contained. Insight is also developed into the parents' and children's problems. The psychotherapist may herself conduct a parents' group. The group conductors, be they child psychotherapists or other workers, are non-directive, attempting simply to clarify problems and identify themes as they develop. Parents (usually mothers, but there are some fathers) both support and confront each other in these groups, expressing their mutual feelings of anxiety and guilt at having disturbed children, and revealing their expectations of criticism. The following example of a parents' group in session illustrates the ways in which a group may support a new mother, who is undergoing an initial crisis during her first attendance at the Day Centre.

## A Parents' Group

Two mothers were discussing, with considerable envy and resentment, Princess Anne's new house. They were completely ignoring a mother new to the group that day, who was looking very tense and suspicious and smoking furiously. This mother offered cigarettes all round, which were refused. Joseph's mother now joined the group and began to defend the allocation of a house to Princess Anne. An argument promised to develop. The psychotherapist commented on the problem of coping with envy of those who are more fortunate. She also suggested that this re-emergence of a very familiar theme in the group, namely that lack of adequate housing is the main cause of people's (that is, their own) difficulties, and their habitual attention to matters over which the group had actually no control, perhaps served the purpose of avoiding immediate feelings and constructive discussion which might lead to change.

The three 'old' mothers responded indignantly to this intervention. They demanded to know what they should discuss. The therapist suggested there might be feelings about the group, in relation to new or absent members. (Apart from the presence of the new mother, several of the usual mothers were missing.)

The new mother was then asked why she had brought her child. She now shocked the group by an outpouring of adverse comments about her boy Jim, ending with her wish to be rid of the child, her inability even to stand the sight of him and her feelings of wanting to murder him. There was a stunned silence. 'Why don't you have him taken into care?' Joseph's mother asked. Laurence's mother then spoke of mothers who 'just don't take to their children' and are better separated from them. Jim's mother said she had tried to get Jim into care but 'they wouldn't do anything'. 'Ah,' said Darren's mother. 'That's just it. They only talk.' That was another frequent group theme.

The psychotherapist commented on the despair expressed and the feeling that there was no solution apart from getting rid of the child. This remark seemed to have the effect of directing the group's activity towards an attempt to support the rejecting mother. They recounted their own rejecting and murderous feelings towards their own children and acknowledged that it was helpful to 'stick around here'. When Andrew's mother joined the group at this point, Andrew was cited as an example of an impossibly difficult and destructive child who had improved enormously. 'Things do change,' said Darren's mother with a smile. 'Although we always do complain.'

Joseph's mother then began to confront Jim's mother with her need to change and to show her son some affection. The group began to discuss the emotional basis of wetting and soiling and children's differing ways of expressing feelings. They emphasized that both mothers and children needed to change but that this process took time.

The psychotherapist was quite surprised at the degree to which this previously complaining group acknowledged in this session the help received in the Day Centre. It seemed that the disturbing effect of a blatantly rejecting mother rallied them, after initial despair, to a supporting and constructively confronting attitude to this new mother. The therapist felt their reaction might possibly help her to overcome the initial crisis in coming to the Centre and might give her a ray of hope. At least she did not walk out that day as she had announced her intention of doing!

**Summary**

The above account of a day centre for disturbed young children and parents, which attempts to provide facilities for extended observation and a supportive, therapeutic environment, is an example of one of the fields of work into which the skills of the child psychotherapist may usefully take him. With these very young children individual psychotherapy may not always be indicated, but the therapist can also act in a consultative capacity to the staff working directly with the children and parents.

# Chapter Six

# *Working in a Hospital*

## by Rolene Szur

This chapter describes further aspects of work in a hospital setting and returns to the subject of individual therapy with both out-patients and in-patients. The functions of a residential psychiatric unit for children are discussed. In hospital, the child psychotherapist may work in close liaison not only with the psychiatric team but also with the staff in other branches of the hospital. M.B., D.D.

---

A child psychiatric department in a hospital may offer certain facilities not always present in a child guidance clinic. The Day Centre described in the last chapter is an example. In some hospitals there may be a residential psychiatric unit for children or adolescents. The close links with other hospital services are important and interesting for the psychotherapist.

Work with out-patients, however, follows very similar lines to that carried out in local clinics. Both see the same wide range of problems – including learning difficulties, school refusal, bed-wetting, conduct disorders and so on. Occasionally, a child is referred specifically to a hospital because the symptoms are very long standing, or are causing severe anxieties.

### Louisa, Aged Six, and her Fear of Death

This bright little girl was an out-patient. She had become excessively distressed when her doll had fallen down and broken, and was convinced that she herself was in danger of imminent death. On a subsequent occasion shortly afterwards she saw a little boy playing with a bow and arrows and began to scream in terror, begging him not to shoot her. Both of these incidents had a delusional quality which was worrying. She was further troubled by frequent nightmares.

In contrast to the patient, her only sibling was a sister less than a year younger, who was said to be a good-natured easy child. The patient was described as quarrelsome, discontented and defiant. Although the girls played together co-operatively much of the time, and were important companions for each other, Louisa may well have found it hard to share her parents with a small rival so early in her life. The expression of jealousy, verbally or in action, tends to put an older or stronger child in the wrong in comparison with a seemingly innocent victim. In this way a gulf between the good approved child and the naughty reprimanded one may become ever wider. As time goes on, the situation can become self-perpetuating.

Moreover, when a particular child's difficulties are the most visible ones in a family, she may come to be seen by one or both parents almost as an adult antagonist, instead of being treated simply as an unruly child. A development of this kind is likely to emphasize feelings of competitiveness towards the mother and father, especially in the case of an ambitious little girl. There were a number of indications that processes of this very kind had been occurring in Louisa's family. As the parents themselves also had a troubled history, it was considered probable that their own difficulties had interacted with problems in the children.

In this case it was agreed by the diagnostic team that the task was two-fold. In addition to individual treatment for the child, the parents, and the mother in particular, needed the help of someone standing outside the situation. A neutral outsider would be able to help both mother and father to approach tensions between the children, and also between the children and the parents, in a more parental, less involved, way.

The case turned out to be just as complicated as had been anticipated. A great deal of ground had to be covered by the social worker in regular interviews with the parents. For the purposes of this chapter, however, I shall describe only the work with Louisa, selecting two incidents which were of relevance to her presenting symptoms. These incidents occurred in the early part of treatment.

As with many very young children, Louisa's transference reactions were both marked and clear. She was openly curious about the drawers in the room, soon trying hard to pull them open. Two cupboards at the sides of the desk, being larger than the drawers, particularly stimulated her jealousy. She demanded, 'Why can't I have those?' Although she was able to acknowledge that she wanted to have more than any of the other children, and indeed to take everything from them, she followed this by asserting, 'You haven't got any children, anyhow.' She said this staring at me with hard angry eyes. It seemed probable that when situations of frustration forced her into experiencing the full measure of her own jealousy, she reacted with a rage that at levels of unconscious phantasy 'wiped the others out'. The way in which this mechanism operated and its dire consequences for her was in fact made very clear shortly afterwards. Louisa was wiping some of her drawings off the board, when the chalk-rubber slipped and fell against her head. It was a slight knock, but Louisa turned pale with shock and terror, wanting to run out of the room. I linked the incident with our earlier exchanges. I explained that in her imagination she might have felt as if she had just wiped out the other children, so that then the hard back of the rubber had seemed to turn into something like a teacher, or a mother, that knocked her down to punish her. Some weeks later when told about the therapist's coming holiday, she first pushed a mother-doll on to the floor, then dangled her from the window.

These and other similar actions, when interpreted, made it possible over a period of time to help Louisa to feel that her murderous impulses could be understood and 'contained' within the framework of a rational formulation. Interpretation made it more possible for her to assimilate her feelings, instead of being driven to projecting them into outside objects and figures, where they then in turn became increasingly menacing.

As mentioned earlier, the child and her family presented a number of complex interrelations. However, Louisa's rather dramatic referral symptoms disappeared, and it then became possible to focus treatment mainly on her character problems and the family interactions.

## Out-Patients

The majority of children coming to hospitals for psychotherapy or other forms of treatment do attend on an out-patient basis. It is generally preferable for children (as for most patients) to continue living in their own homes, and to attend the hospital either by themselves or together with other family members who may be involved in the treatment programme. Appointments for psychotherapy are usually once weekly but may be more, or less, frequent.

Treatment is designed to answer the needs of the particular problem presented, and may consist of one or more of the following approaches – individual psychotherapy for a child, therapeutic interviews with one or both parents, and whole-family interviews. These are all forms of treatment in which the psychotherapist may take part. Other methods which may be used in some hospitals include the prescription of psychotropic drugs by the psychiatrist, remedial teaching sessions or programmes of 'behaviour modification', both of which are carried out by psychologists.

## Differences between Hospital and Child Guidance Referrals

A hospital, particularly a large one in central London, tends to be especially consulted when the symptoms are severe or, possibly, when these have failed to respond to treatment over some years. Sometimes a family has become very anxious and unable to accept local professional advice without a 'second opinion', as in the case of Louisa.

Another frequent reason for referral to hospital is an uncertain diagnosis. Uncertainty often arises when there is the question of an organic basis for the illness. The comparatively greater number of hospital patients whose symptoms include a physical aspect is, in fact, the most obvious overall difference between hospital and child guidance work.

Specific categories include the following:

1 Conditions where an organic element may be present, but it is established that emotional factors

play a part in making the illness either better or worse.
2 Physical symptoms which are the direct result of an emotional state, such as breath-holding attacks, anorexia nervosa, hysterical paralysis and so forth.
3 Disturbances related to a child's difficulty in coping with a serious physical illness or disability.
4 Side-effects which may be the aftermath of a long stay in hospital necessitated by surgery or other medical treatment.
5 Hypochondriachal anxieties, that is, continual worry about illness and seeing signs of this where none or few are present.

Although these types often overlap to an extent in any individual patient, the basic classification given helps us in our approach to the case and in our expectations about the outcome.

**The Hospital Setting**

It will be clear that many of the children whose symptoms have some physical aspect will already have been examined or treated in other parts of the hospital before they come to the Department of Psychological Medicine. A number are therefore already well known in one or other ward. Some children may in fact attend the hospital for almost all their medical care, including, for example, visits to the dermatologist, the dentist and the optician, often travelling considerable distances to do so.

As well as these broad differences in the kinds of patients treated by psychotherapists specifically in hospital clinics, there are also likely to be differences in the way the therapist experiences the work. Especially in hospitals where there is an in-patient psychiatric unit providing for all aspects of the children's needs during their stay, the therapist's feeling of being a member of a team may be strengthened. Similarly, the view of the patient as a 'whole person', whose physical, intellectual and emotional functioning are interdependent, may be seen more clearly and consistently.

**In- Patients**

Sometimes there are special factors which make it worthwhile to admit a child to the children's psychiatric unit. The length of stay can vary considerably. A recommendation for admission is not necessarily an indication of the severity of the disturbance, though in a number of cases this is a principal factor.

Some referrals are in the nature of a consultation when a case has proved difficult to diagnose. The team may then feel that a period of observation of the child in a workaday situation will provide helpful information about social relationships, both with peers and adults. In this respect, as in some others, the in-patient psychiatric unit in a hospital can serve very similar functions to the Day Centre described in the previous chapter.

When a child's particular difficulties have become part of a family pattern which is serving to perpetuate them, it may be helpful to 'break the circuit'. By this means individual members of the family are enabled to sort out their own personal involvements. It may further be possible for the in-patient unit to provide an environment which neither colludes with a patient nor punishes him, but instead helps him to face and to understand his problems. The in-patient unit can also prove to be a valuable learning experience. The hope is that new and healthier ways of dealing with anxiety will be developed, and relationships formed with others which are based on reality more than on unconscious phantasies.

Many cases present complex patterns of psychosomatic symptoms which may respond well to a combination of, for example, psychotherapy together with speech – or physiotherapy.

Sometimes the patient will also be under medication. A residential psychiatric unit may be the best way of providing for such co-operative treatment. This comment applies especially when the patient's home is many miles distant from the hospital.

## Pierre: Combined Physical and Emotional Problems

Pierre came to the psychiatric unit some time after his twelfth birthday, for help with a number of symptoms he had suffered since early childhood. When first admitted to the unit his back was bent almost double, turned to one side, with one foot twisted in the other direction. His voice was shallow and breathy. He spoke little, and then almost inaudibly. The severity of his symptoms had fluctuated over the years. At times he had been in a better condition, though at others had deteriorated to such a degree that he had been unable to walk at all, or even to feed himself. There was evidence that the regressions were linked with situations of stress - particular examples were two occasions when the family had moved house. Although an organic basis for this patient's symptoms could not be excluded, after extensive physical investigations he was referred to the Department of Psychological Medicine and admitted to the unit. Here he was found to have many compulsive habits and obsessions, to be very dependent and full of complaints. Yet despite all this he was often an appealing boy.

In the course of working with Pierre it became apparent that the physical distortions and weakness often signified for him at unconscious levels the emotional conflicts and feelings of infantile impotence which agitated him deeply. This mode of functioning, which might be described as 'thinking and talking through the body', can be seen more clearly by referring to some of the sessions with him. One day when drawing a route map he spontaneously pointed out that a particular conjunction of lines looked like a foot - turning sharply to one side, like his own, in fact. It seemed also quite separate from the rest of the body. Presently he remarked that the roads twisted and turned because they went round different properties. On the basis of this comment we explored together the possibility that he might have a feeling that different parts of his body contained different properties. These, for example, being good or bad, being like father or like mother, or having an adult or a childish quality about them. It might be, I suggested that he felt that these different aspects sometimes pulled him in different directions. This approach of examining possible links or parallels between emotional experience and physical states or postures was developed further when it seemed relevant during the months which followed. The approach proved fruitful. As it brought to light, for example, some of the hidden ambivalent attitudes and phantasy attacks on parental figures, it became more possible for Pierre to acknowledge these in words, instead of expressing them through his body. It was noted that his response to interpretation along these lines also resulted in a freeing of good feelings and of a capacity for appreciation. For the first time he began to talk in ways which had some quality of 'counting his blessings' rather than of listing his complaints. The experience of having his hostile phantasies understood and accepted seemed to have helped to lift burdens of guilt which he could not himself resolve and at the same time deeply resented.

Along with this general improvement he began to be more receptive to increasing encouragement from the unit staff. They now planned special activities directed towards his taking on more adult types of responsibility and more independent ventures. He carried out shopping expeditions and journeys by himself, on which he reported with pleasure and satisfaction.

Simultaneously the social worker was able to discuss in interviews with the parents some aspects of their relationship with the boy which might be reinforcing a tendency on his part towards regression. She was also supportive over situations in which the parents were anxious about Pierre's capacity to function independently.

Gradually the boy's bizarre mannerisms and most of his obsessions disappeared. His voice showed considerable (though admittedly somewhat variable) improvement, and in fact, he became a keen conversationalist. The basic distortion of his frame remained, but Pierre did achieve greater stability and some significant change for the better in his general posture.

Before the end of the year he was able to find a place in a suitable boarding-school which provided an additional impetus to his progress. He continued to visit for psychotherapy, but now as an out-patient, and for fewer sessions. Despite his previous history of breakdowns accompanying any changes and in situations of anxiety, he was able to make the major move to boarding-school successfully. He has continued to show improvement in his new environment, and also at home within the family.

## The Residential Setting

A residential setting provides in itself a kind of 'milieu therapy', with which the psychotherapist's work may be co-ordinated. The co-operation can either be direct, as in the case of a child who is in individual treatment, or indirect through discussions with other staff members about children who are in their care. Psychoanalytic insights can help to adjust the response of the caretaking adult to a child's irrational behaviour. When this seems to make just no sense at all, it tends to spread feelings of confusion, anxiety and anger. A residential unit of this kind can further provide a supportive background when a child is having individual psychotherapy. The unit can take the role of a concerned, understanding and unpossessive parent while the child is away from his actual parents.

At the same time it is important to see that the period of separation from the parents should not begin to create a gulf between child and family or stir up feelings of rejection and guilt among them. There is the temptation for certain children to cling to the protected niche which the unit can to some extent provide. Both of these difficulties are lessened if the children return home every weekend. They can be alleviated also by the work of the psychiatric social workers with the parents.

A large share of responsibility in preventing the development of a breach between parents and child is taken by the staff who directly care for the children. They contribute by establishing a good relationship with the parents which is not felt to compete with them in their major responsibility for good mothering (or fathering) of the child. As well, they structure the patient's activities as far as possible towards individual independence, and direct them outwards. As we saw, this played a valuable part in Pierre's development. Such problems can also be seen as related to difficulties over separation similar to those experienced by very young infants. Thus they enter into the psychotherapist's work with an individual patient in treatment.

At the in-patient unit where I myself work it is noticeable that almost all patients have a strong regard for it, whether positive or negative, as an entity in itself. Quite spontaneously, many in-patients have pointed out the way in which the unit is different in its organization, style and quality of relationships from medical or surgical wards, for example. It is small, catering for a total of eight patients, generally two in one room. There are two further beds intended for mothers to stay over with a child in case this is felt to be advisable.

There is a large group room with kitchen adjoining, in which a fair amount of cooking under supervision takes place. Also a craft room and a roof-top play area. There are six full-time workers, whose training has been either in the field of nursing or psychology. Each child is in the special care of a particular worker, though this is not envisaged as an exclusive relationship. They have meals together with the children and in their interaction combine authority with informality. There are no uniforms or white coats. Although the arrangements are sufficiently organized to give the patients a feeling of containment in a secure framework, the atmosphere on the whole is comparatively permissive. The services of a full-time teacher are available although not a great deal of emphasis is placed on the academic side. Two psychiatrists are concerned, one being the consultant in charge. These take over-all medical responsibility for admission and treatment and also see a number of individual patients on a regular basis. There is also a psychiatric social worker whose principal concern is the families of these children. As in out-patient work, psychologists and psychotherapists from the department are available either to work with the individual children themselves, or to discuss problems with the in-patient workers. Regular conferences and full staff discussions form an important part of the organization.

## Pearl and Jason: Two Cases for Assessment

Sometimes the psychotherapist is asked to see a patient for a few sessions in order to gain additional understanding of the child's underlying problems or to help in assessing which form of treatment is most likely to be of benefit. It may be possible to get a clearer picture of his capacity for change and development over several interviews, as the child's initial anxieties and defences relax.

Both the children described in this section were in the care of the Social Services Department. They were referred to us for diagnostic sessions because in both cases their severe psychological disturbance was associated with a very adverse family history and early experiences. This combination of unfortunate circumstances made it doubtful whether they would be able to make good use of analytic psychotherapy:

Their basic capacity for forming relationships might have been too seriously damaged.

Pearl's mother, who had died some years previously, had been a prostitute. She had neglected and maltreated Pearl in favour of younger half-brothers and half-sisters. The father was in an institution for the criminally insane. Pearl, aged nearly nine, had been excluded from a residential school by reason of her excessively aggressive and uncontrolled behaviour. At times she appeared to be in a state of identity confusion of a psychotic nature. However, she showed a wish to make some kind of good relationship, which was rather appealing. Additionally, the desperate nature of her situation in itself stirred an urge in others to try to find some way of helping her.

In her sessions this judgment of her wish to obtain help was confirmed, as she repeatedly acted games of being rescued from drowning. Another feature which emerged was an aggressive sexual curiosity, sometimes accompanied by masturbation. These games, together with her fierce rages when jealous or frustrated, came through as genuine emotional experiences. A great deal of her method of functioning nevertheless consisted of slipping in and out of alternative, dissociated identifications, or rather simple imitative patches, reflecting current or past figures in her life. On a standardized test she had been rated as considerably below average in intelligence. Persons, places and times were confused and fragmented for her. Her capacity for maintaining an intact process of thought seemed not sufficient for her to grasp experiences in a coherent way. While there were still traces of a wish for, or a concept of, a nurturing parental figure, it became increasingly apparent that the concepts were too weak to hold this girl together. It was as if in her fundamental experience there existed only a starving child and a sexual mother, punitive and deserting.

These many adverse factors did not provide a sufficient basis from which any real personality changes might develop. The therapist felt, therefore, that her most helpful contribution would be to attempt no more than short-term palliative treatment. This therapy would include trying to relieve some of Pearl's separation anxiety, often at the root of her aggressive attacks. She might further be helped to sort out in treatment certain phantasy modes of operating which at times caused her to have conversations with herself, as if she were in fact two persons at once. The understanding and containing environment of the unit also supported Pearl's own efforts towards development. She made some progress, especially with regard to the conversations with herself, although it was still considered necessary to prescribe medication to help control her excessively disruptive behaviour.

A major problem was to find as stable a social and physical environment as possible for her. An elderly lady was, very courageously, acting as a kind of foster mother. She had Pearl to stay for weekends and took her on holiday. The psychiatric social worker was here able to give some help in supporting this often very difficult arrangement. It was considered important that Pearl should have an experience of continuity in at least one personal relationship. Some months later Pearl seemed to have made enough adjustment to justify our trying to look once again for a place in a residential special school. With the help of her local social worker a suitable school was found, willing to accept her. At first we heard good or at least satisfactory accounts of her. But a year later the situation had broken down, mainly because of Pearl's savage bullying of younger or weaker children. Once again, a new place would have to be found.

Jason was another child, a few months younger than Pearl, with an especially difficult background, and with personality disturbances which might be of a border-line psychotic nature. He also was seen with a view to long-term diagnostic assessment. This boy was sent to us from the medical wards when, after some months, a puzzling group of symptoms was discovered to be due to a debilitating drug which was being secretly administered by his mother. She also never left his side and kept him in a wheel-chair with his eyes covered. When Jason was admitted to the in-patient unit, under a court order, this alteration in his physical circumstances quite rapidly removed his organic symptoms. Now however, he displayed violently aggressive behaviour whenever thwarted, was obsessed with themes of poisoning and monsters, and sometimes gave the impression of being in the grip of grandiose delusions about his own strength and powers. We felt that the situation of his being aware that his mother had apparently been poisoning him would be a seriously traumatic event even for the most balanced child, therefore, if on a short-term crisis basis only, psychotherapeutic help should be made available to him. Jason had been tested as only just below average in intelligence and was generally not as retarded as Pearl.

His first sessions had therefore a diagnostic and a therapeutic function combined. (That statement actually applies, to a greater or lesser degree, to most diagnostic and most first sessions.) It soon became clear that Jason was fairly deeply involved in a paranoid type of delusional system, which interlocked with his mother's own disturbed condition. In one or two relevant instances, however, he responded to an interpretation distinguishing between phantasy and reality in a way which made it clear he was able to make use of such a distinction. He also at times engaged in constructive types of activity. It seemed just possible that he might be helped to build up some realistic picture of a mother figure, which would be neither a persecuted though idealized image, nor a totally sinister and terrifying one, but rather of someone who, while 'making mistakes' and being herself very confused, could nevertheless care about him.

On the evidence of these early sessions, therefore, it was decided to undertake psychotherapy in Jason's case with a view to a more basic personality development. While this attempt might mean a very long-term commitment, it seemed that positive elements in his personality were indeed present and that these should be given some chance.

As already mentioned, children with emotionally deprived and seriously distorted backgrounds (many of whom are in care in children's homes and similar institutions) are not generally considered hopeful cases for treatment. They have lacked the opportunity to establish a good relationship with a parental figure in the earliest, formative phase of life. However, psychotherapists are increasingly turning their attention to what can be done to help such children. In Pearl's case, even the minor objectives achieved proved to be only temporary. Hers was one of those sad cases in which one has to recognize that therapeutic resources remain limited and fallible. While always accepting such cautions against assumptions of professional omnipotence, it was still possible to feel justified and not altogether unhopeful in engaging in long-term treatment with Jason.*

Working within the context of a general hospital, one is aware of the long traditions of medicine which have won many seemingly hopeless battles against disease. One recognizes also that in treating an individual case the element of uncertainty can never be entirely excluded. For a comparatively young science such as analytic psychotherapy, this is an important tradition. In working within a team which includes many kinds of specialist, the hospital psychotherapist is part of a setting where the fullest resources are available for the treatment of what have often been regarded as hopeless cases.

One further side to this co-operation is the contribution which the psychotherapist is able to make to the treatment of patients under general medical care. This contribution is most evident in those cases which are considered to fall into the category of psychosomatic disease. Psychotherapy can, however, also be of assistance in the care of children with organic diseases. Sometimes it can mean helping a child suffering from an incurable illness through the painful ordeal of facing an early death. Then there are the children who have to undergo long and stressful forms of medical treatment, or who face the prospect of possible new disabilities arising from surgical intervention. Those, too, who find hospitalization and the sometimes lengthy period of separation from their parents very disturbing in itself. By helping the child to bear the burdens of pain and suffering in ways which do not damage his emotional life, the psychotherapist working in hospital makes a contribution to bringing treatment nearer to the concept of the patient as a total psychophysical entity.

*It is pleasing (about one year later) to be able to give an encouraging report about Jason. He has settled well in a very understanding and supportive children's home. In therapy he proved able to make increasing use of symbolic activities such as games and drawings, instead of the former violent acting out of his phantasies, and gradually also to put thoughts and feelings into words. He now attends for psychotherapy sessions about once a term only. Recently Jason's teacher recommended him for transfer to an ordinary school.

# Chapter Seven

# *Counselling Young People*

## by Isca Salzberger-Wittenberg

This chapter is about work with adolescents, (see also appendix, *Doubly Deprived*). Work with adolescents extends naturally into work with young adults, and in many cases the style of work is nearer to that undertaken with adults than to the work with younger children. In her role as therapist in a university counselling service and with other young people in a National Health Counselling Service, Isca Salzberger-Wittenberg decided to find out what could be achieved within the limits of a few consultations. She gives examples of how some young people were able to make good use of such brief depth exploration. She concludes that limited work of this kind can give clients enough insight to enable them to mobilize their own resources, and to continue working on their problems in ways that help them over a crisis situation. This approach of limited consultation may be particularly suitable for young people who are in any case not prepared at this stage of life to commit themselves to long-term psychotherapy, and with some it serves as a way of exploring their feelings about whether they do in fact wish to undertake longer-term psychoanalytic treatment. M. B., D. D.

---

The work of therapists trained in the analytic treatment of children and adolescents has, during the past few years, extended well into young adulthood. There has been not only an extension in the age range dealt with, but an expansion in the kind of therapeutic activity engaged in. One of the areas to which we apply the knowledge and skill derived from analytic practice is in brief counselling and consultation. It is this particular kind of work which I shall attempt to describe and discuss.

I came to this work ten years ago, almost accidentally, when employed as a part-time consultant psychotherapist in the Student Health Service of Sussex University. As I spent only one day a week there, it did not seem appropriate to take on a handful of students for long-term psychotherapy. I thought that it might be more sensible to use the limited time available for consultation, that is, for seeing students three or four times only. I might in that period hope to be able to help the individual student find out something about the nature of his problems and difficulties – to learn to feel and think about them and generally take stock of himself in the presence of someone not involved in his daily life; someone, moreover, both willing to listen and trained to appreciate emotional distress. There was no selection on my part. I saw any student who asked to see me, but more usually these were students who had been advised to take this step by a general practitioner or a lecturer.

Two aspects of this way of using my time appealed to me. One was that it meant I had the opportunity of seeing a greater number of students and could therefore learn more about the range of problems in the student population. The other was that it provided the challenge of applying my previous experience to a new technique, appropriate to the situation. I found this work both demanding and stimulating, and often more was achieved than I had first dared hope. The time limit tends to introduce a note of urgency which may well lead to extra mental-emotional exertion on the part of both client and therapist alike. When it is made clear that the task of exploration is a shared one, the young person is encouraged to mobilize his capacities to observe and listen to himself and weigh up the evidence. Given the opportunity, the healthy and more adult part of the personality can come to the fore. Here it assists in the process of understanding infantile wishes and of looking at destructive drives and anxieties which are interfering with relationships and the achievement of adult tasks.

The work requires of the client an availability and awareness of feelings in depth and the capacity to reflect about them. The dual task of experiencing feelings and of thinking about them is essential to any therapeutic work. For if there is only an intellectual understanding of the conflict, a kind of theoretical formulation of it, no change can take place. Change can only come about on the basis of learning from an emotional experience. Unless feelings are brought out and experienced in the present, the work remains academic, which may enable the person to present a better facade to the outside world, but does not alter anything in his actual attitudes or his inner world. On the other hand, if his adult faculties are abandoned by the client, he will simply use the therapeutic situation to 'dump' his problems and the responsibility for himself on to the therapist. The onus of working things out is then left to her, with the expectation that she can effect a magic cure. Or the client may hope that, as he is so very helpless, the therapist will yield to his pressures to continue her work for longer than the stated number of times. The study of such expectations, along with the frustrations arising from the time limit, form an integral part of the therapeutic task. It is very important in brief work that one does not in any way encourage dependency on oneself as a person, but on the process of observation and discovery. Feelings re-evoked in the consulting-room towards the therapist are used as live instances of the nature of the client's relationships. These are communications from the client which allow one to study his attitudes towards others in his external and internal world.

The work is, of course, in no way to be thought of as an equivalent but speeded up process of full psychotherapy, a brief intervention which can have the same outcome as long-term treatment. It is no panacea solving the scarcity of, or unavailability of, psychotherapy resources. Nor is it suitable as anything but a part-time activity for the therapist herself. Continuing detailed analytic work is essential in order to keep alive the hard-won emotional sensitivity and openness to unconscious processes in all their depth and complexity, both in oneself and one's patients. It is precisely this basis of therapeutic work in depth which enables one quickly to discern the nature of the problems presented and to have the conviction to face them fully and unflinchingly with the client.

It will be apparent that the therapist engaged in such work

offers something different from what is generally assumed under the term counselling. Career counselling, for example, might include giving advice and guidance on jobs or educational training, and might involve psychological tests. The term consultation, on the other hand, might suggest the medical model of diagnosis without much active participation on the part of the client, followed by a prescription for the correct treatment. Neither of these definitions would cover the nature of our work, for as therapists we are purely concerned with allowing emotions to be fully experienced in order to facilitate self-scrutiny and understanding. This process in itself can bring relief and contribute towards emotional growth. The latter is not aimed for as such, but may be the natural consequence of the client's attempt to discover the meaning of his reactions, the motivation for his actions, and the source of his unease and distress. In some cases, the experience with the therapist provides a model of thinking about feelings, which remains operative well beyond the actual work done together.

While regrettably it is still rare for child psychotherapists to offer brief consultations within the framework of a university, quite a few have undertaken this work in other settings. I am thinking especially of my colleagues at the Tavistock Clinic who work in the Young People's Counselling Service there. This service is a non-treatment, counselling one, staffed by psychologists, social workers and psychotherapists. The other organization I have in mind is the Brent Consultation Centre – linked to the Centre for the Study of Adolescence – at which a number of therapists who were trained at the Hampstead Child Therapy Clinic work part-time. Both services are open to all young people, on a self-referral basis. While the therapists offer their help to a wide age range, from mid-adolescence to mid-twenties, the majority of those who avail themselves of it are seventeen or over.

The need young people have for psychological help of this kind and the actual paucity of facilities available are increasingly becoming recognized. Adolescence is a period of rapid change, outwardly marked by the transition from school to more unstructured educational institutions or to work, from living at home to living outside the close family circle, and perhaps even embarking on marriage and founding one's own home. It is a time of important decision-making in relation to studies, to career and sexual relationships, a time in which the young person's hopes and fears about becoming an adult are put to the test of reality. How well he can manage these various transitions will depend on his previous development, on the extent to which he has integrated destructive and sexual impulses in the service of work and loving relationships; on whether he has reached adulthood by a gradual process of learning from helpful adults in his environment, or taken a leap into pseudo-adult behaviour.

Transition depends also on the outer stresses and temptations with which life faces the individual. At this time of uncertainty about his identity, and about his ability to be creative in work and social relationships, fears, worries and depression abound. These quite readily assume gigantic proportions in his mind. There may be an internal experience of crisis or, if the conflict becomes too overwhelming, it may become externalized and acted out, and may result in an actual life-crisis. Hence a service readily available and confidential, where individuals can discuss their emotional problems, is of particular value to this age group. Where a problem is due to some obstacle to emotional development, an understanding of the underlying conflict can sometimes free the young person to use his abilities and his environment in a more constructive way. Provided he is really concerned about the problem and not just inclined to leave the worry and pain with others (as, for example, delinquents tend to do), a little help can go a long way at this time of rapid maturational development.

The service also fulfils an important function for those youngsters who, wanting the chance to talk about themselves, are yet too frightened to make use of the ordinary psychiatric services. To go or be sent to a psychiatrist can be felt to imply that one is seriously mentally ill rather than merely temporarily disturbed or having a long-standing emotional problem. Youngsters may be afraid, too, of being fobbed off with reassurance, or given drugs rather than understanding. Where a clinic is known to be analytically orientated, they may be reluctant to ask for help for fear of being deemed 'a suitable case for treatment', whisked into psychotherapy and propelled into a long-term commitment. The chance to have a first go at assessing the nature and extent of the problem, the sure knowledge that the commitment is limited, and the chance to be actively involved in deciding whether any further treatment is necessary and desirable – all these aspects are probably of concern at any age, but doubly so for the young person unsure of himself and perhaps suspicious of adults in authority. Where further treatment is being considered by the client, the consultation interviews provide a taste of the nature of the analytic approach, and the hard work it requires. They give both therapist and client a chance to decide whether psychotherapy is something likely to be useful in this instance and moment in time. It is sometimes suggested that youngsters are unable to wait for treatment: our experience has shown that a few interviews are usually sufficient to enable them to contain the anxiety situation well enough till a vacancy occurs.

There now follow case illustrations from the two settings I have worked in, the Student Health Centre and the Young People's Counselling Service. These will allow further examination of the method I developed and some of the considerations which govern this work. I shall, of course, not reveal any personal data which would enable anyone other than the clients themselves to recognize the identity of the individual discussed.

## Feeling Abandoned and Lost

Mr A was in his first term at university. His general practitioner had been called in when this young man felt unusually sick after getting drunk. Mr A mentioned that he often became extremely depressed, and it was suggested to him that he might like to have a few consultations with the therapist on the university staff. Mr A agreed, and was sent an appointment to see me a few days later. He arrived forty minutes late, staggered into my room and sank into the chair opposite me. I wondered silently whether he was drugged. When I asked him to tell me what had made him come nearly at the end of the hour I had reserved for him, he said that he had only just woken up after taking an overdose of sleeping pills; he was still feeling very drowsy. I offered the interpretation that he seemed to want to show me a need to be taken care of, but I did not on this occasion enquire further about his suicidal gesture. I said that I would like his doctor to see him now and that we would talk further next week. Mr A was subsequently sent to the local hospital for a stomach wash-out and stayed there a few days.

When he came to see me the following week, he said that he had been quite happy in hospital and had been visited there by members of his family. I asked him to tell me what had led up to his taking an overdose. He replied that he really did not know what made him do it: he had never done such a thing before. He had been feeling depressed and got drunk. Then when he woke up he felt even more depressed, had another bout of drinking and then took the pills. I commented on his inability to stand the pain of depression, wanting to drown it or put it to sleep so as not to know about it. I asked how long he had felt like this. He said he had only been drinking heavily since coming to university six weeks ago – he had not made any friends and felt very lonely in his digs – but actually he had been depressed on and off for as long as he could remember. This led me to ask him about his home. He said they were a big family because his mother adored babies. He said then that it was 'heaven' to be a baby, you got all you wanted, were cuddled and carried about everywhere. But when the next one came along you were dropped and left to fight for yourself. One's mother just did not care any more what happened to one and gave all of herself to the new baby. I learnt that he had one older sister, and six younger siblings. I commented that coming to university had perhaps felt to a child part of him as if he had been thrown out of the home and his mother's enveloping care, in the same way as he had felt dropped and abandoned by her at the age of two when his brother was born. It seemed that taking an overdose just on the eve of coming to see me was a communication to me that was something like, 'I shall die unless you take me into your maternal care.' Mr A said that this made sense. (On reflection I had doubted whether it had been necessary to admit him to hospital. The admission appeared to be more a response to his emotional than his medical need – he had certainly managed to evoke in everyone the feeling that he required nursing.) We then talked about feeling either totally cared for or totally abandoned. Mr A began to reflect on whether his mother had actually neglected him. She had come down at once when she heard that he was in hospital. She had written to him regularly since he left home and her letters had been affectionate and full of concern: in some ways he thought he was still her favourite. So we established that his mother was not, in fact, so uncaring. Rather, that his feeling rejected arose from his wish to remain the baby for ever and from his acute jealousy of his younger siblings. I suggested that he might like to think further about these issues.

In the next interview he reported a dream. He and his brothers had performed gymnastic antics in front of a female audience and he had outshone everyone and receïved the greatest applause. He gave me some examples of how in reality he still gets favours from his mother by being charming to her. I pointed out that he not only wanted to be fed and looked after by mother but also be the one who filled her with delight, so that she needed neither other children nor a husband. I commented on the fact that he had not mentioned his father at all. We discussed how his rivalry with men for the attention of females had contributed to his loneliness and had interfered with his making friends among fellow-students. He had deliberately chosen not to live in a students' hostel, preferring to be looked after by a landlady – not surprisingly, she had not lived up to his more infantile expectations. Equally, there emerged now a wish to be thought of by his tutor as a specially gifted student, without his having to make any particular effort. The comment on his first essay, 'Shows promise but harder effort is required to keep up with the work,' had annoyed him. I queried whether he felt that he should be able to get by with only talent and charm. He seemed to respond to demands to work harder like a spoilt child who felt he should be admired whatever he does. I also had the impression that, having obtained some relief during our first two interviews, he was reluctant to exert himself to work much further with me. The point raised the question of how much his reluctance was generated by the knowledge that we would only meet once more. This consideration might have been a contributory factor, but I thought nevertheless that there was an infantile part of him which wanted me to do most of the work and which lapsed readily into a passive relationship.

Mr A arrived barefooted and a few minutes late for his third interview. He said he had spent the night at a student sit-in. He was not very interested in the protest as such, nor sure that it was justified, but it had been warm and cosy and he had enjoyed being part of a group. I wondered whether he thought that his own protest at being dropped by his mother and now by me was no longer justified, but that he still felt left out in the cold and lost. I said that he seemed to deal with these feelings by huddling close to others for comfort and warmth, as if wanting to get back inside mother's ken, rather than having to struggle with being outside. Mr A acknowledged such feelings of loneliness and exclusion, but explained that he experienced them rather differently from before: 'I feel more miserable but less rejected.' He knew now that his mother was concerned about him. He also thought that if he got desperate again he would contact me or his doctor rather than take to drink and pills. Knowing how despairing and neglected this young man could feel, I wondered if it might be a good idea if we made an appointment for the beginning of the following term. I said he was, of course, free to contact me earlier if necessary. He agreed to my suggestion and kept his follow-up appointment two months later.

He now reported that he felt better. He had experienced many mood swings but they were less extreme than they used to be and his depressed states did not last so long. He had joined some student societies and had also acquired an older girlfriend. His main worry was now about his work: when he had to write essays he felt anxious and angry. He thought he demanded an awful lot from other people and from himself: 'It has to be all or nothing.' I said this reminded me of how he had felt he got 'all or nothing' from his mother and wondered whether this might result in an internal feeling of a greedy mother, who was demanding that he give everything back. He confirmed this interpretation by telling me that he experienced his tutor as infinitely demanding – which made him in fact want to produce very little. At other times he felt anxious, afraid that 'there's nothing inside my head'. I wondered whether he took in knowledge in such a greedy way – just as he felt he had emptied out his mother – that it was all destroyed inside him, made into nothing that he could reproduce. He was very interested in these ideas and requested another interview in the third term, just before his exams.

It will be seen from this condensed report that a very limited piece of work had been carried out and only a tiny fraction of the problems touched on. The case illustrates that in a brief contact the client tends to present – or rather unconsciously selects – the most urgent problem, and *this* becomes the focus of the joint work of exploration. In a crisis situation, quite primitive affective states and attitudes come to the fore and are relived in the present. Put another way, the crisis has arisen because a happening in the present has re-evoked an earlier, inadequately integrated, anxiety situation. In Mr A's case, leaving home and feeling lost in new surroundings revived the experience of being 'dropped out of heaven' by his mother. These infantile emotions, alive here and now, become available to be looked at and dealt with in a new way. The more adult part of the client in alliance with the therapist can name them – for example, 'feeling dropped', 'rejected' and 'jealous' – rather than just experiencing depression in a generalized way. More than that, internal phantasied reality (a neglecting mother) can be differentiated from external actual reality (a mother having a new baby, but continuing to be concerned about the other children).

This process allows the client to recognize to what extent the internal picture derives from infantile demands and destructive drives. The pain remains – in Mr A's case the feelings of loneliness at being no longer mother's special baby – but it has been divested of a component which previously made it unbearable, namely that of a hostile or uncaring mother. As Mr A said, 'I still get depressed at times but I tend to feel more miserable, and not so rejected and angry.' The possibility then opens up of seeking constructive ways of dealing with loneliness, such as forming new relationships. These are viable alternatives to seeking a way out through angry self-destructiveness, intended psychologically as an attack on the 'neglecting mother'. It could be argued that this young man needed long-term psychotherapy. The possibility was mooted but he felt he had received as much help as he wanted at present. I also privately considered that his pull towards passivity did not augur too well for therapy, that he might in fact exploit a therapeutic relationship and become parasitically dependent.

A particular problem is posed by patients with suicidal tendencies in brief counselling. In Mr A's case the suicidal gesture was primarily meant to arouse anxiety, to prompt me to care for him, not only by understanding but also physically.

It was greatly supportive to myself to work in a medical context which could deal with this aspect and ensure the patient's safety. If one meets such a case in a non-medical counselling service, liaison with a general practitioner or hospital may have to be established.

## A Homosexual Involvement

Mr B had frequently consulted his doctor because of anal irritation and ulcers. He had told the doctor that he was an active homosexual and that he had recently been very upset during his man-friend's temporary absence.

When I first saw Mr B he was reluctant to talk to me. It was not so much that he felt embarrassed, but he was afraid, as he told me, that clarification of his problems might lead to change. Whenever he talked to girls about his homosexual commitment they tried to convince him of his heterosexuality. I commented that he seemed to be afraid that I would not tolerate his preference for men and might want to force a change upon him. He said sometimes he wished he were interested in heterosexual relationships, because he could see that homosexual liaisons did not last forever. The thought of becoming a promiscuous old man was abhorrent, but equally he could not face being all alone in his old age. If one married, one would at least not be deserted; there would be children to keep one company even if one's wife died. I commented on his dread of old age and loneliness. Also that it sounded to me as if he thought parents needed children to keep them company, rather than the other way around. I wondered what his family was like. He said that his parents were very happy together and very close, in spite of the fact that his father had to be away on business sometimes for weeks on end. There were two older brothers and one much younger sister. He was very fond of his sister and had enjoyed looking after her. He could remember how radiant his mother had looked during her pregnancy. I commented that perhaps there was a feminine part of him that would like to be able both to bear and look after children.

He then spoke about his relationship with his boyfriend as ideal – it was a perfect kind of love. Phillip was kind, generous, clever and beautiful and he wanted him 'for keeps'. When Phillip had recently gone to visit another friend, Mr B had been surprised how awful he had felt. He had promptly dreamt of stabbing both Phillip and himself. I pointed out that his dream must make him wonder whether his attitude to Phillip really was so loving. It indicated great possessiveness and quite murderous impulses. Mr B then remarked that he could not visualize Phillip growing old, he could not tolerate any faults and blemishes in him. I said that perhaps he had discovered, and was shocked to realize, that a relationship could be quite sadistic behind what appeared so ideal.

When we came to talk about his childhood, Mr B remembered how dreadfully homesick he had been when he first went to boarding-school – the teachers nearly sent him home because he would not eat or sleep. He also remembered an earlier time of being away from home when he had cried and cried for his mother. His homosexual practices had not started at school. At that time he not only disapproved of such behaviour in other boys but was disgusted at masturbation – he thought it too wicked to indulge in this himself. It was after he left school, during a holiday with his parents, that he succumbed to a young man's seduction. At first he felt very guilty and then came to depend on such relationships. I said that I got the impression that he could not stand the loneliness and jealousy of mother and father together. He affirmed vehemently that he could not stand being alone, and there followed many detailed accounts of feeling panic-stricken. He always thought someone would appear from under his bed, or from behind the curtain, or jump out of the cupboard, knife in hand. He could not go out at night alone for fear of being attacked from behind. In the evenings in his room the fear of 'little people' or a man coming to cut him up was so persistent that he could not work. When he went to bed, he resigned himself to being killed in his sleep. Often he awoke sweating from some terrible dream, and in particular there was one recurrent nightmare. In it he tried to call out for his mother and run to her, but was unable to do either, because he would be killed if he moved or opened his mouth. What I said to him, briefly, was that he was indeed describing real terror, the terror of living in a nightmarish world since his childhood, and of feeling himself to be at the mercy of an extremely hostile father and the other children who barred him from getting to his mother. Unable to face such terror alone, he seemed to have listened to the voice of an 'older brother' inside him who promised that he need not be frightened as long as he obeyed him. His homosexual relationship seemed to be based on his terror of a sadistic attack from a brother/father which he had turned into pleasurable submission.

Two further interviews can be summarized by saying that he brought to me more detailed and extensive descriptions of his fears, and these led to deepening doubts about his love for Phillip, and a greater courage to defy men and seek heterosexual relationships. He actually broke off his relationship with Phillip in the face of the latter's protests. I expressed the opinion that nothing short of an analysis would bring about a lasting change, but this for the moment was unacceptable to Mr B. I do not know what happened eventually, but he came to see me after six months to tell me that he had not resumed any homosexual relationships and was seriously involved with a girl.

I think that Mr B's willingness to come to see me was an indication that he was already wanting to get away from a relationship he had begun to regard with suspicion. All the same, the fears which held him to it were so massive, and of such a terrifying nature, that I was surprised at his ability to make a stand at all. I still very much wonder how permanent or far-reaching his improvement was. But I have been impressed in this, and other instances, by the strength of the healthy part of the personality and the ability to struggle against cruel dominant parts once the underlying anxiety has been understood and partially relieved. One of the factors that has a decisive influence on a client's ability to use a limited number of interviews is whether or not he can build on previous good experiences, and trust in a helping parental figure.

## A Younger Client: Rebelliousness and Uncertainty

Miss C came to see me after hearing a friend talk about how the Young People's Counselling Service had helped her. Miss C herself rang for an appointment, but had her friend accompany her to the clinic. She was small and looked younger than her sixteen years. She darted me a quick glance and I noticed that her eyes were bright and sparkling – an aspect of her which did not match her rather drab appearance and her statement that she was 'extremely depressed'. She was not sure that she could tell me what bothered her. She did not respond to my comment that it must be difficult to trust a stranger, but continued to chew and tear at her handkerchief, looking rather sullen. I commented that she seemed not only afraid to talk, but also sulky and angry, as if she wanted to hang on to her feelings rather than use this opportunity to see if she and I could understand her depression. She again threw me a quick, rather suspicious look, and said, 'What's the use?' I said that although she had picked up enough courage to come to me, she had great doubts about whether thinking and talking would be useful.

When she again retreated for quite a while into herself, tugging at her handkerchief and clothes, I suggested that she was perhaps wanting me to feel useless and no good in the same way that she did. At this she began to tell me that she had been unhappy, getting more and more depressed over the last months. She spent a great deal of time moping in her room and found she could not even confide in her friends. I asked her whether any particular event had started this development. She then told me that 'something happened with a boy' – he was not sure whether he wanted to go out with her any more – which is 'just the last straw when one feels so uncertain anyway'. I wondered whether this event had increased her doubts about herself, made her feel unlikeable and unloveable. I encouraged her to tell me more about herself and her family. Oh, she didn't talk to her parents much, they were strict Roman Catholics and had never approved of her friends. She decided two years ago that she would just go her own way and take no notice of her parents' views. She had gone out with a number of boys of her own age and a few months ago had had intercourse. This information came out jerkily, in half-sentences and rather angrily, as if I ought to know without being told. Having to prompt her, however, made me feel that I was being encouraged to intrude into her private world. I commented that she was treating me as a spying and interfering adult, yet provoking me to force myself upon her . It seemed as if there was very little feeling on her part that we had a joint responsibility to find out what caused her unhappiness. I wondered whether this reflected a general mistrust of adults.

Her sullen way of talking gave me the impression that she was not so much pathetic, as rather a sulking, rebellious little girl who burdened others with her depression, yet frustrated their attempts to be helpful. I drew her attention to these impressions, saying that she seemed more concerned to nurse a grudge than be helped to understand why she was depressed.

She then told me that the sexual experience had been a big disappointment. The two of them just had intercourse to find out what it was like, but she had felt nothing. Nor did she or the boy want to have anything further to do with each other afterwards. She felt cheated and now very uncertain of herself. I wondered whether she had expected some fantastically exciting experience. She said, yes, they tell you so in films and magazines. I said she seemed to feel that this was a personal promise that had been held out to her, and that she had been cheated in some way. As if, perhaps, her parents inside her as well as outside did not allow her to have a fulfilling grown-up kind of intercourse. Perhaps her suspicion that her parents wanted to keep sexuality to themselves and not let her be an adult had made her throw herself into this relationship and to experiment, rather than let such an experience grow out of feelings of real fondness and commitment to a boy. I related her feeling of doubt and worthlessness to having used the boy, and let herself be used by him, in a way that made her feel that she had betrayed a valuable womanly part of herself, as well as, of course, her parents. She agreed that the experience had made her feel more worthless, but as far as her parents were concerned she did not experience any guilt. Her mother was a dictator and wanted her to stay at home just to look after her.

It now emerged that her mother had been very ill during the past two years and might die at any time. I said Miss C sounded as if she did not care at all: I thought that this indifference was related to her feeling her mother's illness was a way of keeping her as a little slave-girl – a plot by a spiteful mummy trying deliberately to deprive her daughter of enjoying her youth. This feeling had perhaps made her turn away defiantly and grab at sexuality. But it had also left her with a feeling of a mummy who was angry and did not support her daughter's growth towards enjoying a loving kind of relationship with a boy.

While I spoke Miss C gradually turned towards me and her expression became far more open and lively. She said she had never thought of it all in this way: she had always felt the injured party. Her withdrawal from her group had evoked concern and attention from the others – yet she had not found this comforting, really. I said perhaps the attention failed to comfort her because it did not deal with her depression, based on her angry uncaring part and her fear that no one, including herself, could tolerate it. Miss C became very thoughtful and, to my surprise, thanked me at the end of the session. She made an arrangement to see me the following week, but phoned on the day itself to say she could not come. For several weeks running, she asked for alternative appointments, only to cancel them again.

One issue which arises out of this case is whether one should pursue a client who is reluctant to come for further interviews. We hold the view that in these kinds of consultations there is no commitment to the therapist, and that the client should be quite free to come back or not. Some would go as far as saying to the client, 'I can offer you up to three appointments,' rather than implying that there is a standard number of interviews. It means that in some cases, as here with Miss C, the therapist has to bear the uncertainty and worry of not knowing what has happened to the client or what use the discussion has been put to. Nor is one able to check on the correctness of one's assessment and interpretations. The only circumstance in which one does definitely take action is when the client is thought to be a danger to himself or others. This aspect would be discussed during the course of the interview. In Miss C's case, I feel reasonably confident that she gained quite a lot of insight and relief from our interview. Perhaps also she wanted me to feel guilty at having hurt her with some painful truths, leaving in me the guilt she found so hard to face. We might also speculate that she kept me hanging on and disappointed, doubting my own worth, in much the same way she had felt disappointed, uncertain and worthless. While I did not feel it incumbent on me to urge her to come again, I wanted to let her know that I was not offended by her absence. I therefore wrote to her, saying that I would be interested to hear how she was, and that if she wanted to come again at some future time, I should be pleased to see her.

**A Suitable Case for Analysis**

Mr D had been complaining to the doctor in the Student Health Service of 'diminution of sexual drive and interest' over the past year. He had had a number of girlfriends of whom he was fond, and had had intercourse with two of them. Once he got sexually involved, however, he lost interest in the girls. When he came to see me he was obviously very embarrassed: he avoided looking at me, and his speech was hesitant. After we had talked about his problem, he was able to tell me that he felt his behaviour to the girls was unfair. He took them seriously but once they became deeply interested in him, he became tense, felt nauseous, could not eat, and fled. Subsequently, he would feel guilty at leaving them in a mess. On one occasion he had discovered blood and pus on his pyjamas, and though he had no reason to suspect his girlfriend, he went to a V.D. clinic for a check-up. When tests proved negative, he felt disgusted with himself.

In this first interview, we talked primarily about his despair that working things out logically, as he had always done in the past, did not resolve his problems; also about his fear of exploring feelings. I said that he seemed to find real involvement terrifying, either because of some fear of a dangerous, poisonous female or else because he was afraid of messing up others. It was obviously very difficult for him to bring himself to talk about these matters and I was impressed by the courage and honesty with which he attempted to work with me in spite of this.

He cancelled the following appointment. When I saw him again he told me that he had had to do some work out of town and it was 'not worthwhile' coming back just for the interview. Anyway we had 'not got very far' last time. He put this down to his fear and tenseness, but then added that he had come with the wrong kind of expectations – he had hoped that I would tell him that he had nothing much to worry about. Yet it was obvious to him that this was not so. He wondered whether he could do what I expected of him. I said that although the adult part of him realized that he was just having a conversation with me, the same anxieties seemed to be cropping up in relation to me as those he described with his girlfriends. There appeared to be some fear of having to give more than he wanted or felt able to give, and some concern about his mental-emotional, as well as physical, potency. After a pause, he said that he had a lot of thoughts about our previous conversation but he supposed they were all rubbish. He was worried that he might have led me to believe that he could get emotionally involved with girls. He now realized that he was all right only as long as he remained aloof. He supposed it was silly but he had often wondered whether he was close even to his parents. He rarely visited them and had, for instance, not gone to see them on his birthday last week. He had first questioned his love for his parents when he was eleven years old. As a test of whether he really loved them, he had asked himself what he would do if something happened to them. What sacrifices would he be prepared to make for them? I asked whether in fact there had been some actual grounds for worrying about their safety or health. Yes, there always had been. His mother had been fragile and ailing as long as Mr D could remember. In fact, she had been sick and generally unwell from the second week of her pregnancy with him, and at first the doctor thought that she would have a miscarriage. He had remained the only child. I said that this circumstance might have made him feel that women were very vulnerable and did not have the strength to cope with him. He said, 'Perhaps.' He could see the point intellectually but could not feel it. I wondered, too, whether it made him frightened of what he did to them, as if right from the start, already in the womb, he had made his mother ill. All this, I suggested, perhaps entered into his decision to stay away last time, in the second week of my pregnancy with him, so to speak. He said he knew he had not been a satisfying and rewarding baby. He had been told that he did not thrive for some months and his mother had tried one brand of milk after the other. When he was three years old, his mother had had a depressive breakdown; the doctor had advised her to go away to rest, but she had not done so. I said he seemed to feel somehow responsible for not giving her enough pleasure and for rejecting the food she offered. I wondered about his feeling worried that too much was expected of him, both then and now – as if he had to care for a sick mother and put her right, rather than finding someone to carry the frightened and despairing parts of himself. (It may well be that I was over-feeding him, but I took the maternal concern he evoked in me as an indication both of his need, and his propensity for tenderness and affection.) It had become clear to both of us that he might want to have treatment, and that we would need to discuss this next time.

Mr D arrived a few minutes late for his next interview, saying he had no watch so did not know whether he was early or late. He commented that it seemed a long time since he had seen me last; it felt much more than a week. He told me that he had had a letter from his girlfriend who wanted to break off the relationship. He added, 'You will not be surprised to learn that I am rather relieved.' He had been considering what he might do after getting his post-graduate degree. He had been surprised how well his examinations had gone and that his tutor thought so well of him. He was not terribly interested to pursue his present line of study; while he was keen on his general subject, his speciality was 'too far removed from life'. He had found that the same thing had happened with his hobby: he used to do life drawings, but lately he had only made abstract designs and they did not hold any real interest for him. I said that he was giving me to understand that he felt despairing about his remoteness from lively contacts and creativity, yet, on the other hand, it was also a relief when a contact with a real live person came to an end. I thought that his pessimism was based on a reluctance to risk failure and disappointment. We talked about his inability to maintain hope over this past week which had seemed so long to him and the fear that no relationship would be good enough. I then tried to formulate his character-structure as it had emerged during these three interviews and relate it to his history. I began talking to him about analysis, as it seemed essential that gaps between sessions should not be too long. He needed someone reliable, dependable, strong enough and available enough to risk getting involved emotionally. He said the thought of getting analytic treatment had crossed his mind since seeing me. We discussed some of the practical issues. As he was about to finish his studies, he thought it might be feasible for him to move to London and apply for a subsidized analysis at the London Clinic of Psycho-Analysis. I offered to support his application, but made it clear that there was absolutely no guarantee that they would accept him. By the following week, he had definitely made up his mind and had already taken some steps to implement such a plan. I heard later that he had been accepted, and found that the analytic experience helped him to get back into 'life' and close relationships.

## Abortion

Miss E was brought by her boyfriend when she was nine weeks pregnant. She told me that she had decided to have an abortion, but her boyfriend was afraid that this might damage her and wanted her to re-think the decision. Miss E looked radiant and exuded self-confidence. She said she had made up her mind, she was just coming to me to please Paul. When I encouraged her to tell me about Paul, she spoke of him in a warm and loving way. He was kind and intelligent and they shared many interests. He was the first person in her life with whom she felt secure and at peace. Last spring they had suddenly had a great urge to have a baby; she had no doubt about wanting to get married to Paul, and he had also decided to marry her. She could not, however, tell her parents about the baby. They would never forgive her. If she faced them with her pregnancy, they would say this proved how irresponsible she was, and so forbid her to marry Paul. The point was that they would have to rely on her parents' financial support, as both Paul and she were in the middle of their professional training. Miss E remarked that she was sure her mother would treat her like a naughty child. She remembered that when she was a little girl, she used to say to her mother, 'Oh mummy, I am sorry, I did not mean to upset you, I shan't do it again.' And her mother would reply, 'It's no good promising, I know you will.'

I took up this aspect and said that it seemed that even now, although twenty-three and living away from home, she still had these internal conversations with her mother. She was behaving as if her relationship with Paul was being a 'naughty girl', defying her mother's edicts and so upsetting her. Although no doubt it would be easier if her parents supported them, so that she too could complete her training, she did not seem to have considered the possibility of sacrificing such plans and taking responsibility for the child she had so much wanted to conceive. Miss E replied that nothing could alter her decision to have an abortion and she had already made an appointment at the hosital. I said that I had no intention of persuading her to keep the baby, but only wanted her to think through her decision fully and consider what it might mean to her and Paul. I wondered, for example, how it might affect their future relationship. She replied that the appropriate time for me to help her was after she had had the abortion. I said that sounded as if she expected to be upset and depressed afterwards. She answered rather petulantly, 'Maybe.' I then commented that she was assigning to me the task of picking up the pieces after the event, rather than helping her to examine her feelings so that she might know on what basis she took this step. Also I drew her attention to the fact that she talked about the baby as 'it', as if she did not want to think of the life inside her as the first of her children. At this she stalked out, saying that she was not sure she would come again because by next week the abortion would probably have been fixed up.

Indeed, it was only on Paul's insistence that she did come for a second interview. She said she was definitely not keeping the baby and nothing could change her mind now. I pointed out that unless she was at least willing to entertain the opposite notion, she would never be sure on what grounds her decision was based. I said I had the impression of an obstinate little girl engaged in a personal vendetta with me, just as if she were still fighting with her mother. She wanted to have her own way, rather than consider the decision in an adult and responsible fashion. Miss E then said she had never been close to her mother – in fact, she had spent a good part of her early childhood at her aunt's home. The reason was that her mother had become pregnant again almost immediately after giving birth to Miss E. When the second child was born, he was weak and difficult to rear, so her mother was fully occupied with him. Miss E had never got on well with this child, Joseph. She always fought with him, to the extent that at one stage it had not been safe to leave him with her. I thought that this suggested that she had felt quite murderous towards him – perhaps she had never forgiven her mother for giving so little attention to her and so much to Joseph? I wondered whether the baby inside her might be felt by a child-part of her not to be her own at all, but confused with her mother's little boy that she wanted to throw away. She listened in silence and then said rather sneeringly, 'That's all fairy-tale stuff.'

She came to see me once more, and announced that she

was keeping the baby after all. This, of course, had 'nothing to do with our talks'. She was planning to marry shortly and Paul was coming home with her this weekend to tell her parents. She thought that her mother might, perhaps, be not all that unreasonable. In a dream the other night, her mother had looked at Miss E's swollen stomach and after chiding 'just a little' had embraced her. It was hard for me to hide my pleasure, but I did so, knowing that it might have been misunderstood as my satisfaction at my own ideas – my 'mental babies' – rather than at her achievement of arriving at a thoughtful decision. I have indeed no certainty that the interpretations I made helped Miss E to keep her baby, but I tend to think that the shift in her feelings about her mother were not unrelated to her experience in the consulting room. I suspect that the undoing of the confusion between her own child and her mother's was important. Also experiencing me as a mother who, knowing about murderously jealous feelings towards a brother, still allowed her to have a baby of her own, made it possible for the forgiving aspect of her own internal mother to come to the fore. This disentangling enabled Miss E to make a choice based on a better appreciation of internal resources.

It might be thought that I should have seen this client together with her fiancé. However, not only was it Miss E's wish to come on her own, but it seemed that there must be some conflict inside which interfered with her having the baby that both of them so much desired. The unearthing of such very private feelings embedded in the client's emotional development seems to me most appropriately dealt with in individual interviews.

It might also be questioned whether I was not making deep interpretations on too little evidence. This is admittedly a risk in a situation when the therapist feels pushed for time, and where the client is about to take an irrevocable step. It should be borne in mind that the analytically trained therapist relies not only on the verbal communications the client makes, but is guided by the feeling-tone and the responses evoked in herself by the many non-verbal communications. It is important to let one's mind wander over all these possible clues. But equally, it is important in brief counselling to put interpretations and comments tentatively. These are offered as a possible way of understanding what has been stated explicitly and implicitly, rather than implying a degree of certainty. This tentativeness encourages the client also to consider matters from different angles and join in exploring further.

While the way the client relates to me is part of the evidence of the nature of his attitudes to others and to himself, it is something that one is wary to verbalize. I tend myself not to draw attention to positive feelings because I would not wish in any way to strengthen a personal attachment to me, that would be bound to increase dependency and make it difficult to end the series of interviews. On the other hand, where the client's feelings towards the therapist are hindering the work in hand, either because they are negative (as with Miss C) or too parasitically infantile (as with Mr A), I find it essential to verbalize them.

## Summary

I hope that the five examples presented here in brief form convey some idea of the variety of problems that clients bring to a counselling service. The way the young person entered into the relationship with the therapist was different in each case, and so was the outcome of the consultations. The latter was not dictated by any specific goal the therapist had set, but was the result of examining what the client expected or wanted from these interviews. A further factor is the client's capacity to use the actual help offered. The help given involves the therapist's capacity to listen and to question, in order to enable the client to take stock of himself and to face his feelings and attitudes, sincerely and in depth. It will be evident that the work is not only brief but tends to be very intense.

This intensity arises from the fact that the therapist neither blurs over the conflicts, nor gives reassurance, nor sees her role as necessarily confirming the client's view of life. Instead she is interested in helping the client discover the truth about himself however painful the process may be. The client thus finds that ready-made solutions are questioned, vague feelings brought to the light of day, their nature examined and possibly traced to their childhood source. While the adult part of the client is encouraged to join with the therapist in the task of exploration, quite primitive feelings can come into the open and be experienced acutely. Unconsciously, the client selects some pressing anxiety and with it brings details from both his past and present life-situations. These make it possible for the therapist to propose meaningful links. This leads to clarification of what the problems may be about and what underlying conflicts might have led to the present impasse. The experience enables the client to feel that infantile demands and destructive drives can be looked at and borne without necessarily being condoned. This sincere enquiry, and the discovery that strange or confused feelings are meaningful, can encourage the client to continue to do 'homework', scrutinizing and wondering about his relationships and learning from that experience.

Certainly I as a therapist have learnt a great deal from this brief work, and I am constantly amazed at some clients' capacity to make such full use of so few interviews. For therapists mainly engaged in long-term treatment, such counselling can make a real contribution towards their appreciation of the strengths in some of their patients. This knowledge helps to mitigate too much timorousness and over-protectiveness. Such attitudes can lead therapists (and others) to encourage undue parasitism and dependency in their patients, instead of helping them to use their inner resources and take greater responsibility for getting on with the work. Brief counselling, as here described, leaves one with a sense of gladness at the flexibility of many young people's mental structures and their drive for understanding and growth.

I am anxious to acknowledge my debt to my colleagues in the Young People's Counselling Service. The discussion of our work over a number of years has helped to clarify the concepts of brief counselling presented in this chapter. While I myself take responsibility for the views expressed here, they are in the main shared by us all and we tend to follow similar lines in our work.

# Chapter Eight

# *A Study of an Elective Mute*

## by Pat Radford

We now turn to a more detailed case study of a younger child. This chapter describes in detail the course of psychotherapy, over a period of years, with a little boy of six who did not speak outside the home. We are shown the vivid phantasy play of this child and the events leading up to his first words in the treatment sessions. The case well illustrates the therapeutic process and the complex dynamics behind this unusual symptom. Above all, we see the careful, painstaking work over a period of time which a child psychotherapist may undertake with an individual child. M.B., D.D.

---

### The First Sessions

Rob was just six years old when psychotherapy began. My first impression was of a little marionette, a puppet on strings – pale-faced, clumsy, uncoordinated in all his non-stop jigging, feverishly giggling while he pressed his fingertips together, walking on tip-toes. His odd appearance was not helped by his particularly large head, nor by his exaggerated miming – his only method of communicating with me.

The intensity of his anxiety, however, forced him to elaborate his mimes in the first few weeks of treatment, until I could verbalize what he was acting for me. Frightening, exciting intercourse scenes culminated in him constantly placing a baby's bottle to his penis, which he also tried to suck as if performing fellatio. I was at a loss to understand the significance of this miming, which had an immediacy to it either indicating a current trauma totally out of keeping with the assessment of his parents' sexual relationship, or a frightening failure of the normal repressive processes of childhood amnesia. If the latter were the case, he was having constantly to re-live old, anxious excitements which his immature personality was unable to master. I was bewildered both by the scope and range of the material. Typically, in session after session, he would present me, through his vivid actions, with five or six themes, as if he must pour them all out. I found myself thinking of a constipated child having diarrhoea.

In one session, endlessly jumping and giggling, he ran into my room, grabbed the chalk and drew and mimed lorries being bombed, crashing to fall in pieces into the water trough. I said it sounded as if there were explosions which could damage. His response was to charge to the open toy cupboard, pick up a naked female doll, look at its bottom excitedly, and then fling it into the water with the lorry, deliberately knocking them together as if in a sexual act. When I commented that the doll seemed so excited with this game it might want to shout, Rob immediately picked up a toy crocodile from the cupboard. But he was terrified of it and dropped it as if afraid it could literally bite him. Frantically he then kicked it out of the room. I wondered why he had done that. Could a crocodile harm us? Rob responded to my clarification by showing his wish to be as destructive as a crocodile. He grabbed an Indian chief and a squaw with a baby. The chief violently attacked the baby but the baby retaliated. Rob, without a sound, made the baby attack the father and throw him out. Then it attacked the mother, and threw her out. Rob found more crocodiles and tried to make them and the adults eat each other. When I warned him of the end of the session he chewed and tore at the teat of the baby's bottle.

The different components of Rob's emotional disturbance were clarified through this material. The crashing lorries represented his angry explosions. The female doll represented his overt sexual curiosity and the Indian episode his jealous rivalry with his father. Finally, the biting crocodiles and the gnawed teat represented his fury with the unsatisfactory mother-therapist. It was as if there were no security or pleasure in any aspect of his relationships, only fear and hostility from his own feelings and his projection of them on to objects. With these feelings now transferred to me, he obviously expected my hostility, as he became increasingly provoking and demanding in his silent-behaviour in sessions. He was reliving his primitive longing to be as one with mother and so avoid the sadness and anger aroused at having to share her.

## The Background

Rob, at six years of age, was referred to the child guidance department of a hospital by the paediatrician who had known him since he was three years old. He had been referred to her at that time because he was not talking to anyone, although his parents reported that there was some inarticulate speech in the home. The paediatrician recognized that the child was socially isolated by reason of his family's problems and recommended that Rob should join a nursery class. Rob separated easily from his mother, but he did not talk or play with anyone during the entire two years he was at the nursery. This pattern was continued when he then moved to primary school. However, the impact of the move to the larger unit broke down some of his resistance to speech. He began talking in a compulsive manner with his parents at home, when they were alone. The paediatrician was now concerned about the increased size of Rob's head. Nevertheless, on investigation no evidence of hydrocephalus or other brain damage was found. She became convinced that emotional disturbance was of greater significance in the causation of the symptom and so referred him to the Department of Child Psychiatry.

At her diagnostic interview the child psychiatrist found Rob's behaviour and appearance most odd, agreeing with the parents' report. Rob was an unplanned and unexpected pregnancy for his mother, aged thirty and his father, aged fifty-five, eight years after their marriage. Labour was difficult. The baby was in an unusual position. Reports from the gynaecologist, however, showed no birth damage. His early development was not markedly slow, yet he was not a contented baby. He did not enjoy his bottle and from two months he was banging his head and scratching at his cot.

Eczema began at the same time, and this still appears on his legs under stress. His mother said she 'toilet trained' him from birth. When he began to walk at eighteen months he rebelled against his mother's regime and had violent tantrums. He was not clean and dry until he was four years of age. Speech was delayed. He was managing a few words at three, when his mother unexpectedly had to go into hospital for a few days. Rob meanwhile was looked after by father. He was most distressed by the loss of his mother, and both parents thought that he did not speak again until he was around five.

There had always been a question mark over Rob's physical condition. His head was large from the birth and it was wondered whether there was any parietal lobe damage, although no factual evidence of this has been found. His muscular co-ordination was poor and he had an extremely stiff gait. Weight and general growth were, however, satisfactory. Nonetheless, he was a faddy eater, refusing all foods which had to be chewed. Mealtimes, like all other behavioural areas, were a battleground between the parents and the child.

## The Parents

It was hard for the parents to see behind Rob's belligerent facade the terrified child which the psychiatrist recognized. This was a child whose life was dominated by fears – of dogs, of stairs, of traffic, of being hurt, of falling down, of being alone. Above all, of noise. He maintained such an aggressive cover for his anxieties that his over-anxious parents were totally unaware of his need for an exceptional degree of their protection.

His mother, Mrs B, the third of six children, had lost her own mother when she was four years of age. Although she had had an efficient stepmother, she had lacked sufficient loving. She married a father figure, a man twenty-five years older than herself, from whom she expected loving care. Mr B, however, was an extremely rigid, meticulous person, who could not adapt either to his wife's or his son's demands. He jealously resented his wife's excessive attention to Rob, while feeling quite inadequate to meet the child's needs himself. It was inevitable that the child was be a pawn in this pathological marriage. As in the work of Browne and his colleagues (1971), here too was the problem not just of individual, but of family psychopathology, which we had to try to deal with in its totality.

**Diagnostic Assessment**

There was no doubt, whatever the parental contribution, that Rob had a neurotic conflict in his own right. At his diagnostic interview his frantic play, flitting from smashing cars to jumping away from devouring crocodiles, had indicated an intense degree of anxiety associated with any show of aggression towards, or from, the parent-dolls. He made no contact with the psychiatrist, but his manner of play gave more evidence of average intelligence than psychological testing had been able to assess. In the testing session he had been totally uncooperative, even on non-verbal items, effectively illustrating his attitude towards school, where he seemed to be learning nothing. He presented a paradoxical picture, a child with severe controlling inhibitions which would suddenly break down into uncontrolled impulsive behaviour – though never to the extent of allowing himself speech. Every aspect of his personality was involved in his psychic conflict – his relationships, his drives, both aggressive and libidinal, and his ego.

**Further Sessions: Jealousy**

Rob's jealousy of his parents' relationship was very soon demonstrated when, having seen me talking to another patient, he grabbed a large toy dog from the waiting room. Like the crocodile he wished to be, he bit the dog and attacked it in a most brutal way. I interpreted his displaced wish to attack the person to whom I had been speaking. Breathing heavily, but still without words, he at once drowned the dog, smearing dirt all over it, gnashing his teeth violently. I verbalized his wish to bite and mess on me to stop me talking with others. He confirmed this interpretation by picking up the toy telephone, at the same time grabbing the small mother-doll and pulling off its head. Then, drawing my head on the board (he gestured that it was meant to be me) he tried to bite it. I said he looked like a crocodile. He drew one on the board but then produced a terrific fiery dragon which devoured the crocodile. I interpreted Rob's intrapsychic conflict: the infantile crocodile part of him which greedily wanted me for himself was attacked by his powerful conscience, his dragon, punishing him for such wishes.

Before the next session he had nightmares. He illustrated these on the blackboard – a witch (myself) whom he bit and ate. By projection of his hostility I had become a dangerous witch whom he tried to control by incorporating. He was trying to master his anxiety by identifying with me, the aggressor. He brought me to the father-doll, indicating it was ill and weak, and then threw it away. Then he drew a mother/boy witch whom he would marry and make into one person; a man witch who never opened his mouth. He seemed to think he had found the way to become omnipotent and not fear attack from adult male or female figures.

Now feeling so powerful, he dared to show overt anger to me. He began many sessions gnashing his teeth, drawing my car being destroyed by a thunderstorm which he, the powerful god, had started. But this material was inevitably preceded by a panic attack on the stairs, when he seemed unable to mount until I had verbalized his fear that I would have disappeared. I interpreted his anger with me at the weekly wait between sessions and he confirmed the interpretation in silently drawing three vivid paintings: a picture of the hospital in sunshine (the kind Miss Radford); one of himself with two extremely large mouths (hungry for more time with Miss Radford); and a third in which the hospital and Robby were destroyed by a storm (angry Robby). This last drawing was accompanied by more of Robby's vicious gnashing of his teeth.

My acceptance of Robby's need to feel more loved and wanted helped him to accept his guilt about his ambivalent feelings. He introduced, through a comic, benign, reparative figures: Thunderbirds International Rescue. This group was used to protect us against Rob's angry feelings. On one occasion he drew the Rescue Ship to make sure I understood and then forced me into a corner with himself and the toy Humpty Dumpty and Teddy Bear, which we had already identified as the damaged and baby parts of himself. Thunderbirds must come to rescue us from the 'shouting' monster who wanted to destroy me and the hungry, angry boy. I identified the silently shouting monster as yet another part of

Robby, the part of which he was most afraid, since he did not feel able to keep it in control except by silencing it completely. He had now illustrated his anxiety that his weak, disintegrated ego could be overwhelmed by his powerful aggressive drive, unless he maintained the device of his elective mutism to avoid conflict. He had made it clear how his terror of noise and avoidance of speech were defences against his hostile wishes, by which he would destroy his beloved objects.

## Separation Anxiety and the Fear of Anger

We soon experienced Robby's fear of his own destructiveness very dramatically in session. We had had a week's holiday. Rob would not look at me in the waiting room and he fell on the stairs – recognized indications of anger and fear. I accidentally knocked over a tin noisily. Robby ran out of the treatment room in sheer terror and was unable to return, until I directly linked his fear of the noise with his fear that his anger had killed me. Timidly he stood looking at the tin as if it were a live bomb. I asked why the tin seemed so dangerous. At once Robby jammed his hand over my mouth. He could recognize, helped by my verbalization, how he equated speech with explosions. He insisted we must call in Thunderbirds – the kind, powerful figures – which could guard us against explosive feelings. We alone (mother and Robby) were not strong enough to cope – realistic assessment of his mother's inability to keep them both safe from his explosive anger when he was small.

The psychiatric social worker in her weekly interviews with the mother had uncovered a frightened woman whose own reality testing, too, seemed impaired. Mrs B had brief psychotic episodes in which she seemed slightly depersonalized. These, of course, added to her uncertainty about herself and her son and their relationship. Her husband's carping criticism was as devastating to her own self-esteem as it was to Robby's.

*The parents' inadequacy in solving the problems of their relationship only intensifies the child's helplessness and feelings of hostility. The mutism becomes an omnipotent weapon to offset the helplessness and to punish the inadequate objects. But the neurotic interaction of the family is such that it preserves the symptom indefinitely.* (Browne *et al.*, 1963)

Robby now brought a large, stuffed monkey into the treatment to represent the aggressive aspects of himself. His symbolic process was obviously developing. The monkey clearly showed that Robby wanted to talk, for he made its lips move. As monkey, I yelled on its behalf (of course, Rob's) that I was tired of keeping silent. Rob immediately collapsed on the floor in abject terror, crawling away with monkey to the cloakroom. I took up the monkey's aggressive wishes hidden under Rob's fear of noise. Rob immediately became the 'good' monkey, making me tea and scrubbing the floor, while he introduced a more perfect mother – Lady Penelope. Lady Penelope was the heroine of the Thunderbirds, who could help him more than I did when he showed he wanted to be a great chief. The part of Lady Penelope was played by one of the stuffed dolls.

The real mother who collapsed at the sound of bangs, as Rob demonstrated in the session, was of no use to offset the fears arising from his competitive wishes. Only the ideal mother, Lady Penelope, could protect him. And he held Lady Penelope while I had to read from his chosen book, which vividly portrayed his own problems. It was an illustrated adventure from *Huckleberry Finn*, in which Tom, Huck and Becky had to escape from the evil male, Injun Joe, into a make-believe land. This proved equally beset with dangers, until the prince found his lost love and all ended happily. For session after session I had to repeat the story with no deviation, and Rob remained calmly, silently peaceful. But the idyll could not last. I was unexpectedly ill and missed a session.

## Trauma and Speech

At our next meeting, Rob effectively relived the trauma occasioned when his mother had unexpectedly gone to and returned from hospital, when Rob was three years old. Rob did not look at me on my own return, but drew a complicated picture of what he indicated was my house, perhaps being bombed by a little spaceman called Robby. I said I could not understand the drawing. Robby made the monkey cry and pushed him at me to comfort it. I commented on Rob's sadness last week. He put his hand over my mouth. I was only to be the ideal mother reading Huck Finn's adventures, having to repeat the prince's despairing call for his beloved Marna. But I was allowed now to identify the prince and Marna as Robby and myself. Sadly, as the prince in the story, I noted the passing time. Robby joined in and for the first time in his life spoke to someone other than his parents. He said 'cuckoo' like a cuckoo clock. I continued to read. The prince called to Marna, 'Where are you?' and Rob, now shouting, repeated it. I went on reading. The prince found Marna, as I said Rob had found me today. Rob angrily yelled at me, 'Shut up!' And then for the next twenty minutes *he talked.* He poured out, with entirely appropriate words, a commentary on the activities of the family dolls in the dolls' house.

He made a man he called the father try to mend the drainpipe. The woman, the mother, verbally criticized him: the father was extremely angry and turned on the little boy, who was told to go upstairs. The boy protested loudly that he could not go because he was frightened and there were ghosts. The father said sarcastically, 'Yes, and I am Jesus Christ the Saviour and I'll deal with the ghosts.' The boy now dashed to the safer world of the TV. The father yelled that the boy was a stupid imbecile and, 'Go back to bed!' I commented that I was sorry for the boy who seemed frightened. Rob at once displaced the problems on to me. He told me that I was a stupid idiot who had not understood his drawing. It was about snow, not bombs and there was a snowman who would become a ghost, who would disappear into nothing. I wondered if Rob had been bothered last week that I had disappeared to become a frightening ghost. Rob said I was stupid. No one was disappearing. All the family were staying together in the house. I once again warned him of the end of the session. Reluctantly he left the treatment room and stopped talking. I said he had again stopped speaking because he was angry with me sending him away, as he had been with Mummy when she went away. He quickly said he was coming back to see me.

Since then Rob has talked at all his sessions – first only in the treatment room, but gradually wherever he was with me. Provided his mother did not see she was allowed to hear.

*Why could Rob talk?*

My absence and safe return after a week's intense anxiety – Rob had had nightmares and soiled – undoubtedly precipitated a reliving of the old experience at three years when his mother was in hospital. I had verbalized Rob's feelings for me of sadness, loneliness, anger and sense of loss, which his mother had been unable to tolerate when she came back from hospital. But the vital preparation which had made it possible for Rob to abandon the elective mutism with me had taken a year's treatment. We had together understood how he feared that his explosive anger and his faeces could destroy the mother who had left him. He had relived these feelings in the transference; but with the help of my interpretations he could recognize he had not killed me. In reality I remained a reliable, safe object whom his powerful noisewords could not make dead and turn into a frightening ghost to hurt him. He no longer had to maintain the mutism in the treatment situation as a self-protective reaction to a hostile, rejecting environment. He did not have to relive the phantasy outcome he had elaborated in which the mother was unwilling to protect the boy either from the powerful father who wished to destroy his son or from his own terrifying nightmares, wishes and fears. In the safe relationship with the therapist he no longer needed the omnipotent control of his speech to counterbalance his overwhelming feelings of helplessness.

## The Problem of Concrete Speech

Despite the breakthrough, I quickly discovered that speech for Robby was not the normal ego-organizing agent, but that his misunderstanding and misinterpretation of words actually added to his feelings of helplessness. I appreciated for the first time that concrete thinking dominated his thought processes. The social isolation forced on him by his major symptom, as well as his environmental deprivation, prevented him from questioning the meanings of words. He could not test reality through speech, to help himself make the move from concrete to abstract ways of thought. His literal interpretation of everything heard filled him with an all-pervasive dread of a dangerous world where whatever was spoken happened. 'If he speaks,' said his mother, 'I'll die laughing.' For Rob, this meant his mother would die.

I now had to learn the meaning of Rob's speech. This was not only concretized, but frequently based on a primitive type of thought, in which condensation of ideas and lack of time-sense excluded reality testing of the here-and-now. As far as therapeutic treatment was concerned, it was irrelevant how far his aberration was the result of minimal brain damage, with a resultant ego defect, or whether his elective mutism had psychologically worked against the development of thinking along normal lines.

It was my task to find my way through to his ways of thinking in order to help him understand the real world about him. The immensity of my task was spelled out for me when I realized how Rob has misinterpreted his name - Robert - to be Robot. He thought this identity must be him. His stiff-legged gait, machine-like movements and staccato speech were the robot's - a puppet out of its own control. His frantic attempts in his miming to establish a more satisfying identity, a more acceptable self-image, for example through his transient identifications with TV characters, could now be understood in the context of concrete thinking. There, in those identifications, he could escape from the identity of the stupid robot existence which he thought his parents had assigned him: 'They gave me my name.'

## The Puppet

The unfolding clinical material showed why Rob had gone along with this identity of a blithering, silent puppet. Through it he avoided the 'evil' consequences of his greedy demandingness. He wanted me, the mother, entirely for himself. But others might challenge this claim and he, the boy, would not be powerful enough to keep me unless he maintained omnipotent control - that is, by keeping silent. He elaborated this wish through his interpretation of the story of Peter and the Wolf, a record he had memorized at school while still totally silent. Rob assigned the roles. Rob-Peter began as a little boy driven away from his home by the greedy wolf. But then he grew into the big man who changed the wolf into a little poodle with harmless, round eyes which could never pierce you and gobble you, as the greedy wolf had gobbled the duck. I clarified that Rob fitted into all these roles. Accepting my interpretation, he elaborated his theme. The greedy wolf was killed by the big man and cut open. Inside his tummy was the duck with its legs and arms torn off, its lungs pulled out, and unable to talk. Rob insisted that I should be called in to make the poor duck whole again. I interpreted Robby's wish that I, as the all-powerful, all-kind mother-doctor would get rid of the greedy part of Robby, which, like his shouting monster part, would make him castrated and impotent. Rob screamed at me that I must get rid of the greedy eyes. Beside himself with terror, he could not bear my acceptance of his greed. It was too dangerous for his vulnerable ego to allow this instinctual wish. He screamed that I must say the wolf was dead and could do no more harm. I clarified Rob's fear that he would not become a man if he did not destroy his greedy, infantile wishes. Rob yelled he didn't want to be a man, but a footballer like Georgie Best – a man hated by his father. I said that I was delighted, as that meant it was safe for Rob to be greedy in the way Georgie Best must be greedy for goals. Rob, startled, accepted that greed itself might not be bad, but for him it was not safe. Greedy eyes were ghosts' eyes, ghosts who tried to eat you up with their eyes. (We were later to link this statement directly with his death wishes towards his father.) We must not talk about it, we were to go back to the comforting Huck Finn.

For the first time now Rob was held up by the picture of Injun Joe. He said that Injun Joe had greedy, greedy eyes, and we must shut the book. I said I was sorry to shut out Joe. Rob thoughtfully wondered whether Injun Joe was greedy because he felt cold and hungry and nobody loved him. But did I know that poor Tom Sawyer had lost his willie because he was a baddie? This wasn't because he had greedy eyes, it was just because he wanted to get rid of Injun Joe.

Rob could hardly have put more clearly or specifically the intermixture of his oedipal and oral wishes and the defensive use of his mutism to avoid the consequences of them. I brought together all aspects of the phantasy to interpret his unconscious castration fear. If he were greedy for me, mother, and wanted to get rid of the Daddy/husband, the man with the bigger willie might also be greedy, a wolf who could destroy the little duck, Robby. He would not be able to defend himself unless helped by the 'omnipotent' Mummy/therapist, but he knew she was not strong. She did not have a willie.

Rob confirmed the interpretation and his disappointment in the mother. He told me that he once had a full baby's bottle but his Mummy had thrown it out. That had made him feel very cross, so cross he wanted to shit on her. He thus introduced the anal aspect of his psychic conflict to complete the developmental picture of disturbance. The infantile wish to incorporate the mother and so keep her for himself was frustrated by his own explosive hostility, as he was forced to recognize the existence of the father-rival powerful enough to render the child impotent. He had to find some ways to control his internal conflicts. His elective mutism had seemed able to contain all aspects though to the detriment of his development and growth.

## Progress and Insight

We had to continue to try, through psychotherapy, to resolve these internal conflicts and enable Robby to continue to develop through his own strengths, to find more economic ways of growing in his unsupportive environment. Psychotherapy had enabled him so far to become aware of some of the underlying motivations for his unhappy, disturbed behaviour – his powerful, aggressive impulses, linked with his fears for his own safety in a world made hostile by his feelings and reinforced by the reality of his unprotective parents. Rob told me: 'If a father and mother dies, the child must die too.'

However, in the protected setting of regular psychotherapy sessions, Rob had regained the minimum basic trust built up in his early childhood months. Here he could relive his conflicts in the safe relationship with the therapist and test the effects of his and his environment's hostility in reality, not terrifying phantasy.

Interviews with the parents by psychiatric social workers had underlined their problems. The father's insistence that his son was an incapable imbecile was found to hide his own fear that he must become a decrepit, useless old man who would die if Rob grew in strength. As Rob now refused to maintain the role of the idiot child, the father's health deteriorated. He began to have trouble with his ears – 'noise hurts them' – rising blood pressure and, for the first time in twenty-four years, time off work. He openly blamed Rob for his troubles, and made no attempt to protect the boy from the mother's neurotic anxiety which prevented Rob going to school. It became essential to overcome the mother's fears by transferring Rob to a school where he could spend each whole day and have an opportunity to become part of its community – no longer, therefore, to be brought home by mother to eat and defecate, because she was sure it would damage him to stay at school. Rob accepted the change with relief. The new school became a place of safety where, although still refusing to speak, he participated in the life of the class, not only taking in knowledge, but also reproducing it for his teacher through mimes and writing. It was as if he extended to his new school the positive feelings that he had towards treatment, rather than the intense ambivalence he currently felt to his mother.

## Competition and Castration Fears

Rob was openly acknowledging his wish to be clever, to be better than father/my husband. He insisted he was a good decorator, and demanded to know whom I had let decorate my home. Then he immediately said that he didn't want to hear about a man with greedy eyes. I noted that he didn't want to know anything about the man in my home. He responded by remarking that his father was going into hospital to have his ears treated because they had been hurt by Robby's shouting. The doctor would be my husband and he cut off tongues. I interpreted Rob's wish to hurt my man and his resulting castration fear that as a consequence he would lose his penis/tongue. Robby recalled that when he was a little boy he had been to this hospital and my doctor-man had put something down his throat and so injured it that Robby could never speak again.

Rob's identification of his tongue with his vulnerable penis had only strengthened the need to maintain his control over his speech. This control was, moreover, a double-edged tool. Retention of speech not only protected him from attack, it enabled him to maintain his phantasy that he was powerful. He would only have to speak to destroy his rivals. This phantasy was still reinforced by his concrete thinking. He actually believed his parents' remarks that his talking would deafen them and send them mad.

Rob was helpless, yet powerful, and he did not know how

to reconcile these two images. He tried to puzzle out how the powerful Jesus Christ (father) who was God could also be the son of God who was crucified. I underlined his speculation, how could a boy so powerful as to stop himself talking be in danger from a powerful father? Rob responded with vivid, confused phantasies of competition and death in which it was only too easy to see how partially understood comments and scenes had complemented his phantasies, turning the real world into a bewildering place.

For many sessions I had to participate in a re-enactment of a TV show, 'The Golden Shot'. Any attempt on my part to question what role I was supposed to be playing, so that I could understand the phantasy involved, inevitably resulted in a physical panic-attack on me. When I objected to being hurt, Rob would immediately become Robert the Robot who was not responsible for what he did. I clarified the anxiety behind this defence and learned that Rob was convinced that in the show the man with the loud voice was my husband and that he was aiming the shot out of the screen to kill Rob, who was sitting looking at it with me. Having interpreted the castration fears, I commented on Rob's wish to share things with me and his jealousy when I was with my husband. He responded by drawing a picture of me with enormous breasts which the Robby-puppet was trying to suck, while he yelled, 'Shit, shit, shit.' I commented that greedy baby Robby wanted to shout shit at me if he could not have me for himself. He quickly told me a shitty baby should shut up. If it speaks it will be walloped on the bottom. When I wondered what the baby had done wrong, Robby said it was obnoxious. They, the parents, would not want an obnoxious baby. But they liked puppets on strings – a justification on his part for maintaining the role of Robert the Robot. I suggested that Rob thought no one could hurt a wooden puppet no matter what it did. He responded with one of his seemingly chaotic phantasies which was so condensed as to be unintelligible unless I went along with the roles assigned to me until the light began to dawn for me.

Rob told me I had to make some coffins and lie in one, dead, with my face covered with a towel, so proving I could not speak when dead. I eventually triggered off Rob's intense anxiety when, although dead, I asked why I was dead. He screamed at me that he was by my side in a grave and we couldn't talk to each other, could we? I pointed out that we could not be the dead ones as we were talking. Who ought to be in the coffins? His father and my husband should be dead in coffins like the people from the Black September catastrophe he had seen on TV. But there were no lids on their coffins, so the father's mouth would open and eat Robby. And this was like Tutankhamun, a dead king, a living Mummy inside several coffins who would stop him eating anyone, including the king himself. When, as always, I had first clarified the specific aspects of the phantasy, I suggested that this was his old conflict. Robby wanted to get rid of the Daddy/husband but he was afraid that even dead in a coffin, or dead as a ghost, the man could still hurt him. He could do so especially as Mummy/me did not help, perhaps because we had gone away.

These interpretations did not, however, seem able to relieve his anxiety sufficiently to allow him to resolve the conflict. In a series of devastating sessions, he showed me why. He changed the Lady Penelope doll to a deaf and dumb mother/girl called Rina. Robby, as father, swore at her for talking to others. He threatened her with imprisonment, tore out her hair and chopped off her tongue. But then, overwhelmed by his own castration fears, Rob abandoned his attempt to identify with the adult father/rival. He screamed there was a black monster ghost in the room who had been Jesus Christ dead on the cross. Rob was not sure if he would stay dead: when, before his next session, Rob saw me speaking to a male doctor, he became convinced Jesus had come to life again. He acted out his phantasy of what the angry, powerful father would do to the rival son. Robby attacked Rina/mother, cursing, telling her she would never talk again but nevertheless demanding she stay with him. Then quickly the punishing father intervened. Rina became the castrated, damaged boy whose mother had gone to hospital to a doctor. Robby, enacting father, told Rina in the most violent tones that she was wetting her pants, she was dirty and she was talking too much. Every insult was accompanied by a slap on the face and always the threat of, 'I'll shut your mouth for ever.' He stuck Sellotape over Rina's mouth so that she would not only be unable to talk but also unable to breathe and so die.

It is impossible to over-emphasize the violence that Rob

used in these sessions. Certainly from his own fears he had introjected an appallingly sadistic representation of a father, furious with him for demanding the mother the little three-year-old thought had left him. His only safety lay in not talking. The power of this terrifying, internal, alien introject could not be mitigated, because of the continuing reality of a father given to violent outbursts of rage. Robby's own projected hostility on to the father intensified his fear of reprisals.

However, Rob learned to realize, through the comings and goings of sessions, that no doctor took me away for ever any more than Mummy had been lost indefinitely. He coped even with the second three-week summer holiday. He told me I should not have gone as he was lonely and had had no one to talk to; however, he remained an integrated personality. His improved physical co-ordination was maintained. His achievements at school continued, and he was even willing to talk to others in order to make me as jealous as he himself had been.

Rob began another session sure he had seen me talking to the doctor. He slapped Rina very hard and then he decided he was going to use the telephone actually to speak to the secretary in the office. I was to sit there and not dare to speak. He put his hand over my mouth while he carried on a long, involved conversation with the secretary, including pungent criticisms of me. I interpreted this behaviour not only as a wish to make me as mother jealous, but also, in his family's triangle, to make father jealous. From observing Robby in the waiting-room, when he deliberately stopped talking or reading to me (he was now reading competently) as soon as his mother appeared, I had noted the provoking collusion between them as if each were daring the other to make a third in the conversation. When I commented on this, his mother would giggle like a flirtatious teenager, as if she were enjoying a familiar situation when, feeling cheated and neglected by her impotent husband, she used Robby as her sexual object. She had no wish for a third party, and clearly she was as jealous of him talking to me as he was of his mother talking 'in secret' to the psychiatric social worker. Both of them were frightened that if they verbalized this jealousy to the third person, they must be rejected and treatment would be stopped. The mother's conviction that treatment must stop if Robby talked to others was clearly a reflection of her pathological reasons why she could never encourage Robby to speak. She could never say to the child that he had the right to talk. So Rob had to do it himself.

**The Symptom as Loss**

Certainly, Rob was beginning to appreciate the secondary drawbacks of his elective mutism. He told me that he, the little monkey, was lonely, sad and had no friends. This was because he couldn't talk. When I returned after having flu he told me that John, the little boy in 'Thunderbirds', was lonely, unhappy and in despair. He was alone, needing someone to take care of him and talk to him: I must go at once to rescue him. I said John must be three-year-old Robby with Mummy in hospital. He dashed to the adjoining cloakroom and noisily defecated, yelling at me that he wanted to kick me right out. Later I could take up how he had turned this anger against himself, by drawing attention to his scratching his bleeding legs. The eczema had reappeared during my three weeks' absence. I interpreted that he was punishing his legs – part of his self – for wanting to kick me for not being with him. As the shouting started, the scratching stopped, and the eczema cleared within two weeks. Robby could stop using his body to express his affective loneliness and anger with his mother, but he still found it difficult to cope with his anxiety arising from his projected hostility on to the father-figure.

Rob demanded to know what doctor had looked after me while I was ill, and then immediately went into a panic state, giggling, uncoordinated and screaming in his anxious, falsetto voice. He insisted I must act the man who shot the cord which released the cascade of coins in 'The Golden Shot' programme. The panic was so acute that it seemed that Rob was showing fears of disintegration (the cut cord and the falling coins representing the losing and emptying of his body), as well as of anal explosiveness and castration. I asked if he thought he might fall to pieces if the doctor took me away from him. He clutched at my hand, demanded I should carry him as the stairs were collapsing – a return of his old phobia of stairs, which we had worked through previously as part of his worries over masturbation and castration. I said he seemed to think the whole world was collapsing, and only I, the omnipotent mother, could save him from danger. But where was the danger? Rob confirmed my understanding of his behaviour as a regression from his own oedipal fears by yelling at me that I was a clumsy, stupid idiot. Interpretation of this displacement on to me of his father's denigration of Rob, and Rob's need to identify with it to avoid further conflict, freed him again to verbalize his wish to be superior to father.

## Masculine Identification

Rob found new ways of achieving this superiority in finding a strong masculine figure with which to identify. He dared not identify with a father whom he felt would destroy him. His earlier method of taking on the identity of TV characters no longer satisfied him – with his improved reality testing, he knew 'it's only pretend'. So he attempted to find another way to feel loved and to build up his self-esteem.

He was like a boy called Tom who wanted to become a mermaid. He longed to do this because he hated being a boy. He thought nobody liked boys, so he would be a mermaid sitting on a rock, and he was happy. But didn't I realize there was something wrong – he'd still got a boy's voice. I must change it and give him a girl's sweet voice that everybody would like to hear. I wondered if Tom thought his parents preferred girls' soft, sweet voices to boys' strong, powerful ones. He nodded sadly. But indignantly, he said, a mermaid had no willie! A new voice was no good without a willie, and he threw the girl Rina doll out of the room. I applauded his determination to stay a boy with a powerful voice/penis. But, he told me, men damaged women. He, a boy, had torn Mummy's tummy when he was born and that was why she had left him when he was three years old! He had seen a man hurt a woman with his willie and she then bit it off. He reminded me that he had shown me this when he first came to treatment, how he had peeped in at the activities of his neighbours. His verbalization of this really seen or imagined trauma, and of his sadistic wishes generally, enabled him to rejoice in his masculinity and to move forward rapidly in his development.

Rob took on a challenging adult identification with my

man. He was Dr Rob, an extremely clever person. He knew the answers to such questions as why a boy had to stop talking and appear stupid. It was because he had felt jealous and angry. The solution was easy. At five the boy could not talk because all he wanted to say were rude and nasty things to his father and mother. But now he was big and strong, aged ten, and he would be able to stop himself saying rude things to anyone! I thought that was a funny way to use his strength, to stop himself saying things. Dr Rob was not so sure, he had better examine my odd head. With my interpretation, Rob could now recognize how he had used his mutism as a defence against his own angry wishes, because he had thought such feelings made him mad and he would be sent away. Rob handed me the stethoscope. The patient was all right - and did I know he was going to talk to everybody on his tenth birthday? I suggested he was like a little boy who was holding on to his faeces until he was ready, even if it gave him a tummy ache. That was silly, Robby said, he would tell his teacher. But would he then still be able to tell me?

With Rob's acceptance that he, too, could have more than one loved object, he is moving towards complete resolution of his conflict and his symptomatology. He has an integrated personality, still with the vulnerable areas but with enough inner strength, based on an adequate reality testing, not to be overwhelmed by instinctual urges or external traumas. The diminution of concrete thinking and the now preponderance of rational thought has made speech an asset to clarify, not distort, the world. He has learned to differentiate between phantasy and reality, between his own fears and his mother's, between thought, speech and action. No one dropped dead because he thought or said so.

## Factors Contributing to Progress

Many factors have contributed to change this child from the pathetic puppet who started treatment to a physically co-ordinated, intelligent nine-year-old boy. First, significant changes in the home and later the school environment were vitally important in making the real world in which Rob lived a factually less hostile place. The painstaking work of the psychiatric social workers with the parents reaped its reward. Rob was allowed to develop when the parents achieved other ways of working out their problems. His teachers supported his growth, supplying him with the appreciation of his achievements which his parents withheld.

None of these environmental changes would, however, have been effective by themselves if our psychotherapeutic efforts had not succeeded in clarifying, and changing, Rob's psychic reality. The phobic, panic-stricken, bewildered elective mute, uncoordinated physically and mentally, lacking the psychic means to understand the discordant noises which terrified him, would have been incapable of making use of the most understanding environment. That he later did so was the outcome of the insight he gained into the unconscious basis of his symptoms. This could then be examined in the light of his more mature, reality-orientated knowledge, and readjustments made to his developed ego strengths.

## Summary

We had slowly unwound the strings of the puppet to find the greedy, jealous, hostile toddler who felt unloved and rejected for these very feelings and who angrily responded with omnipotent control of the hostile world. The omnipotence itself manifested in his elective mutism. His belief that his anal explosive wishes, which he equated with noise and speech, could and should destroy the objects on which he depended for his safety showed his uncontrolled ambivalence to them. His terror of the castrating father emphasized the strength of his oedipal longings to destroy the powerful man who could take the mother from him. Rob's longing to gobble him up intensified the equation of his tongue with his penis and made retention of speech the only safe course to avoid becoming the actually preferred girl. It was only in the safety of the transference relationship with the therapist that he could relive and resolve these all-pervasive psychic conflicts. He could consciously accept his sexual and aggressive wishes without being so punished by his sadistic super-ego (the introjected parents) as to submit himself to the massive secondary defects latent in his chosen symptomatology. The world was no longer a hostile place peopled with avenging ghosts of those killed by his omnipotent thoughts. The consequences of thinking and speaking had become differentiated from action. It was safe to emerge from social isolation.

His negative, sadistic attitude was no longer required. People wanted to hear him speak and speak he could – as Rob sang for me, 'We will overcome one day.'

**Clinical Data and Review of Literature**

This clinical material, obtained from a boy undergoing once-weekly psychotherapy for a period of three years from the age of six, may at least help to show how many of the factors concerned were interrelated. Their psychic relationship integrated the major, presenting symptom into his personality. My psychoanalytic understanding of the dynamic, economic and genetic origins of the factors followed the unfolding of the clinical material in sessions with the child and his parents. The therapeutic technique used was based on my understanding of the material the child brought in phantasy, play and, later, speech. This material was clarified and interpreted through the use of the transference phenomenon, which I understand as a reliving in the here-and-now relationship with the psychotherapist the unconscious conflicts surviving from former relationships, and other psychic events which have affected development in the past.

From a study of the literature (see page 317) it is clear that most authors are puzzled by the complexity of the symptom of elective mutism and its poor response to a variety of methods of treatment. Several theories are put forward on its causation and long-term effects. The extensive observations of Von Misch (1952) led him to argue a galaxy of causes. He considered that environmental factors can precipitate mutism; that it may occur when there had been a sudden separation from the family, especially at the time of entry into school; and that whilst factors of heredity and intelligence must play some part, basically the disorder was psychogenic. In all cases which he examined he found exaggerated ties to the mother. The selection of mutism as a symptom might possibly, he felt, be related to a traumatic event at the time that the child was developing speech. These various theories have all been upheld in turn by successive investigators.

H. L. Wright (1968) considered that in all cases of elective mutism there was an underlying dominant neurotic problem.

Halpern *et al.* (1971) were of the opinion that a combination of factors, such as a traumatic experience during the critical period of language development, or conflicts within the family involving talking, openness or dependency, were vital. Wyatt (1964) felt we should look at the early mother-child relationship for lack of feedback from the mother's communication with the child as a basis for the symptom. He thought that if the mother were withdrawn or inadequate, the child's capacity for word-finding would be disturbed. Then the child would react with anger against the mother at his own feelings of helplessness and at being unable to communicate with her. Further loss of contact with the mother would follow and the child's hostility could then be shown by its witholding words. Adams and Glassner (1954) certainly subscribed to this view, namely that the mutism in the child was a self-protective reaction to the hostile, rejecting environment provided by the mother. Browne *et al.* (1963) thought that the children who choose this symptom appear to be either fixated at or regressed to the anal stage of development. They seem to develop an intense negativistic and sadistic relationship towards most adults. They then utilize their muteness as a weapon to punish people who have offended them. This study found that parents of such children are unhappy in their marriage and that the mother may use the child to attack the father.

Clearly, there is a considerable breadth of opinion on what causes or may cause this particular symptom. All these views, however, do involve some aspect of the parent-child relationship. Interestingly, many of the theories advanced could be equally specific to other neurotic disturbances – for example, to encopresis or stammering, with the recognizable witholding of faeces or words. It may well be that only in looking at the complexity of the many internal and external factors seemingly involved can we find an answer to the question why elective mutism in particular, with its many secondary disadvantages, is chosen as the compromise solution to the child's neurotic conflict.

I wish to acknowledge my indebtedness to my colleagues – Miss J. M. Barton and Miss A. Burton – with whom it has been my pleasure to work.

# Chapter Nine

# *Beginnings in Communication: Two Children in Psychotherapy*

## by Jess Guthrie

What happens if a child not only does not talk, like the one described in the previous chapter, but cannot even play? Jess Guthrie, a psychotherapist with long experience, who has died since this chapter was first published, gives a sensitive and illuminating account of a psychotherapist's attempt to get into contact with two very disturbed children, who could not communicate in an ordinary way. M. B., D. D.

---

In their everyday living children naturally express themselves through their play. By this means inner feelings, fears, wishes and phantasies find form in relation to the outside world. Their expression helps to relieve anxiety and contributes to the child's growing ability to discriminate between inner and outer reality. If, however, anxiety has become more acute than a child can satisfactorily manage, he may come into psychotherapy for help with his emotional difficulties. Then, if he is able to play, that self-expression can be used as a medium of natural communication between himself and the therapist. At the same time, of course, one is in touch with the child through spoken language, absorbing what he says, at times conveying one's understanding and helping him to put his thoughts and feelings into words. Some children, through no lack of intelligence, come into treatment unable to speak, or with their speech restricted to certain persons to the exclusion of others. Many of these are children who have achieved speech development appropriate to their age, but whose use of language has become impaired through some experience which has proved traumatic. They may nevertheless be well able to relate to their therapist, and to communicate, in other than verbal terms, until the use of words is again freely available to them both in treatment and their daily living.

The two patients with whom I am concerned in this chapter were in a very different predicament. In both the illness had its roots in very early infantile experiences, which had seriously interfered with emotional growth. Not only had the children failed to develop adequate speech, they had been unable even to experience coming into meaningful communication with another person, usually established between an infant and mother long before the development of speech is maturationally possible

In the beginning such communication is by no means the later two-way process involving a common language. It seems rather that the baby's early sounds and cries act as a discharge of tension before he is able to direct them at a person outside himself, and use them as communication. These cries are, however, picked up by the mother who learns to recognize them as signs of various needs. As she comes to know which need is indicated she responds with such care of her child as feeding, changing and holding. In his early stage of diffused tension and discomfort such attention to specific areas helps the infant to become aware of the parts of his body where the tension is most acutely felt. Certain of the sounds he makes therefore begin to be associated with particular needs and they gradually become signals which both the infant and his mother understand. When both partners recognize the signal, and the response meets the need, the foundations for communication are laid down. This two-way communication contributes to the child's gradually growing awareness of himself as a continuing and separate entity.

He is further helped towards this awareness by the limitations of the situation. His mother cannot invariably respond in a way that provides a complete fit between herself and her child's needs. The inevitable frustration of waiting, and of incompletely satisfied need, aids recognition that help comes from outside himself. If no adequate help comes within bearable time, however, then the child is flooded with tension so acute that it may blot out the possibility of any other awareness. But as long as there is on most occasions a sufficiently good experience of relief and satisfaction, the need becomes manageable. A need which the child can contain, for a time, encourages the sense of his own continuing existence. As the infant, again and again, sends out his signals and these evoke a good enough response, there is gradually established a communication between him and the mothering person. She can be reached, but is no longer experienced as an inseparable part of himself.

Jane came into treatment at five years of age when she was markedly unable to express needs of her own, and gave the impression of being a child with little sense of herself as a person. She was brought rather reluctantly by her parents, on the advice of a doctor who had been consulted on account of her persistent diarrhoea. Although it was clear that Jane sometimes understood what was said, her own speech was incomprehensible, consisting of a meaningless and apparently undirected jumble of words. Her only real contact with adults and with other children was through physical aggression. Nevertheless, her parents could not accept that she was ill – instead they saw her as much more advanced in development than other children of her age. To illustrate their belief they described how very secure and independent Jane was when, at a much earlier age, she would wander off on her own for quite long periods in a crowded department store. At these times she would show no signs of the anxiety or feeling of loss usual to very young children in this situation. Her parents said that she had always been healthy and normal, although they could give few details of her early developmental history. They thought that she had not been a 'cuddly' baby. They saw no significance in the fact that, during her infancy, she had never been held in her mother's arms to be fed, or on her lap to be changed, but placed away from the mother on a table. It was striking how well this arrangement for the minimum of body contact fitted with the personalities of both her parents, who were withdrawn and anxious people, little in touch with their own feelings or those of their child.

When I met Jane in the waiting-room she was a white-faced child who seemed to have little connection with her parents. She wandered around making waving movements with her hands, like a pale little ghost. She came with me with no sign of realization that she was leaving her mother and father. In the treatment room she sat down at a table and covered several sheets of paper with drawings of spidery-looking shapes. Meanwhile she kept up a flow of jumbled words which I could not understand. These did not seem to be aimed at me. She did not appear to notice when I sat down beside her, and throughout the whole session I could make no contact. I could only be there and wait. As this pattern repeated, week after week, I found myself feeling very much alone, with that quality of isolation peculiar to being in the presence of another person who seems quite unaware of one's existence.

Then one day we came into the room when I had omitted to turn off the tap after my previous patient. The flowing water immediately seemed to fascinate Jane and throughout the hour she stood silently watching it. Thereafter, each day when she arrived, she would turn on the tap and stand, silent and immobile, watching the water running from the tap into the sink and away. She still seemed unaware of my presence beside her. As time went on, my feeling of isolation became acute – until I could begin to sort out what was being touched in my own experience. This allowed me to realize that the child's aloneness had become part of me, that I was feeling the isolation that Jane was experiencing. Then I could feel closer to her in watching the water with her, and this left me more open to the water's essential quality, the continuity of its flow. I began to put this feeling into words, again and again. First just the simple observation that the water went on and on. Then that this was something that she needed to feel was happening. After a time, I added that she needed to feel that she, too, had a part in this continuous flow. She needed to feel that she had a part in her mother being there for her, and in her own going on being Jane.

Eventually I put all these observations together with the fact that there really was something she could do about her situation. She was the person who turned on the tap each time she came and needed to watch the water, just as she could do something about letting her mother and myself know something about what she, Jane, needed from us. Whether the specific words of this interpretation meant anything to Jane it is impossible to know. I think it is unlikely that they did. It is more probable that what she experienced was some sense of my change of feeling. Instead of letting her isolation get inside me and cut me off, I had been able to make a move in my understanding of her need.

The only change in Jane's behaviour showed in an apparently new awareness of the sound and vibrations of the trains below us. At moments her concentration in the water could be interrupted while she listened. Later she could turn her body in the direction of the sound and, eventually, she crossed the room to the window to look. We were working in a building where my room was anything but quiet, being almost directly above a busy underground station. Jane's sessions coincided with the rush hour so there was a train arriving or leaving about every three minutes. As we balanced uncomfortably on the window ledge, I had to make a considerable effort to keep my mind on the repetitive coming and going below, till I realized that we were again involved in a watching contact with a process of continuity. This time there were interruptions, but still the process went on.

Again, I began to put into very simple words what we were watching and experiencing together. When one train went out another came in. There was always another train. I verbalized for Jane how much the sequence of the trains was like her coming to see me at the clinic. When she left me on Wednesday there was a space, till she came back on Friday and we were together again. After a few weeks I noticed there was a slackening in Jane's body tension. This relaxation suggested that something was being taken in. So I went on to link this experience with me now with her own repeated experience of finding that her mother was there again each time she felt she had lost contact with her. At these times it was as if neither she nor her mother were alive any more, but her mother could be found again. Soon Jane began to show for the first time that she was in direct contact with me by leaning her body against mine while we watched the trains. This contact was repeated at intervals until Jane was able to get down and take a much more active part in making continuity happen. She did this through using the blind on the window. She would pull down the cord to lower the blind then release it to spring back and away out of sight. She repeated the whole monotonous process again and again, session after session, until she could take in the meaning of what I was saying. Just as she went on finding me each time she came to the clinic, so she could do something about finding her mother each time she felt she had lost her. It was Jane who pulled the blind down towards herself each time it had gone out of sight. She had let me see how much she needed me to know how alone she felt, and now she could do something about getting what she needed from me, and from her mother.

In her next move Jane showed still more clearly that she had begun to experience me as a person outside herself, with whom she could make contact and find a response. She no longer left me to pick up her clues indicated through the blind, but brought from the waiting-room to each session a book which she had never appeared to notice before. This was called *Anybody Inside?* and she sat in my chair beside me while we went through it page by page, week after week. On each alternate page was the picture of a container which was empty till one turned the page over and there was the occupant safely inside. There was a bird in a nest, a car in a garage and, appropriately enough, a train in its shed. Jane was sitting comfortably close to me. There was also a feeling of contact between us as I repeatedly put into words what she was finding for herself and showing me. I said that she now felt that she was a person with an outside and an inside. She was not like the empty shed, she had a real body which could be safely close to mine and real feelings which she could let me know about. At first hesitantly and then more surely, Jane began to speak, naming the objects inside and outside as we went through the pages. 'Nest-bird, garage-car, shed-train.'

With her new awareness of herself and of me Jane could begin to use words in a meaningful way. The words which she had previously only recognized could now be used in communication concerning the objects and the feelings they represented. Improvement in general use of speech came only slowly. Jane first had to make contact with me by hitting and biting me each time she left the clinic and when she arrived again. Her need to be in touch through her aggression could then be expressed in its appropriate context. She could now feel, and let me feel, her anger at the interruption in the continuity of our being together.

It was noticeable how Jane used not only her hands but her mouth once she could express her rage and fear at the inevitable separations from me. This is understandable in the light of her feeding experience in infancy. Lying separately on her cushion, the only contact available to her was that of her mouth with the teat of the bottle. In this way her mouth functioned in isolation as an organ of feeding. There was none of the security of being held, nor the warm body-closeness, which is part of the very intimate experience of nursing where more than food is conveyed and received in the satisfaction of instinctual needs in both of the partners. At first the mouth is indeed the main centre of feeling and sensation. But in the infant there needs to come a gradually growing awareness of the mouth in its relation to other body organs and their functioning, and to body surfaces. In the early life of the child the mouth plays a dominant part not only in feeding and sucking but as an organ of contact. Contact cannot be achieved in isolation.

The importance of the mouth as the area where not only contact but the beginnings of perception take place is described by René Spitz in his paper 'The Primal Cavity' (1955). He points out that the first co-ordinated activity of the infant is in sucking. This action brings into play the lips, cheeks and tongue whose muscles are therefore the first to be brought under control. Their surfaces are also the first to be used in contactual exploration. Various other senses are also involved in the act of sucking. There is not only touch, but taste, smell, temperature and pain. Added to these is the deep sensitivity in swallowing. These activities all take place within the one body area and are rooted in the infant's early state of undifferentiation. They continue throughout his growing awareness of his body parts, the localization of his body sensations and the gradual discrimination of what is inside from what is outside. Spitz sees the mouth as the organ wherein the beginnings of perception take place. It is characteristic of the mouth that it not only receives stimuli arising from inside the body but stimulation from without when the nipple is placed in the mouth. The oral cavity lends itself as does no other organ of the body to bridge the gap between inner and outer perception. These general observations contribute much to the understanding of the condition of children like Jane. They give added weight to the fact that the mouth, with all its history and its associations, is to become the vehicle for speech through which both inner and outer perceptions are communicated by, as we say, word of mouth.

In some children there seems to have been a failure in the satisfactory functioning of the mouth as a 'bridge' to subsequent development. It may be that, as infants, they have been particularly sensitive and more than usually limited in their ability to bear frustration. In some instances the mother has no recollections of early feeding difficulties. It may, however, become clear during the treatment process that the baby had experienced the feeding as predominantly unsatisfying and painful, or so fraught with anxiety as to have been felt as near annihilation. Therefore, instead of being mainly a source of comfort and satisfaction, the mouth has become a source of danger – a danger that is increased by the strength of the aggression accompanying the pain.

Such an infantile experience was vividly re-expressed during the treatment of a very ill little boy, Martin, who first came to the clinic when he was three years old. He was described as being unable to relate to other people. His parents found him quite uncontrollable, constantly active and extremely destructive. He would tear the wallpaper, empty drawers and cupboards and throw things out of the windows of his home. He had gained no control of his bowel or bladder functions so he was soiling and wetting by day and night. Potting had been consistently attempted. As he was unable to chew any solid food, Martin was still on an entirely soft milky diet. He was showing no attempt to speak, except for the use of three baby words, and it was indicative of his condition that these included no word for either himself or his mother.

Although this child had not had an easy start in life, it does seem that some children might have been able to weather similar difficulties and move on towards more healthy personality development. Martin was born in a hospital which seems to have been a particularly rigid one, with a constantly changing series of nurses for feeding, changing and putting the infants down. He was slow in beginning to make any gains in weight and so was kept in hospital for some weeks, before being taken home by his mother. She was an anxious person, and unsure of her own ability to care for Martin. He had a hernia which, after three months, became acute and very painful, necessitating separation from his home for surgical intervention. When he was eighteen months old there was yet another separation from his mother, on account, this time, of her illness which lasted for nearly two months.

When I first started working with Martin he ran around in my room in a rush of aimless activity. Almost at the end of the second session, he stopped in his tracks and stood looking at an open tin of plasticine on the table beside me. Among the fragments in the tin were some little round pieces which he carefully picked out and laid on the table. Then he took my hand, placed it in the tin and stood silently watching while I rolled more plasticine. During his next session he extracted all the balls and again lifted my hand and put it in the tin. Instead of doing the work for him, I softened a small piece of plasticine and put this in his hand. He drew his hand back sharply as if he had been burned. His anxiety became less acute as I went on rolling the plasticine in his hand so that he could feel it there and between his hand and mine. After a time he was able to go on rolling his own balls without my help. As he laid each one on the table he asked tensely, 'Ball?' Then he stood, with a worried expression, holding a small piece of plasticine in either hand. It seemed that he wanted to join them but was too anxious to do anything about it. So I placed the two pieces together and took his hands, helping him to fuse them into one. When this was done he patted the product with satisfaction and, for the first time, he used two words, saying, 'Big ball.' These two words spoken together suggested that he had a greater understanding of language than he had as yet shown in speech. The whole incident seemed to express his need to be in contact with another person, as well as the dangers which this need held for him.

Having made his tentative move, he withdrew from me and again spent the time running around exploring the room as if I were not there, although he occasionally used my hand, as though it were part of himself. It seemed that unless I made some impingement upon *him* we would go on being in the same room together without any real contact between us. So I refused to have my hand used except for things that were too difficult for him to do by himself. This was very frustrating for him. He would begin to cry or stamp his foot, but at the first actual expression of emotion his anger would be shut off, and he would move away from me, fixing his gaze on some object in the room. It was as though he had erased the whole experience. He showed no further interest in the plasticine, but his attention was caught by any round object, by marbles, saucers or the pattern on the curtains.

I felt that at this point he needed some very fluid material, so I left out for him each day a bucket of fine dry sand and some beakers. Soon he began to use the sand, filling and emptying anything he had brought with him, a tin, a bus or a tiny model of a typewriter. This became an endlessly repeated activity, session after session, filling and emptying as if he were alone in the room. I felt useless and could do nothing but watch, until it became obvious to me that in this continuously repetitive movement nothing was ever 'contained'. I began to put into words what was happening: when one container was emptied another got filled, only for this to be emptied too. He felt that nothing could be held inside. Although the light was not switched on, he would occasionally look up at the bulb in its round shade and say, 'Ball'. Then on three separate days the character of this action changed. He said nothing at all, and as he silently gazed at the shade he appeared to become completely absorbed in it. He stood motionless for minutes on end and seemed quite unaware of me and of his surroundings. He showed no response when I touched or spoke to him, and when I once held my hand before his eyes he stood still and unblinking. This condition had the quality of an hallucination, with the obliteration of the awareness of any boundaries between himself and the outside world. In his absorption in the circle of the shade it seemed he could have some re-experience of the 'oneness' with the mother which, in the infant, precedes the awareness of her as a separate person outside himself. It was clear that in this child's condition there was very little establishment of boundaries within the self, and between the self and the outside world, although there were islands of ego development. These were seen in his recognition of shapes and in the beginnings of speech.

Allowing for the fact that nothing could be known of this child's constitutional endowment, it seems that his early life experiences may have contributed much towards his faulty development. These included the lack of establishment of a warm rapport between himself and his mother; the prolonged association of the act of feeding with the discomfort and anxiety of vomiting; the pain of the hernia; the separation from his mother and the surgical operation; and the further separation from her at eighteen months. In all this the situation seems to have been that there was too frequently a predominance of discomfort, pain and frustration over the good experiences of instinctual satisfaction. One possible effect of this may have been a premature awareness of the separation of the self from the infant-mother-unit before there was sufficient maturation or development for objects to be felt to be under the infant's control. David Rubinfine describes the situation in his paper 'Maternal Stimulation, Psychic Structure and Object Relationships' (1962). He goes on to suggest that the result can be too early a differentiation of the aggressive drives out of what he calls 'the undifferentiated energic reservoir'. Martin's illness seems to have come about much on the lines described by Rubinfine. It was clear that his aggressive drives had become extremely active before there had been sufficient pleasurable instinctual experiences for contact with another person to be felt as anything but predominantly dangerous.

A few weeks after his periods of absorption in the roundness of the lamp shade, some gradual changes were seen in Martin's use of the sand. As his filling and emptying continued, and I went on giving words to what he was doing, he would occasionally, and then more frequently, select and use only two containers out of his collection. I began to liken these to Martin and myself and to Martin and his mother. When she fed him with milk and he took it from her, he felt that none of it could be kept inside him – just as he felt that I gave him nothing he could keep and use for himself. Martin did not appear to notice my words, but after a time there was yet a further change. He discarded the whole medley of objects he had brought with him, and used only the two beakers, one bigger than the other, which I left ready for him each day. Eventually he held out the bigger one to me calling it 'Nannie', which proved later to be a newly found word for his mother. I asked if the smaller one was Martin, and at this he nodded his head and looked directly at me. This was the first time that his eyes had come into contact with mine. Also, although these were minimal on his part, words had been used by us both, in communication together. It seemed at this point that at least some of my interpretations had been taken in, and not only at the level of empathy. Something of the actual meaning of my words had been grasped and used.

During the following months Martin became less tense and also more aware of me. His interest spread to other objects in the play room. His mother reported that he was settling more easily to sleep at night. His use of speech increased both at home and with me, although most of his enunciation was babyish with the beginnings of his words cut off. In his play with the sand he now used a doll which he called 'Baby Martin', but he made no attempt to feed it through its open mouth. Instead he would make a hole for feeding by pulling off its head or an arm or a leg. He enjoyed scribbling with coloured pencils. To do this at the table he would sit on my knee – although he could now safely use me for the convenience of his purpose, there was no feeling of warmth of contact between us. It was as though I were felt as an extension of the chair. Gradually his scribbles changed from straight lines to spirals, and then to circles. I understood these circles as being associated with some at least temporary awareness of himself as a whole, in the sense Michael Fordham describes in 'New Developments in Analytical Psychology' (1957).

Two months after the emergence of the circles, Martin drew a face, first with his finger in the dry sand on the floor and then with a paint brush on paper. This was not drawn as children usually draw a face: the features came first and were named eye, eye, nose and lastly mouth, which was continued in one sweeping line to form the whole boundary of the face. In whatever way one understands this first picture of himself (illustrated on page 198), it does underline the importance of the mouth and the intensity of feeling Martin invested in it. It could be that, at times, the whole face was experienced as mouth. Or that the mouth was felt to carry such dangerous feeling that it had to be denied. It is likely that both views were in part true for this child, whose speech had been so limited and who was still unable to use his teeth in eating.

Ten days after this picture was painted Martin again drew a face. This time he began by drawing the outside boundary to the shape and inside this the features were added. He immediately went on to make a large circle with his finger in the sand on the floor, saying decisively, 'Big one.' I agreed that it was a big one and asked what was inside it. He walked into the circle and stood with his feet firmly together in the centre saying, 'Martin middle.' I agreed that he was in the middle of his circle and said that he knew he was Martin. I took his hand so that he was both within his own boundary and in contact with me outside of it. After a moment he stepped out and made with his finger two little squiggles on the outside edge of the ring. One of these he called Nannie and the other Baby Martin. Following this session there were several others when his wish to be inside and to come into touch with a person outside was played in close contact with myself. My lap was used as a container for his sand and the face was made with beads either buried inside the sand or placed out on the surface. When he could bring his mouth into touch with the sand which made an extension of my stomach, he could climb on to me and be in affectionate contact.

Several years of further work were necessary to allow the opportunity for the consolidation of this human contact and the development of a real relationship between us. There were stormy patches as his anger became more openly and sometimes very violently expressed. And there were fleeting moments of sadness. For long monotonous months he did nothing but paint, with the paint poured on to the paper and spread everywhere so thickly that it cracked as it dried. At times this was a way of trying to come to terms with his need to contain his feelings; at others the painting expressed his strong anal aggression, which was further associated with sharp, biting teeth and showed his confusion between anus and mouth.

When Martin was five-and-a-half years old, that is about two-and-a-half years after the beginning of treatment, he started to attend part-time at a day hospital. This experience gave him the much needed contact with other children which he lacked, as no nursery had been able to keep him for more than a few days. Attendance at day centre also gave his mother a much-needed break from the continuous presence of this over-active, uncontrolled and demanding child.

When Martin joined the day group his concentration was extremely limited except when he was enjoying something which he had chosen to do. He was talking a great deal and had a good vocabulary for his age. His enunciation remained babyish, however, until, in treatment, his anxiety had been expressed and met. Then he spoke quite clearly. He was using his intelligence well in endless enquiries about reality matters. He was clearly ready for a learning situation carefully geared to his individual needs. He was fortunate in having an experienced and wise teacher who never in her behaviour or her attitude was anything but honest with the children. She acted on sound intuitive judgment and could be very firm, as well as warm, without losing sight of her role as a teacher. As she slowly increased the limits she felt she must put on his impulsive and aggressive behaviour it became more frequently and strongly directed towards me. His attacks of hitting, biting, scratching or butting with his head often came as a surprise, by their suddenness and apparent lack of association with what we were doing. At times I had to restrain him physically, and it was very difficult to do this without a resulting increase in his violence.

Eventually he settled down with me to another long spell of painting with every available shade of paint, producing a rich and colourful mess which he repeatedly called 'rainbow-coloured'. After some months, form began to evolve out of this mass and he painted pictures of actual rainbows. In every rainbow he made, each arch was separated from its neighbours by an empty space. This gave them a disconnected, unrelated appearance which was at first puzzling and then prompted me to remark on the difference between these and real rainbows. This very realistic observation brought a strong denial from Martin, but it helped me to clarify, for myself and for him, how much the empty spaces were expressive of the quality of his contact with me at that time. Although he was lively and active there was again a lack of real feeling between us. So I put into words how he was again afraid of being close to me. The arches of his rainbows were like the anxious, frightened Baby Martin who was afraid to be in close touch with me and with his mother in case he would damage or be damaged by his anger. He looked apprehensive but gradually relaxed as he painted, until two arches, as if by accident, had joined together. 'Look,' he said in excitement, 'they've run into each other.' I said he seemed to be feeling that it was less dangerous to be close and he replied, 'Yes. As if they are mixed up together.' Although he had been able to allow the arches to join, his expression 'mixed up together' seemed still to carry some fear of losing his identity in the face of real closeness to me as another person. At the same time, this was his first use of the phrase 'as if', and it suggested that a beginning was being made towards the development of symbol formation. He could make some distinction between the picture he painted and the original experience it represented. This development prompted me to make an active move in drawing a simple picture of an open mouth whilst he covered his hands with paint. He stopped to see what I was doing. Then he said, 'I'll paint a mouth.'

The second picture on page 198 shows his painting of a mouth consisting of a multitude of black and red shapes. When I remarked that it seemed to be made up of a lot of spots, he told me in quite definite terms what the picture represented. 'No,' he said. 'It's a broken-up mouth.' At this I again put into words his feeling that his mouth had been broken up when he was a baby and angry with his mother and afraid he would break her up too. While he now felt he had a broken-up mouth, he could say only words with their beginnings broken off. In response to this interpretation he took a tentative little bite at the edge of his picture. He agreed with a smile when I remarked that neither his mouth nor his picture had got broken. Then he went across the room and brought back the remains of a broken toy telephone. Only the base was intact and he had previously used this for pouring paint into the round hollow which he called the mouth. This was adjacent to the two teeth-edged discs and the little lever which sticks out like a tongue. On this day he fed in little bits of broken up chalk for the teeth to grind and so, for the first time, he could play at chewing up food. In this play he could also make the symbolic connection between chewing and speech, two restricted functions of his mouth. He could bring these elements together in the broken telephone which looked as if it had a mouth, teeth and a tongue, and which he knew to be part of an instrument for verbal communication.

When Martin came for his next session I had inadvertently left out a quite sophisticated painting of a rabbit done by an older child. He looked at this saying, 'That's nice. I did that well.' I made it clear that we both knew that he hadn't really

1

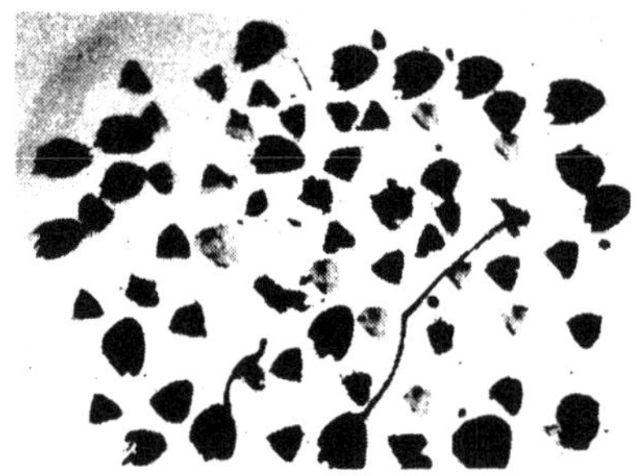

2

painted the rabbit, although he could make pictures like his rainbows and his broken-up mouth. To this he responded, saying, 'Yes. I'll paint the broken-up mouth again.' Then out of a whole assortment of colours mixed ready on the table he selected the black and began a series of five pictures, one straight after the other. These are reproduced on page 200. The first shows the mouth in sixteen fragments. Then in the two following pictures there is a decrease in the number of fragments, which become larger and closer together. As he painted Martin told me with quite clear enunciation what was happening. 'The bits are getting bigger,' he said, 'because they are joining up. There aren't so many bits and they're getting bigger because they are joining up.' He needed only my attention and agreement to allow his own processes to continue. In his fourth picture the mouth is painted as a single round of black. This could be seen as a joining up of all the fragments, but from what I knew of Martin, I felt doubtful that this item was now established as a complete and manageable mouth. It seemed important to avoid falling into the possible danger of glossing over his deep anxieties by accepting his achievement too readily. So I put into words my understanding of it as the empty black hole which had, for so long, been frightening. We stood looking at the black hole together. It seemed that his ability to face it to this extent with me had brought him one step nearer to coming to terms with the mouth-hole when he painted his last picture in the series. This shows the outline of an open mouth with teeth inside it, and one small black spot outside. To my enquiry about the separate spot he replied, 'That's a little bit that hasn't got joined up yet.' I suggested that when he felt he could have a mouth with teeth inside it, like his picture, he could also have a tongue and could use it. At this he brought his face close to mine and gave a long drawn-out 'Aah', like the sound that goes with a satisfying discovery. I responded by saying that now he could feel close to me and he could say something to me. He answered with great feeling, 'Mmm, Me, Mummy.' In very simple terms I verbalized for him how the good experience with his mother expressed in the satisfied sound 'Mmm' could be felt in close contact with me and with her. We could each be identified as separate, yet related, people, and we could each remain intact.

Martin arrived for his next session announcing, 'I'm going to paint a mountain.' His mountain was a fiercely erupting volcano, isolated in space with no base to stand on. Its two upright sides were outlined in green and from the whole width of its top came piercing shafts of colour. This seemed to depict very vividly the attacking, destructive quality of his experience in the feeding situation. The good experience was also expressed when he again drew his mountain a few sessions later. This time, though still precariously balanced, it was shaped like a breast and from the nipple only came five green and yellow streams. He held up this picture for me to see and said quietly, 'It's not spurting out so much.' He smiled when I agreed that it was a much less angry and dangerous mountain and linked it with his last picture of the mouth with teeth that seemed to be safe. Although a very important move had been made, it was clear that a great deal more work needed to be done in helping him to come to terms with his fear and aggression, so that further personality development could become possible.

About four months later it seemed that Martin was ready to begin to use his teeth in eating – but that he would not be able to do this on his own impetus. With the support of his mother and teacher, he agreed to eat one course of solid food each day. During the following months, with a great deal of understanding and firm support, this venture was carried through. Together with his pride and sense of achievement it was very hard for him to give up the baby position. There

3

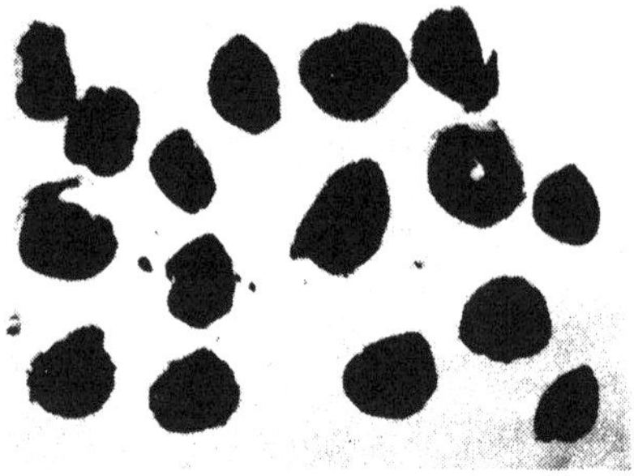

4

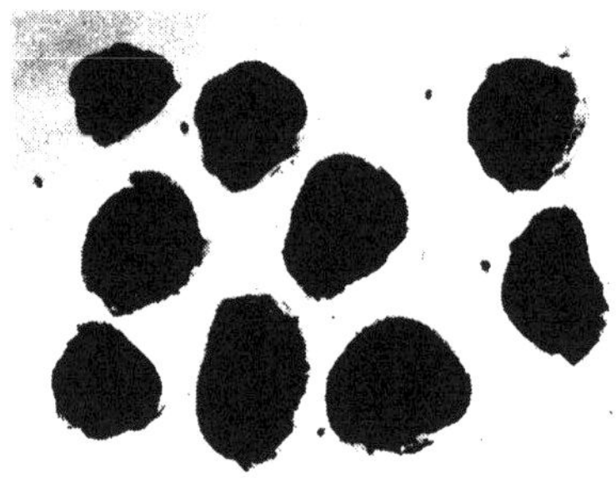

5

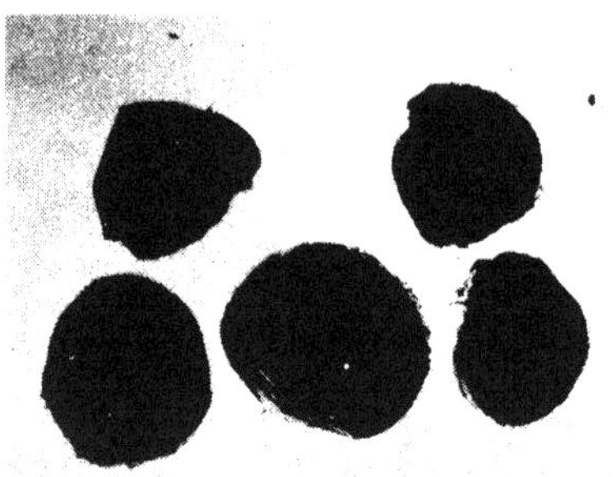

6

7

was consequently an increase in his violent behaviour towards both me and other people. It was a long time yet before he could gain any control over his impulsive hitting out and kicking, or take any responsibility for his actions. He would either deny what he had done or assert that other people liked it. Later, when he had hurt somebody, he would cling over-affectionately to someone else. There were many difficult months before he could bear the pain and guilt which go with genuine concern for others, and which usually begin to be experienced much earlier in a child's life.

In both Martin and Jane the illness had its roots in the very early months and years of life. Both had missed the firm establishment of the sense of the self as a continuing entity with the gradual distinction between the self and the outside world, first met in the mother. In the early stages of treatment neither could make any communication with me as a person separate from himself. However, their quite different use of the material to hand showed something of the predicament of each. Jane's absorption in the constantly running water and in the repeated presence of the trains gave a clue to her isolation and her need for a continuing experience of herself and her mother. Martin's repetitive emptying of any object which got filled with sand was expressive of his inability to contain feelings, urine, faeces or food. When so little could be contained, little could be fully felt, or linked with what had gone before to provide a continuity of experience. Notwithstanding their severe illness, it seemed that both children had after all met a sufficiently good response often enough in infancy to allow for the beginnings of continuity to be felt in the specialized situation of treatment. For continuity to become a permanent reality they had first to be helped to become aware of a separate person who went on giving a response which they could use. In this shared experience, what was happening with the therapist at the moment could then be linked in a meaningful way with what had taken place in the past. From these beginnings the children's capacity for real communication could develop.

This chapter is based on a paper read at the Inter-Clinic Conference of the National Association for Mental Health.

# Chapter Ten
# *Play and Communication*
## by Shirley Hoxter

The previous chapter traced in detail the connections between patterns of behaviour and communication shown in the therapeutic situation and the kind of infantile experiences which the children concerned had probably had. These infantile experiences had not, of course, actually been observed, but were inferred from the patient's session material, along with information and impressions gained from the parents.

In this chapter something of the theoretical basis of the assumptions involved is explained. They derive from Freud's work and its development by Melanie Klein. We are first given some direct observations of an infant's behaviour. Then the development of play and of symbolic thought from earliest infancy onwards is traced. We are shown how such understanding is used in the Kleinian technique of child analysis and psychotherapy. We also see a further case study of a boy for whom normal methods of communication and interaction with the mother had not been available in infancy. As a consequence the child had developed almost no powers of symbol formation. M.B., D.D.

---

**Development Observed in Play**

An example of observation of a developmental sequence in a child's play leads us to consider what we mean by 'play'.

The following account, covering a period from the age of

four weeks to over eight years, is necessarily highly condensed and selective.

*Infant play*

Ricky, from the age of four weeks onwards, when ending a feed from a bottle in a calm and contented way, used to mouth the teat repeatedly allowing it to slide a little way out of his mouth and then retrieving it. His mother allowed him a little time for this activity before the bottle was taken away, sometimes humming or rocking him in rhythm with his mouthing. A month or so later, when being settled to sleep (with a kiss from his mother) he often used to look at her, shut his eyes, then open them again to look into her eyes. He repeated this several times before she left him. Later on, when he was able to use his hands, before being left to sleep he used to pull a little sheet over his eyes, then pull it down again and look at his mother, often with a gurgling smile, then hide his face again. Together with his mother's responses this activity developed into 'peep-bo' games. Subsequently these were not reserved for bedtime but took place on many occasions. Father and others were now drawn to play their part as companions in this game.

*Mobility and expanding from the family*

As Ricky became more mobile the peep-bo games were gradually developed into other hiding games. At first he hid only his head (apparently believing the rest of himself to be out of view as young children do); this then led to slightly more effective hiding and invitations to be chased.

As a toddler Ricky often seemed precariously balanced between his wish to be so cleverly hidden that he outwitted the parental seeker, and his fear that his hiding might be so successful that he would never be found. If the seeker took too long he would jump out of his hiding place to give her a shock. Games of 'ambush' – springing out from the hiding place to surprise the passing adult – soon flourished. From about two-and-a-half years companions of his own age joined the hide-and-seek games and games of ambush. Gradually more adventurous areas were chosen – the garden, the park, the countryside and eventually the house in the dark. For several years the children preferred to hide in pairs and to have an adult as the seeker. Before they were six it was rare for one of them reluctantly to accept the more lonely role of the seeker.

*Laws and legends of childhood civilization*

By the age of six and seven such games were elaborated by variations and rules: long discussions (and sometimes fights) over rules and fair play entered into the activities. Less structured games also continued. Into the themes of hiding and seeking, ambushing and chasing, there was woven another theme: that of the hunter and the hunted. From about four to six years of age this frequently took the form of dramatic play concerning animals. Later it increasingly focussed upon themes of the cruel oppressor versus the courageous resistance hero. The scenarios included Robin Hood versus the Sheriff of Nottingham, Hereward the Wake being hunted by the Normans, the Cossacks ambushing Napoleon's retreating army and the French Resistance versus the Nazis. The children's reading of fiction, nature study and history and the dramatic games were mutually enriching and stimulating. They also provided a means of expressing and confronting their own experience when playing on the edge of fear and triumph.

At seven and eight years, between the close friends, such games could be continued for hours at a time without the immediate presence of an adult – provided that they knew that a trusted adult was readily available. Every now and again aggression and fear could not be contained within the dramatic outlets of the game. One or more of the children would really become the tyrannical oppressor and the oppressed would become terror-stricken – or resist with all his might. The 'make-believe' broke down, feelings of real danger took over and an adult would be sought to cope with the ensuing fight, to ensure that the feelings aroused were once more restored within the limits of safety. If it was felt that the adult could not cope with such situations (that is, was as overwhelmed by the release of hostility as the children were themselves), they tended to avoid such games altogether, preferring television or individual activities.

**The Psychoanalysis of Children**

The study of observations of young children at play is likely to lead to more questions than answers. This process is by no means without value, as the observer gains conviction of his need to question his understanding of what he perceives. A full realization of the inadequacy of pat answers and interpretations is essential. First-hand conviction of the infantile origins of the older child's play can be gained and understanding of the mental development of the child increased.

An early example of detailed observation of a young child's play and a discussion of its significance is found in Freud's *Beyond the Pleasure Principle* (1920). Here, in the context of a book which is for the most part highly abstract, philosophical and controversial, Freud's contemporary readers may have been taken aback to find a down-to-the-nursery-level description of an eighteen-month-old child at play. We have an account of how this child repeatedly threw his toys under the furniture and played with a wooden reel attached to a piece of string, which he could throw into his cot and pull out again. Freud's account of the child's activities is detailed. He notes the context in which they occurred, the emotions and the half-formed words which accompanied them, the background of the child's current life, especially his relationship with his mother and his reactions to her absences and returns. The scope and limitations of the child's other achievements are also noted. Freud links all these diverse observations in making his interpretation of the meaning of the child's play. Later he discusses the reel-and-cot game in relation to a major theme of the book – the 'repetition compulsion'.

What is especially striking is Freud's respect for the child's play activity. This forms the basis of his search for an understanding of the child. He does not regard playing simply as a pastime or as a developmental achievement. He regards it as essentially meaningful in respect of the child's attempts to come to terms with emotional experience. Moreover, the emotions in question are seen to be directed towards the child's mother, although the play occurs in her absence.

In this brief account we perceive many of the key approaches used by contemporary child analysts and psychotherapists. Freud himself, however, did not undertake the psychoanalysis of children, except indirectly and in collaboration with the father of 'little Hans'.

The adult patients with whom he worked could of course communicate verbally, but Freud focussed his attention not only on their rational statements, but also on their 'free associations' and their dreams. By observing the 'free play' of the mind he was able to perceive the workings of the unconscious.

## The Transference Relationship

Freud also came to pay increasing attention to the strong feelings which patients developed towards him. These feelings were inappropriate or disproportionate to the current doctor-patient relationship, but poignantly appropriate when perceived to have been 'transferred' to the doctor from the patient's past relationships with those who were closest to him in childhood.

Gradually it was recognized that the 'transference relationship' was also not just a recovered memory of how matters had been between the child and his parents in the past. It was rather a dynamic and current reliving of feelings and phantasies, which in early childhood may never even have been demonstrated or acknowledged. These nevertheless had coloured the child's way of experiencing the parents and shaped the images of them in the child's mind. These images now persisted unconsciously and largely unaltered within the adult. They determined (for better as well as for worse) much of the adult's current subjective experience and relationships. Although usually manifested indirectly and in disguised ways in the adult's present life, in the analytical setting the infantile phantasies and feelings could be demonstrated and repeatedly experienced much more directly. A study of the patient's free associations, dreams and transference relationships therefore enabled Freud and his followers to increase their understanding not only of the origins of the patient's illness but also of the general childhood desires and anxieties which form the origins of all of us.

These initial findings have since been greatly extended by

the psychoanalysis of children themselves. Anna Freud and Melanie Klein made the greatest pioneering contributions in this field. Developing their views independently, their different techniques and approaches led to theoretical divergences of significance. Some aspects of this divergence will become apparent to readers of this book. In this chapter I am attempting only to indicate something of the approach of Melanie Klein and her followers.

In her *Techniques of Child Analysis* (1932), Melanie Klein is particularly concerned to stress the similarities between child and adult analysis: 'The difference is purely one of technique ... not of principle.' Of particular importance to her is the similarity of the nature of the transference relationship in both cases. With the transference parallel goes the similarity of the analyst's function. This is to endeavour to understand and to share the analyst's understanding of the positive and negative feelings, the anxieties and phantasies, shown by the child both directly and indirectly in his relationship with his therapist.

The child has a strong, continuing bond of relationship to his parents and siblings. These family relationships and the significance of the part they have in his life are aspects of a continuous developing process. The process is influenced by the feelings and behaviour which the family members show towards him. The analysis of the transference relationship does not intrude upon or replace these family relationships. It is concerned rather with those unconscious phantasies of a more infantile nature which may disrupt the development of current family relationships, or which may prevent the child from making full use of such beneficial opportunities as provided by the parents, by teachers and by others.

## Facilitating Communication in Child Analysis

### *Play technique*

The techniques of child analysis differ from those of adult analysis mainly because the child communicates his thoughts and feelings differently. He makes far less use of verbal associations and more readily expresses himself in play, in actions and other direct behaviour. In the play technique described by Melanie Klein the child is provided with a variety of small toys, little human figures, wild and domestic animals, cars, small bricks, houses, fences and so on. He also has paper, scissors, pencils and nowadays usually also paints, plasticine and access to water. The toys selected are not educational or constructional. They lend themselves to being used in an endless variety of ways according to the conscious imagination and the unconscious phantasy of the particular child. They are not provided to reassure the child or to give him a joyous time, or to provide a creative or an abreactive outlet – although they may function for him in all these ways. Primarily they are there to provide the child with a vocabulary, as it were. They are a means of facilitating the expression of his thoughts and feelings and clarifying their exploration. Klein considered that the child's play could be understood and interpreted in very much the same way as the psychoanalyst interprets adult dreams. She stressed the need to consider the child's play in the context of his total behaviour in the session.

Some children plunge themselves into play with zest and rapidly become immersed in the 'stories' and conscious fantasies* of their activities. However, not all children can play. For that matter, not all adults can dream. Many of the young patients described by Melanie Klein were too inhibited or too overwhelmed by anxiety to be able to play. She describes how by interpreting the underlying feelings of hostility, fear or guilt in a child, the youngster could experience initial relief – and so begin both to face and express his own feelings in play.

Some of the children we work with, however, are too severely arrested in their development to be able to use the symbolism of play at all, as we saw in the last chapter. Their communications are not only non-verbal, they are even of a 'pre-play' nature.

### *The setting for child analysis*

Part of the role of the child analyst or psychotherapist is to establish a setting in which the child can communicate. For each of her patients the psychotherapist provides a place and a time. The room is arranged to be as free as possible from everything which is extraneous to the child's needs – therefore

*The spelling 'fantasy' is used to denote conscious fantasy and 'phantasy' to denote unconscious phantasy.

from intrusive evidence of the therapist's personal tastes, her other occupations and evidence of other patients' use. Whenever possible communal toys are avoided but an individual drawer or box is provided containing the toys which are for each child's use. These are also safeguarded from the raids of other children. The therapist provides an appointment time, be it daily or weekly, which the child can depend upon being available for him, for his exclusive use. This appointment is uninterrupted by any other claims for the therapist's attention, but subject to cancellations for holidays and the like, for which the therapist will give the child a period of preparation. The sequestered area provided also entails the keeping of boundaries and limits. A child is not allowed to intrude upon the place, equipment or time which is not his own. Some children find these restrictions extremely frustrating and will constantly beat themselves up against the boundaries or insidiously try to coax their way through them. In meeting the frustration of these set limits in the course of therapy, they reveal a repetition of the difficulties experienced in coping with the frustrations of home and school life. So they encounter and reveal all that arouses their anger or jealousy within the family situation. Earlier infantile feelings about being unable to invade the mother and possess the whole of her body, heart, mind and life from within are also revived.

*Receptivity to the child's communications*

The most important part of the whole setting lies in the receptivity of the analyst's mind. Easing the impact of the child's anxieties by reassurance, guiding his instinctual drives along educational or creative lines, stimulating him with our own ideas, attempting to civilize his hostile impulses by control or by presenting him with our own values, and providing safe outlets for 'letting off steam' – all these aims can be undertaken by adults in sensitive *rapprochement* with a child. Yet all these form no part of the technique of Kleinian child psychotherapy. These have the effect of closing unconscious doors and redirecting that which is unacceptable.

A source of danger to the therapy and to receiving the child's communications are the closed areas of the therapist's own mind. There are blind spots in all of us, especially regarding the aspects of ourselves that we wish to disown and deny. The ideal of creating within ourselves an internal, mental space which can receive *every* aspect of *every* patient can never be attained. But the personal psychoanalysis which the analyst and the therapist undergo as a fundamental preparation for their work can greatly expand the areas of acceptance within the self, and therefore of the receptivity to patients.

The therapist makes herself available to the child only in her role and function as therapist. Many children try to discover the weak spots in their therapist through which they may enter into her mind and life and seek to make a liaison with a non-therapist part of her personality. They may try to seduce her into being an idealized parent, a playmate, a teacher or an ally against the parents. They may involve her as a source of sexual excitement. Or by use of destructive and aggressive behaviour they may aim to force her into the role of a punitive, authoritarian figure against whom they can battle. The therapist seeks to maintain her true role whenever she recognizes such tendencies being aroused in her. She is then able to perceive the real motives of the child's attempts and wishes. She is then strengthened in her function of interpretation and not led into acting-out with the child. To aim to be receptive to every aspect of the child is, of course, not the same as being all-compliant or all-indulgent.

The art or 'gift' of the therapist appears to be related to the extent to which she is able to provide an 'internal mental space' for the patient. Just as the play room and the appointment time are cleared for the use of the patient, so too must be this mental space. In addition to diminishing the closed areas of her mind the therapist also seeks to be able to free her mind from irrelevant preoccupations, so that the child may occupy the mental space which is his by rights. This entails attempting to exclude, for example, thoughts about the previous patient, thoughts about what her analyst, her supervisor (or students, for those in teaching positions) will think about her work, or the temptation to produce 'brain children', that is, interpretations remarkable for their brilliant originality rather than their relevance for the patient. To be receptive to the child with an open mind, the therapist may even require to suspend from attention her own previous interpretations of the child's behaviour. For even if these were correct on a former occasion, they could now become prejudgments obscuring her view of the present one.

Yet memories of the past behaviour of the child and of past interpretations to which he may be reacting need to be readily available to her, if she is to be able to make integrative links. Few are able to sustain such a state of mind for long. However, by recognizing her own limitations and by tolerating imperfections and uncertainty, the therapist may be 'good enough' to enable many a child to find a place in her into which he may put himself, and then find and recover himself.

Melanie Klein explored, together with a child, the changing concepts that the child has of the place he occupies within the life-mind-body of his mother.* Klein's receptivity to the infantile aspects of the child's inner world enabled her, in her later work, to lead the way to the understanding of the most primitive forms of communication. However, the further clarification and conceptualization of the significance of the receptive mind which can contain the impact of infantile anxieties was undertaken by her followers.

Donald Meltzer (1967, 1973), developing the concepts of Wilfred Bion, discusses the establishment of the setting for child analysis, in particular the part played by 'internal mental space' in the analyst's mind.

Taking a somewhat different approach, Donald Winnicott (1971) has also contributed to our understanding in this area. In addition, he turns our attention to consideration of the nature of play itself and stresses its role as a creative mental activity.

## The Significance of Development Observed in Play

### *From separateness to separation*

At what point in the observed sequence at the beginning of the chapter might we say that 'play' commenced? Was Ricky's 'play' with the teat just a desire to continue the sensuous enjoyment in his mouth? That is, was it an auto-erotic activity with no accompanying mental imagery, however rudimentary? Might he have been at least fleetingly aware that the teat (the extension of his mother) was not a

*Melanie Klein, *Narrative of a Child Analysis* (Hogarth Press, London, 1961). For those wishing to know more of Melanie Klein's work, this book is of particular interest: it records a very detailed account of the analysis of one child, a boy of ten, and also illustrates the writer's fine receptivity.

part of his own mouth (himself), that he and the feeding mother were separate beings? If so, was his mouthing something akin to a goodbye kiss, that is, sensuous, but also loving, and a wishing to part with the loving feeling kept safely within him? Or did he perhaps believe that by his mouthing he could control the comings and goings of the feeding mother? Did he so protect himself from the pain of more fully realizing their separateness and the possibility of loss of that which he depended upon? Later, when before being left to sleep he covered and uncovered his eyes with the sheet, there can be more certainty that this was a preparation for an anticipated parting. It suggests that a degree of separateness had been acknowledged, and was in the process of being coped with. But was this concept of 'self' and 'other' still very tenuous? Did he feel that he could really make his mother disappear and reappear at will? Did his smile express relief, or triumph, at her reappearance? Or could it at least sometimes have been a smile arising from the shared make-believe joke of the game? Probably in this extended sequence leading to the establishment of the more developed peep-bo and hiding games, there came by imperceptible and fluctuating steps a diminishing of belief in the phantasy of having magical power to control the mother by mouth and eyes. Simultaneously there was an increase in the use of the game as a symbol for the experience of losing and regaining the mother.

Throughout the whole sequence there is a marked tendency to reverse the situation, that is, to play the active rather than the passive role. The child is the one who determines when mother leaves him (goes out of view), and in hide-and-seek there is a strong preference that it should be the parent who faces loss, and has to seek the child.

The earliest examples refer to the little weaning which occurs at the end of each feed, to the little step into the dark which occurs at each bedtime. This is the time when fears and persecutions must be faced. Then it requires loving courage to hold fast to the memory, the internal image, of the mother as the protector and the provider of good experiences. Time and again during development contact with this source of internal security is swept aside and lost in the wave of hostility to a mother who is felt to have abandoned him. Hostility is also experienced to the rivals (father and siblings) who unjustly deprive him of his rights and form an occupation army in possession of mother. This is, briefly, the thread of thought which leads me to link not only the structured games of hide-and-seek but also the later dramatic games with the early babyhood activities.

*Containing rivalry and maintaining friendship*

It is very evident, however, that the later games have become enormously enriched and complicated by the interweaving of many other strands of phantasy and other surges of development. A few of these emerge with some clarity: the children's enjoyment of one another's company for example, and the development of their capacity for social relationships. But to achieve this stage it is necessary for the children to devise means of dealing with feelings of aggression and rivalry which are barely below the surface. These threaten to destroy the companionship which they clearly value and wish to preserve. Typical of their age, and like citizens of a state, they can devise laws to ensure that justice prevails: if self-restraint is required then it must be equally imposed upon one's rivals. Or they fight out matters more freely, but still within the limits of safety, by having an enemy group as the legitimate target for aggression, towards whom no guilt need be experienced. Stories of the little or lone hero who stands up to a powerful oppressor have a universal quality – the same theme occurs in Jack the Giant Killer, David and Goliath and, in a more complex form, Oedipus Rex. But each child within a group enacting such a theme will use the game as a vehicle for his own individual unconscious phantasies. Indeed, for the same child the same game may have a different significance on different occasions. The casual observer of such games is unlikely to be able to perceive the individual nuances of significance. In the course of sessions, however, the psychotherapist is in a position to do so. For the therapist might well, for example, be cast in the role of the oppressor in such stories, and thus be on the receiving end of the child's feelings. By using her understanding of the transference relationship, and by following the to and fro of interpretation and response, she can gain an understanding of the significance of the phantasy in greater depth and detail. In such situations she would aim not only to unravel the projections of hostility and rivalry, but also eventually to help the child to make less use of projection – to face the enemy within himself, to battle against his own aggressive impulses and to conquer his own tyrannical desires.

*The accessible adult*

The therapist in session also plays a role akin to that of the adult in the background, whose accessibility is essential for the game to take place. The children turn to this adult when the symbolical nature of the play breaks down and they are overwhelmed by the force of their own feelings. Here it is less important for the adult to minister justice than it is to provide containment for the overpowering fear and rage. The children need to re-establish contact with a parental figure who has the firmness and authority to set limits but who is *not* the oppressor. He has greater strength than they have to withstand the emotional onslaught. Contact with an adult who is felt to be able to contain their aggression can (by introjection) reinforce both their own capacity to contain it and their ability to differentiate between inner phantasy and external reality. If the capacity to contain mental pain or danger (aggression, in this case) has not been developed to some extent and is not accessible to them internally (or, of course, externally through the presence of an adult who has this capacity), the game cannot take place. If such lack was a major rather than an occasional feature of the children's lives, it is likely that frequent real warfare would take place. That is, constant fights and bullying with real intent to harm and a use of projection which might later lead to gang warfare or delinquency. Faced with such a situation some children might shun play in groups and withdraw from social relationships.

## Communication in Infancy and Some Functions of Play

The use of the adult as the container for painful states of being is the prerequisite for development within the self of one's own capacity to bear the pain of thinking (Bion, 1962). The earliest forms of communication take place without any mediation by verbal or non-verbal symbols. In a direct and often raw, compelling way the baby conveys its feelings to the mother. If the baby is alarmed or distressed, what he does about this is to arouse alarm or distress in the mother. He causes the mother to experience in her own feelings what he cannot yet bear to keep inside himself. And the mother has to cope with these feelings of alarm and distress in *herself*, before she is able to respond appropriately and give relief to the baby. The mother who is not too immersed in her own difficulties replies to the infant's behaviour, his varied cries, his kicks and screams, his inertia or limpness, his smiles and gurgles, as though she believes that such behaviour is a meaningful communication which requires to be understood and responded to. Her response is probably an essential prerequisite enabling the baby gradually to build up some form of realization of his own that behaviour is meaningful and communicative. Such experience accumulates from innumerable little daily incidents. I will give an example of one.

A three-day-old baby girl is lying asleep in her cot by the side of her mother's bed. She wakes up and cries a little; the mother speaks to her and the baby immediately stops crying. The baby is then quiet for a few minutes, after which her face puckers and she begins to whimper. Again she stops crying, apparently as soon as she hears the sound of her mother's voice. She remains quiet for a few moments while her mother is preparing to pick her up. When held in her mother's arms she continues to be quiet and apparently contented until she dozes off again.

It would probably be mistaken at this stage to say that the baby's cry was intended as a call for mother, as an older child's cry may often be. It might be more nearly correct to say that the cry was an expression of distress (in more severe states an expulsion of pain) which was received by the mother as *though* it were a call or communication of need. Being held in contact with her mother seems to meet the baby's need at this moment and the baby has the experience, or at any rate the opportunity of the experience, of being made sense of by her mother, of being treated as a person with communicable feelings. But, for this experience to be possible, the mother has first to be in touch with the baby. If the mother had been absent, or too drowsy or depressed or busy to respond to the baby, the opportunity would have been missed. If the mother had been lacking in confidence about her capacity to give good mothering, she might have responded to the baby's cry with her own anxiety and distress. The baby's experience might then have been not that her distress was accepted, understood and coped with, but that distress is met by the repercussion of her mother's own not-understood, not-coped-with anxieties.

## Developments Towards Symbol Formation

For the purpose of studying the origins of symbol formation and thought, it is of particular relevance to observe very closely what the baby does at times of delay between the experience of a need and the satisfaction of the need. The baby who is wanting to suck at the breast may for a while cope with the frustration of his need by sucking something else instead, for instance his thumb or one of his favourite toys. Used in this way, the sucked article can be the precursor of a symbol. It has some of the features of symbol. It is used in place of the wanted object and it serves to bridge the separation between the baby, with his experience of need, and the feeding mother, who gives satisfaction. Like a symbolical object, the sucked thumb differs from the object it replaces in important ways. It is ever present for example, and, from an early age, it is under the baby's control. It can be made to enter and leave his mouth as he wishes. To a slightly lesser extent, the same applies also to toys. At first the substitute articles are very unlikely to be true symbols, because the young infant probably makes no differentiation between the substitute article and the wanted object. That is, the baby is not making any differentiation between the part of his own body, the sucked thumb, and a part of his mother's body, probably the nipple or breast. To the extent that the sucked article is not differentiated from the nipple, the absence of the nipple and the frustration of its absence is not experienced by the baby. In such a case we could not say that the sucked thumb helped the baby to *tolerate* the frustration, we would have to say that it was used by the baby to enable it to be *unaware* of the frustration. Often this unawareness means that both the baby and mother are spared the experience of hostility aroused by frustration. If too extensively present, however, it can impede the baby's ability to distinguish between self and non-self and affect his later ability in symbol formation.

To some it may seem strange that I have given the example of the sucked thumb, being a part of the baby's own body, as an instance of a precursor of a symbol. Both baby observation and psychotherapy with very young or very immature children highlight the great part played by body imagery in the earliest stages of symbol formation. The expression 'He plays with himself' is often used by parents when referring to their child's masturbation. Various parts of the body – the mouth, anus, genitals, hands, fingers and so on – are among the child's earliest playthings and are especially likely to be resorted to in the mother's absence. Inanimate objects such as rattles, beads, cuddly toys, blankets and nappies are also 'played' with very early in the life of many infants. Early toys are likely to be things which can be sucked, smelled, stroked, cuddled or poked into; also things which can easily be moved and controlled or which have movements which may be followed with the eyes. It is likely that in the early stages of their use these inanimate things are barely differentiated from parts of the child's own body and parts of his parents' bodies. The making of such differentiation is probably a very gradual process, proceeding by hardly perceptible degrees.

In the ordinary course of development the baby gradually accumulates experience of his mother as a person who is receptive to his communications of feeling and need; equally, as a person who can tolerate his hostility and anxiety. He gradually finds that when he is angry with his mother, she can bear it, survive it and help him once more to regain his good feelings. If the mother can contain the baby's hostility without denial or excessive guilt and anxiety, the baby is so helped to make the first steps in doing likewise. When the feelings of anger themselves are experienced as being less catastrophic, it becomes more possible to acknowledge the frustrations which arouse anger. On the occasions when his needs are not met with speedy gratification, the baby can then begin to bear to realize that he and his mother are separate beings. At this point of tolerating a degree of separation and distinction from the mother, it can also be tolerated that the sucked toy is not the same as the breast. It is then sucked *instead* of the breast, it stands for and represents the breast – or, in other words, is a symbol for the breast. The toy is in turn used to help the baby to tolerate further, and come to terms with, his experience of frustration. More elaborate play can develop, less directly tied to the infant's wishes for bodily gratification. The substitute objects become more like the toys they are, representative objects which can provide interest and enjoyment in their own right.

## Play as a Bridge Between Unconscious Phantasy and External Reality

When we recognize an activity to be a play activity, we are implicitly recognizing that the activity is not 'the real thing'. As an example, we may consider the play of a little girl who baths her baby doll and carefully tucks it into bed. The activity of the little girl is not the 'real thing' in terms of external reality. It is not care for herself or her own baby. Neither is it 'the real thing' in terms of unconscious, *internal* reality, the direct phantasies of rivalry with mother, or feelings concerning a new baby sibling, for example. The play is an activity which lies between the two areas of reality, external and internal, and which in such a case forms a bridge between them. This bridge or in-between area of play can be used by the girl to express, work over and sort out her rivalry with her mother and perhaps to reach a good identification with her. It is also an area in which she can develop and acquire practical knowledge and skills which will later enable her to achieve competence in her external environment. The symbolical area of play is a relatively safe area. When it can be used, anxiety can be experienced in a modified way. The child does not have to face the full blast of the anxiety, guilt and other consequences which he would experience if he directly expressed and imposed upon his parents the full force of his conflicting instinctual urges. On the other hand, he also does not have to face the full responsibility and consequences of the *limitations* of his capacity to cope with dangers and difficulties of his external environment.

## The Use and Impairment of Symbol Formation in Child and Adult

Play is of particular value to the child, as it provides possibilities for anxiety-provoking situations to be faced in a symbolical way. The anxiety itself is then reduced to tolerable and manageable levels. But if the anxiety is nevertheless too great, the child will break off his play at the point of danger. This also can be seen in everyday observations. Let us suppose that a little boy is playing in the garden, pretending that it is a jungle and that he is an intrepid explorer facing unknown dangers. At one level we can see his play as an attempt to cope with the anxieties attendant upon his leaving the safe familiarity of home and the safe protective aspects of his mother. While the garden remains the *symbol* for the dangerous unknown all goes well. The child, however much absorbed in his play, knows that he is still in the garden, and that he can return to his mother. This awareness enables him to spend a period playing away from her. He can explore and extend his knowledge and understanding of the garden and its contents. He can enjoy the garden. He may also develop actual skills and learn to cope with real, if minor, hazards in the garden. But if his anxieties become too great, the garden is no longer experienced as a symbol for the jungle. It is felt to be in actuality that particular aspect of the unknown, of the 'not-protective mother' of his unconscious phantasies, for which the jungle had stood. The dangers then threaten to become ones with which he cannot possibly cope. He breaks off his play and runs indoors to mother.

A similar situation may be experienced by an adult. For example, if an adult has to make a journey to a country unknown to him, he also has to prepare for it in imagination before he can achieve it in reality. Within his mind he requires to foresee many contingencies and prepare to meet them. He needs to imagine what he will have to take with him, each stage of the journey, where he is going to stay, and so on. As with the child, a moderate degree of anxiety may serve as an impetus, leading him to extend his knowledge. He may get time-tables, maps, read books, study the language. If his anxiety is moderate the adult, like the child in his play, can in his conscious fantasies obtain pleasure from imagining himself in a variety of novel situations. Alternatively, the more anxious adult may, in conscious fantasy, face again and again the many different mishaps which could occur on his travels. If he is really excessively anxious, that is to say, if what the journey symbolizes in his unconscious phantasies is associated with overwhelming anxiety, his capacity to make realistic preparations will be impaired and he may even decide not to travel. The journey no longer symbolizes the unconscious danger situation. It has become equated with it and must be abandoned.

In these examples both child and adult are faced with situations which require a degree of independence. In both cases this is likely to be associated with whatever unconscious anxieties each may have concerning separating from the person or place, upon which they have previously depended for their sense of security. For each this is a testing occasion of the strength of their inner security, the strength of the psyche for the containment of anxiety. Both adult and child prepare for novel situations by the use of conscious fantasy. But with the adult these conscious fantasies are contained within the mind as anticipatory thoughts and plans. They are largely of a nature which could be communicated by words, though generally it is not essential to talk about them in order to think them. But the young child's conscious fantasy, the jungle game of the example, is not contained in his mind, as is silent thought. It exists and is experienced in his play activity. To a large extent, the child is actually compelled to play in order to think the situation out. Play is behaviour, an active externalization of mental experience, which makes use of symbolical objects and of dynamic, dramatic interaction with these objects.

The adult uses his verbal ability, his system of word symbolism, to express and communicate to others his thoughts and feelings. But he also uses words, to a great extent, for inner thought, for the actual process of thinking. The mature adult has considerable capacity to contain his thought processes in his mind. But from time to time the adult will find it useful, perhaps even essential, to clarify his thoughts by externalizing his mental imagery in the form of talking, writing, doodling, and so forth. It appears that children have a similar but still stronger need to externalize their mental experience. The young child does so by creating a three-dimensional play situation into which he can put himself, or at least a toy representing himself.

In the examples of play observation discussed, when anxieties became overwhelming the symbol formation broke down. However, the children were able to return to the mother (or her representative). They could return to those aspects of their mother and life experience, which had retained the significance of a safe area into which to put anxieties. But what happens if the child has been insufficiently able to establish contact with such safe areas? If, for whatever reasons, he has been unable to experience his mother (or her substitute) as a person sufficiently available, sufficiently receptive and sufficiently strong to bear with the forceful inrush of his unbearable feelings? Some of our patients show us very vividly such consequences. In extreme cases symbol formation has hardly developed at all. From this it follows that every aspect of the child's surroundings continue to be experienced as in the earliest of days of infancy. The world remains a world composed of parts of his own and his mother's body. Without symbolism, there is no way that his interests can develop beyond the goals of the instinctual urges of his infancy. Play is impossible and every aspect of the child's mental development is arrested.

Giles was in this condition when he first came to me for psychotherapy, when he was three years and nine months old.

## Giles

Some of the points I have been making are illustrated by the first six months of therapy with Giles, a child whose development was severely arrested.

Some of this material is unavoidably of a disturbing nature, partly because it is exceedingly primitive. But perhaps it disturbs mainly because Giles's way of communicating his feelings of distress was to arouse such feelings in me; these, in turn, I may arouse in the reader. If we find his material repulsive or disturbing we may at least have a distant realization of why his mother had difficulty in accepting him.

Giles was the youngest of three children. His young mother, highly intelligent but somewhat superficially gay and brittle, appeared to have coped well with the elder children. With Giles, however, there were difficulties from the beginning. He was a weak, sickly infant who suffered throughout his first year from frequent illness. His mother described him as having 'perpetual diarrhoea'. Thinking that this must be due to the quality of her milk she weaned him after a couple of months, but his symptoms continued. He remained frail and slow to gain weight. 'He could not keep anything inside him,' his mother said. From about six months he had frequent colds and bronchial trouble. He must have been a very unrewarding baby, perpetually arousing anxiety, needing great care to keep him alive and yet never thriving. He seems to have aroused in his mother the feeling that she could do nothing good for him. Her own need to defend herself from depression seems to have become more pronounced. She reported that he 'seemed not to have much personality' and that she increasingly handed over his care to others. There was quite a long period of separation in his ninth and tenth months. On returning to his mother's care, Giles seemed now to reject her and for a long time he appeared withdrawn, spending much time just gazing into space. During his second year his health improved, although he remained frail and small for his age; his main physical symptom was then constipation. As he approached the age of two, his mother was able to recognize that all was not well with him. She became very concerned and began to look after him entirely herself. He then became more affectionate and responsive to her and a little more alert and interested in his surroundings. For a while it seemed that he might be able to make further development in response to his mother's changing attitude. However, between the age of two-and-a-half (when I first saw him for assessment) and three-and-a-half, he seemed to have made no discernible progress, apart from obtaining saliva control.

Giles commenced therapy with me, attending four times weekly, when aged three years and nine months. He did not talk at all and his only vocalization was a sound like 'eh, eh, eh', which was varied to 'ar, ar', apparently when he was referring to cars. He had never developed the varied babble of an ordinary baby and until he was two he only grunted or screamed. From time to time he responded to what was said to him in a way which suggested that he understood speech, but one could not be altogether sure of this. He looked frail, very undersized for his age and his walk resembled that of a much younger child. Although he could only toddle with unsteady gait, he was sometimes nippy and unpredictable, suddenly darting to a cupboard or drawer and emptying out or destroying its contents. At home he made his needs known by using gestures and pulling his mother's hand. If he was not understood rapidly he tended to become very angry, screaming and flinging things about or sitting on the floor shrieking and banging his head. If offered food which he did not want, or even seeing it prepared for others, he screamed violently. He refused or flung away food if it was not given to him as soon as he wanted it or in the precise way in which he wanted. For the most part he continued to wet and soil, and he had intermittent bouts of severe sleeping difficulties. His main interests concerned cars – he liked collecting, holding on to and lining up toy cars, but rarely made them move. His other interest was in doors and door knobs; in particular he would spend long periods opening and shutting the doors of the kitchen cupboards and taking out and lining up the saucepans and tins. He also liked to tear up paper and sprinkle it all around his cot. He had a number of cuddly toys which he liked to carry about with him, 'hugging and biting them just as he does me', his mother said. Out of keeping with this general picture was his isolated and relatively advanced ability to do jigsaw puzzles.

At first he gave me the feeling that he was more like a primitive creature than a real human being. Like his mother, I was sometimes aware that he aroused in me a faint chill of repulsion. From the first, however, he did show signs of being very much aware of me and of eagerly seeking contact. He varied the emotional tone of his 'eh, eh' sound in a communicative way, brought toys to show me or took my hand and tugged me about the room to do what he wanted. His use of toys showed little discrimination. He picked toys up in a haphazard way, examined them but soon dropped them and turned to something else. Often he seemed about to play or to develop some sort of theme or pattern in his handling of the toys – then he would perhaps stumble over another toy, become distracted by this and pick it up, only to leave it a few minutes later when some other chance stimulation came his way. At other times he would hurl the toys one after another out of his drawer, and stamp and bash them or tear them to shreds with his teeth, laughing gleefully as he did so. All paper and cardboard boxes were quickly bitten up in this way and the fragments strewn about the room or mushed up with water. Occasionally he seemed briefly to show something more systematic in his play. He would, for instance, line up a row of cars or bricks, or make some other sort or arrangement which seemed to be deliberate and meaningful to him. He always showed special interest in the toy cars, often clutching one in his hand as he went about, or putting a little car inside a larger truck.

I tried to understand his activities, to regard them as meaningful and to put to him in the simplest words possible what sense I could make of them. Often, however, I could not follow the meaning of the details of his activities. I could understand, nevertheless, that he was filling the room and myself with his own inner chaos, his own feeling that everything was hopelessly meaningless, that nothing remained good for long enough to be of use, that everything lay in destroyed, unrelated bits, which he could only desperately throw about from one place to another. Occasionally he seemed to follow what I was saying. By the end of the first fortnight he had used three words, apparently in response to interpretations. He spent some time opening and shutting the carrier part of a little tip-up truck, and when I interpreted this as a biting activity he laughed and tried to use the truck to 'bite' or pinch my finger and cheek, saying 'nip-nip, nip-nip' repeatedly. Another time when he was pushing a stick in and out of a plastic bottle and listening to the noise it made, I used the word 'pop' after which 'pop-pop' was added to his vocabulary. On one occasion when he was making a particularly ferocious attack upon a little car taken from his drawer, I interpreted this as standing for a rival baby felt to have been with me during his absence. He then put the car into my lap and hit it, saying 'smack' in a vigorous voice. These words, the first he had ever spoken, remained with him and were frequently used.

From about the third week of therapy his play became more focussed and concentrated. But what he concentrated upon for several months was endless water play: almost daily he drenched himself, me and everything in the room.* He very often filled a mug with water, took a little drink and then flung the rest of the water away. Then he refilled the mug and repeated his behaviour over and over again, saying 'rubbish' or 'nasty' as he splashed out the drink. Or often he flung the mug away and took a drink from a bottle instead. Then this, too, would be thrown away and a series of hollow cubes used as mugs, each in its turn to be rapidly discarded. Even when he began drinking eagerly, as though finding something good, it rapidly changed to something 'nasty', and either the liquid or the container was rejected. When drinking he did not use his lips but opened his mouth and

*Some limits were set, but in view of his urgent needs and extremely limited means of expression I restricted Giles's messing far less than I would have done with a more mature child.

tried to pour in the water from the mug or bottle, dribbling out most of it. But he did use his teeth, and sometimes spent a long while holding the neck of a plastic bottle between them, chewing and worrying at it like a puppy with a rubber bone. Most of all he just stood at the basin with the plug in and taps running at full force and simply baled the water out all over the floor and all over me too if he had the chance. Things which might have helped to cope with the mess, like floor-cloths and dusters, were especially attacked. Occasionally he urinated or defecated. At this time, also, he had several tummy upsets and frequent colds. He deliberately drenched or tore up the handkerchiefs provided by his mother, and preferred to wipe his runny nose up against my shoulder or on the curtains.

Altogether he could hardly have shown more directly his need to find in me someone who would be inexhaustibly absorbent of his tremendous outpouring of angry wretchedness. When I interpreted that he was filling me with his wee-wee he chortled with delight. Very soon the words 'splash, wee-wee, plop-plop, nice, nasty, rubbish, drink', were being used. Sometimes he would trickle water into my lap saying, 'Wee, wee, wee, cry, cry, cry.' Tottering around the room through the puddles and debris on the floor, his clothes drenched and his nose running, he looked a pathetic little scrap of misery, unable to find anything which remained solid or usable for more than a few moments. Yet it seemed that it was I, not he, who felt unhappy about this. With an unreal triumphant laughing he would soon return to more flooding, leaving me to feel helpless and lost.

There were also more hopeful moments. He began giving me mugs of water as well as himself; at first these would soon be snatched away from me and drunk or splashed out by him, but then he would place a little chair close to the side of my chair. We would each have a mug or bottle of water and he wanted us to have a quiet drink side by side. Often he showed that we should each have exactly the same things or sit in exactly the same postures. He began to use phrases like 'your cup, my cup, your chair, my chair, here you are'. At home his mother reported that he played similar games with her, particularly concerning parts of the body, saying, 'your nose, my nose, your mouth, my mouth' and so on, and these also entered into his sessions. Previously his mother had made several unsuccessful attempts to teach him words, but now he was really keen to get them from her. At first he sometimes just echoed whatever she said, but increasingly he obtained words and short phrases which he could use meaningfully. As may be imagined, this was a very rewarding experience both for his mother and for myself, and had the effect of increasing our confidence and ability to help him. Although water play continued for a long time to be his predominant activity, gradually his play became in every sense more formed, coherent and substantial. He could contain things for a longer time, in a more solid form, and there were more indications of memory.

From this general therapeutic picture it may be useful to pick out one line of development. From the first it seemed that cars were of special significance to him. When a child like Giles is clutching in his hand a little lump of painted metal we have to forget that to us it is immediately recognizable as a toy car. To understand what it may mean to the child we have to observe carefully how he uses it. Early on, Giles used the tip-up truck to 'nip' me with. He also used another car as something to be put into my lap and smacked. He almost never pushed cars about on their wheels. Some days he did everything while holding a little car in his hand. If he turned on a tap or threw something away it was as though these actions were not being done by him but by the car. I began to refer to his favourite as 'the Giles car'. He quickly took this idea up and after a while other cars were named 'Hoxter car', 'Daddy car', 'Mummy car' and so on. The cars had been used as things to line up or throw away, but most of all as things to hold, without life or action. Now they began to become more alive. They crawled up the sides of bottles to have a drink, they perched across the top of a hollow cube, like a pot, to make wee-wees. They lay on their backs and went to sleep. They fought and kissed and bumped and climbed on to and into one another. They began to follow after one another, to part and to come together again. At the beginning of many sessions, the Giles car would violently crash into the big Daddy lorry and knock it off the table, and then go around with, or inside, the Mummy truck. Weekends and the first holiday break from psychotherapy could be talked about more meaningfully when the Giles car was made to run to and fro from the Hoxter car. A

Giles house and a Hoxter house also came into the play.

He sometimes used two or more cars to represent one person. Early processes of splitting and differentiation began to be shown. If he had made a destructive mess, it was the 'bad Giles car' (or a brother or Daddy car) who was to blame and who had to be thrown away and a car representing a remaining good part would take its place. When he was angry with me a 'bad Hoxter car' would be punished and thrown away – but there still remained a good Hoxter car and all was not lost.

He began to introduce words which I had never used with him like 'horrible', 'naughty', 'greedy', 'dirty'. In the fourth and fifth months it was typical for him to come into the room, see that one of the floor-cloths was already damp and say, 'Who did that? Horrible boy did that.' Then pick up a car saying, 'Horrible dirty bottom boy! Rubbish! Rubbish!' and fling it into the waste-paper bin. He would then turn to me saying with a soft whimper, 'I'm not horrible Giles, don't throw horrible Giles away.'

There was a curious quality about his use of the cars. There was very little about them that was really car-like – they were named as people. But what nature of objects were these 'people' to him?

Some light was thrown on this question in the course of another kind of play which occupied many of the sessions of his fifth and sixth months of therapy. He often used to get me to arrange two easy chairs on the couch in such a way that they formed a sort of tunnel. He pushed cushions into this and then crawled in himself like a mouse into a hole. Once there he would suck his fingers and scratch his bottom. This I interpreted in connection with his wish to get into my body (the mother's body) through the anus. One day he put two cushions on the floor in front of me, saying, 'Your bottom, my bottom.' Then he put a car on each cushion saying, 'Your toy, my toy.' He then put the cushion and car into the little house of chairs and crawled in himself. Then he fingered the car and pushed it in and out of the tunnel. He emerged to collect a bottle, calling it 'a wee-wee toy', and took it back into the house with him. The nature of the car-people then became clearer. Often they did not stand for people in the external world, but for part-objects incorporated in his internal world, sometimes literally equated with his faeces. His symptom of constipation, his way of holding on to cars and keeping them immobile, his early word at the commencement of therapy, 'ah-ahs', said to mean 'cars', all could now be related together. Giles was still very close to the baby whose first substitute objects are parts of his own body. To Giles his toys were the things in his bottom, and there he 'played with himself'. But these were also felt to be aspects of people, or bits of people, held concretely inside him. There were many other examples confirming that he felt his faeces were good or bad bits of people inside him, but the most vivid illustration was one reported by his mother. One weekend, when using the lavatory at home, he said as he defecated, 'There goes little girl Hoxter!'

When Giles began psychotherapy I did not know whether he was able to understand anything that was said to him. Nevertheless, I used verbal commentary and interpretation from the outset. Sometimes I wondered whether this was an inappropriate act of faith, but in talking to him I was sustained by the consideration that a mother talks to her baby long before he is able to understand what she says. If she does not do so, his speech will never develop. In fact, Giles's rapid development of speech suggests that, before commencing therapy, he must already have had a good deal of speech within him, although it was unavailable for use with normal meaning. Although the main situation in retrospect seems adequately clear, it is probable that the actual details of my interpretations were often incorrect. With most patients interpretations would not be made until a much fuller stage of understanding had been reached. With Giles, however, mistakes were a risk that had to be taken in order to convey to him the message that was of prime importance – namely, that I was trying to understand and that I was consistently regarding his behaviour as meaningful. It seemed that as his behaviour was received, understood and given meaning, so he became increasingly able in fact to behave more meaningfully and to communicate this to me also.

At the start, Giles was unable to play in any ordinary sense of the word. His activities appeared to scattered, fragmented, haphazard. He behaved as though he were surrounded by meaningless bits and pieces which he could only pick up, throw about and attack. These activities seemed to be an expression, or rather at first an evacuation, of his own inner feeling of everything being chaotic, senseless and fragmented. I saw his behaviour as that of a baby who is in a state of frenzy, screaming, kicking and trying to throw himself and the contents of himself about. The first stage of therapy was to attempt to receive his behaviour as a communication of the state of mind which he was trying to fling out of himself into the room, into me – a process which resulted in his environment becoming a chaotic mess undifferentiated from his internal state. But there were probably enough times when I was felt to be different from the rest of the environment. These would be the occasions when he could experience me as a mother, who neither shut out nor was overwhelmed by what he was putting into her, but had a place within her which could receptively contain his states of disintegration. The mother normally returns these to the baby in the form of responses which appropriately meet his needs. As a therapist, my responses took the form of interpretations by which I attempted to transform his senseless evacuations into communications which made sense of him. The first few words occurred, perhaps, when he felt that words could be fitted to his experiences, when he felt that I was talking about things that meant something to him.

The long months of flooding activity were, to Giles, a vital stage when he really got down to using me as a lavatory-like container for his outpourings of misery and rage. One can see how closely the actual bodily experiences of urinating, defecating, drinking and biting were related to his emotional and mental states. He seemed also to be re-experiencing the condition of his first year, when he had 'perpetual diarrhoea'. He demonstrated vividly how closely related at the infantile level are the physical processes of taking and keeping in the mother's food as a source of nourishment for growth, and the mental processes of introjection and integration. As his mother had reported, 'He could not keep anything inside him.' He had a mind and body like a sieve. He had been unable to find within his mother a place which could retain his states of 'wee, wee, wee ... cry, cry, cry'. He desired to evacuate and flood his way into her through every pore of her being. Her withdrawal from him took the form of allowing his crying to go through her unheard and the psychic significance of his somatic condition to pass through unattended. This could have reinforced in him his concept of her as a porous object and the establishment within himself of a porous mind, where nothing could be held together in a cohering or coherent form.

Gradually he did develop a rudimentary capacity for containment within himself, a small area of internal mental space, so that he was no longer compelled to spit and fling out his experiences immediately. He could savour them a little. He could begin to recognize them for what they were and begin an elementary differentiation between the good and the 'rubbish'. He then began to use me more in association with feeding and a more reciprocal relationship developed. He wanted to be like me, but at the same time worked out, both with his mother and with myself, a small awareness of separateness and some sense of his own identity. The game he developed with his mother at the age of four (getting her to say 'your nose, my nose, your eyes, my eyes' and so on) is one that commonly takes place around the turn of the first year.

Giles showed other indications of becoming more able to bear, to face and recognize his own feelings. As the time approached for ending a session he often played bedtime games, pleading pathetically, 'Put the toys away. Don't put Giles away.' Or he would play-act that he was in his cot and that I was the mother who went 'out to a party'. He would then stretch out his arms and say, 'I can't reach you. I can't reach you.' There were also indications that he was in touch sometimes with the feelings of others. One day when I was feeling rather despondent he sat beside me and said, 'Don't be sad, Mrs Hoxter, have a sweet.' Although the sweet would not have cheered me up, his being able to say this had the effect of a real act of reparation. From his mother's reports it appeared that she also felt that her capacity to respond to him was being healed and restored.

The phantasies accompanying anal masturbation which Giles showed in his house play in therapy suggested that, at this stage, the mother was no longer felt to be a porous object. She now had an orifice through which he could enter an enclosed space and into which he could place himself in a less fragmented form. This change was also accompanied by an increase in the coherence, the meaningful content and retentive qualities of his own mental functioning. At a slightly later stage he worked upon increasing the structure and differentiation in his own mind, in terms of phantasies concerning the discovery of the structure and different parts of the mother's body. This internal work was shown in a more symbolical form of play in which he frequently drew maps of road routes. He placed special emphasis upon providing the cars with ample parking places and with petrol stations to supply the sustenance they required.

By this stage a play language had developed, a mode of communication suited to what continued to be very concrete body-mind experiences. The long process of psychotherapy for his severe condition of psychopathology could then commence.

## Conclusion

One of Freud's greatest contributions lay in his refutation of the dichotomy of body and mind which had dominated so much of previous and contemporary thought. By understanding the nature of unconscious phantasy and by following the principle of genetic continuity, Freud and his followers replaced the dichotomy with integrative insight, revealing the complex interrelationship of body and mind. The child psychotherapist may sometimes feel that her work is like that of an overburdened charwoman. That what the child needs is a nappy, and not someone with many years of post-graduate training. Nevertheless, she is in fact dealing with the crudest somatic elements of infantile experience and the most sensitive and subtle processes of mental growth. Within herself she requires to be in touch with infantile sensations and emotions and to integrate these to the fullest extent of her intellectual and conceptual ability. She is then able to follow and accompany her patient along the path of communication – which begins with expulsions of pain, anger and fear, conveyed in yells and violent action. It proceeds to expression conveyed by the increasing use of the symbolism of play, dreams and words. Finally it arrives at the integrative stage of internal communication, the forming of links which give birth to sublimations and creative thought.

# Chapter Eleven

# *Psychotherapy with Psychotic Children*

## by Frances Tustin

The preceding chapter described vividly the course of psychotherapy with a little boy whose communications were at first of a very primitive and chaotic kind. A therapist with a great deal of experience in treating psychotic children gives us now a further glimpse into the psychotic layers of the mind and the awful 'black hole' feeling which these patients experience. The nature of childhood psychosis is discussed and the problem of diagnosis. We see the extremely difficult, dedicated and firmly disciplined work which is necessary for getting in touch with these children. In it, agonizing primitive feelings have to be shared with the patient before psychotherapy proper can be begun and established. The parents of psychotic children need great sympathy: the task of the psychotherapist is to try to heal the formidable break between mother and child. M.B., D.D.

---

In this chapter I want to describe the conditions I have come to regard as necessary for the psychotherapeutic treatment of a psychotic child. My account is based on over two decades of experience with such children. I hope it will warn the reader of the pitfalls inherent in work with these children, and perhaps also save him from the holes I have dug for myself.

Since my comments about necessary conditions arise from the views I have formed about the nature and origin of childhood psychosis, a brief résumé of these has to be given. These views are in turn based on a great deal of clinical evidence, which I have not sufficient space to discuss in detail: for a full exposition the reader is referred to my book *Autism and Childhood Psychosis* (1972).

## The Nature of Childhood Psychosis

Psychotherapy with a psychotic child presents special difficulties, of which the most outstanding is that of working with a patient who to all intents and purposes has almost no psyche. Clinical experience has convinced me that such a child lives in a sensation-dominated state - and in some children further pathological processes have developed which even deaden awareness of sensation. These pathological processes are also body-centred, therefore the psychotic child habitually reacts to the outside world as if it were an extension of his body - although, paradoxically, in his state of relative undifferentiation (or scanty and blurred differentiation), he is not aware, or only vaguely aware, of his body as such.

In the course of normal development, sensations become organized into percepts and concepts. Once such organization occurs, true psychological functioning can be said to have begun. Except in narrowly restricted areas, that pyschological functioning is not typical of the psychotic child. Therefore, in the early days of therapy, the main task is to encourage and enable continuous psychological processes to be set in train. In this endeavour there needs to be some understanding of what events have apparently led to such restriction of psychological function.

## The Possible Origin of Childhood Psychosis

I have come to view childhood psychosis as being a protective measure against the unbearable shock of feeling disconnected from the mother. In *Autism and Child Psychosis*, I have offered evidence indicating that the breakdown of normal attachments to the mother results in the infant being seized with enraged and grief-stricken panic. The mouth seems to be the prime focus for early attachment processes: crisis comes with awareness that the nipple is not part of the mouth. Realization dawns that vital supplies cannot be taken for granted. There is a power and energy crisis.

Yet, for the infant, the experience seems to be far more

dramatic and intense even than the last statement implies. As the experience in the mouth is spread to other sensitive bodily orifices, the infant becomes aware of his body and of discomforts to his body. Everything is now shot through with destructive tantrums of rage, which thunder through the body, as awareness of the lack of an everlasting bodily connection is forced upon the infant. Due to his relatively unorganized psychological state, these sensations are excessively intense. Frustration seems to be experienced as a disconnecting mutilation. Endings and separations are not just a fact of existence but an explosive catastrophe. Doom is in the air. The child is in the grip of a threat of annihilation which is worse than death. 'To be' brings in the notion of 'not to be', in a manner which is excruciating. The child feels hurled into an agony of consciousness from which he retreats.

The foregoing is an attempt to put intense non-verbal states into words – an attempt which distorts their essential nature and power, for they were experienced only in a bodily way. However, it is necessary to verbalize them if we are to have some inkling of what awareness of bodily separateness seems to have meant to a psychotic child. Workers who have been deeply in touch with psychotic children confirm how 'real' such states are to the children and how constant are their efforts to avoid re-experiencing this 'psychological catastrophe' (Bion, 1962), this 'psychotic depression' (Winnicott, 1958), this 'basic fault' (Belint, 1969), this 'place of critical hurt' (as I understand some Jungians have termed it). Body-centred processes proliferate and perseverate to divert attention from this basic unbearable situation. These processes also divert attention from the outside world. They produce the consequent lack of commonly agreed constructs of reality which characterizes the psychotic child, and makes him so difficult to reach. And to reach him is a necessary pre-condition for psychotherapy.

## Getting in Touch with Psychotic Children

To reach such a child we have to share his anguish, his rages, his terrors, the bodily 'flop' of his disillusionments, without being overwhelmed by them. For most of us, such states are inexpressible. Poets and artists, however, lend us conviction and help us to communicate to and about them. Emily

Brontë, for example, was in touch with these depths when, in a poem concerned with 'being' and 'becoming', she wrote:

> Oh dreadful is the check – intense the agony –
> When the ear begins to hear, and the eye begins to see;
> When the pulse begins to throb, the brain to think again;
> The soul to feel the flesh, the flesh to feel the chain.

The psychotic child has retreated from too sharp an experience of 'being' and 'becoming'. He lacks the balance-wheel of assimilated nurturing. Instead he has an impulse-driven, body-centred artefact which collapses at the first hint of strain. Thus he is at the mercy of spiralling states of bodily excitement which are succeeded by the 'flop' of despair. The latter comes when impossible expectations, whipped up by the crescendos of excitement, are not fulfilled. The only way in which these oscillations have been controlled is through massive counter-reactions which diminish or nullify responses to stimuli. Thus, the first aim of treatment is to help the child to turn sufficiently from the excesses of his body-dominated world, and to live over again the failed crisis of becoming a developing psychological being. This time he will have skilled help in bearing the anguished disillusionment aroused by this 'new birth'. To reach this re-birth itself, accompanied by depression and bewilderment, often takes a long time.

The psychotic state was well illustrated in a poem dictated to me by a boy who had been psychotic. He had had three years of psychoanalytic therapy five times a week, and at the time of dictating the poem was eleven years old.

*Leslie's Poem*

> Why am I so wonderful?
> Why does the rain fall to the ground?
> To the ground? To the ground?
> And why? why? why? why?
> Does the rain made us sad?
> And why should we be so sad?
> Why are we so sad? sad? sad?
> And why don't we take the sun
> And be happy all over again?

In his state of feeling 'so wonderful' Leslie finds it difficult to make contact with a world which, because he cannot control it, makes him feel helpless and a failure. The situation makes him feel excessively disillusioned and sad. He desires the comfortable state he terms 'happiness'. Comfort and discomfort are primal elementary distinctions.

D. H. Lawrence's comments on the pitfalls of striving after the illusory comforts of such 'happiness' are very apposite. He writes:

> The more you reach after the fatal flower of happiness which trembles so blue and lovely in the crevice just beyond your grasp, the more fearfully you become aware of the ghastly and awful gulf of the precipice below you into which you will inevitably plunge as to the bottomless pit, if you reach any further. You pluck flower after flower – and it is never *the* flower. The flower itself – its calyx is a horrible gulf, it is the bottomless pit ... But the end of the rainbow is a bottomless gulf down which you can fall forever without arriving, and the blue distance is a void pit which can swallow you and all your efforts into its emptiness and still be no emptier. You and all your efforts. So the illusion of attainable happiness.
>
> D. H. Lawrence, *The Fox*.

The quotation illustrates vividly the crisis through which the psychotic child has to pass during therapy. It also emphasizes that this crisis is not peculiar to the psychotic. His development has in fact been stopped or become seriously distorted by it, but it is a crisis through which we all have to pass, with varying degrees of intensity, on our way to individuation. If we are in touch with our own psychic depths, we find we have feelings we can share with these psychotic children who at first sight seemed so bizarre and strange.

Thus, we find a psychotic child lamenting about 'the black hole with the nasty prick' (Tustin, 1972), and Luther writing 'I'm afraid of the darkness and the hole in it and I see it some time every day' (Dare, 1969). Luther wrote this in a time of anguished spiritual doubt – it may be pertinent to remember that he had broken away from the 'mother church'. Perhaps the heretics, the originals, the creative artists, the inventors, the innovators, the eccentrics, the exiles, the outcasts and the 'drop outs' suffer more acute pangs of individuation than most because, in their various ways, they have broken away from an established order. Perhaps most of us who are drawn to work with psychotic children have much in common with one or other of the types of people cited above. If this is so, we can draw from the situation the comfort that may help us in our quest to understand and reach these often seemingly unreachable patients.

But to get deeply in touch with them we have to:

> Descend lower, descend only
> Into the world of perpetual solitude ...
> Internal darkness, deprivation
> And destitution of all property
> Desiccation of the world of sense
> Evacuation of the world of fancy
> Inoperancy of the world of spirit ...
>
> T. S. Eliot, *Four Quartets; Collected Poems.*

And, again to quote T.S. Eliot, who seems to know well these ultimate depths of human experience, we shall have to go through states in which we feel we are ...

> Whirled in a vortex that shall bring
> The world to that destructive fire
> Which burns before the ice-cap reigns.
>
> T. S. Eliot, *Four Quartets, Collected Poems.*

It seems that to be in touch with the awesome poetry of human existence is a necessary pre-condition of psychotherapy with psychotic children.

We also need to be in touch with the intense and passionate feelings which pounded through muscle and vein before they were bridled by an attachment to a civilizing and nurturing situation, the co-operation and sharing with the mother. In psychotic children (and in a 'pocket' in the depths of many of us) the frustration aroused by this 'bridling' has stirred up such violence that attachment has never been established, or only established in an insecure way. This attachment is as to an external psychological 'placenta', which brings to the child a sense of belonging. In normal development this sense of belonging arises from the use that is made of the nurturing ambience of breast (or feeding-bottle experienced as a breast), the parents, the family and social groups. It will be noticed that the emphasis is on *the use* made of nurturing agencies as well as their availability. The latter has been much considered in the literature, whereas when working with patients in a therapeutic setting, it is the capacity of use we endeavour to foster and release.

Psychotherapists themselves need this sense of belonging to a nurturing and supporting group. For therapists who work with psychotic levels 'belonging' is even more of a necessity, and more than usual strain is likely to be put on such a group by the therapist. Thus, in my view, therapists need to commit themselves to an attachment to one of the psychological schools. Such a commitment entails acceptance of the limitations and inevitable partiality of our views as finite human beings: it means giving up the desire to see things from all sides at once in a timeless universe. On the debit side, the technical language of the theoretical schools, if over-used, can cease to be a vehicle for communication and become instead an encapsulating protection which cuts us off from contact with fellow workers of other schools and from our fellow human beings.

G. K. Chesterton seems to offer good advice to child psychotherapists, particularly to those who work with psychotic children, when he says:

> Stand up and keep your childishness;
> Read all the pedants' screeds and strictures,
> But don't believe in anything,
> That can't be told in coloured pictures.

It seems to me, that for pyschotherapy with a psychotic child to be effective, the therapist needs to be both warm and responsive, and not afraid to express thoughts in 'picture language'. This expression will be meaningful to children who have little capacity for abstract thinking.

However, on a more severely practical level, before psychotherapy can begin, intelligent, informed and careful diagnosis is a first necessity.

## Diagnosis

In the past much unnecessary hurt has been caused by

attributing undue blame to the mothers of psychotic children. Sadly, this has often come from psychotherapeutic quarters, where the aim should be to understand rather than to blame. In moving papers on his work with the parents of psychotic children, Tischler has pointed out that these parents, and particularly the mothers, are often in a state of acute distress due to years of living in close proximity to a psychotic child. He shows that this condition is far more upsetting than living with any other sort of handicap (Tischler, 1971). It is important for the clinician to appreciate this aspect when making diagnostic assessments.

In my opinion, phrases such as 'refrigerator mothers' and 'schizophrenogenic mothers' have distorted our approach to psychotic patients. Each case is different and needs to be studied in detail. Generalized conclusions based on global and unrefined diagnosis can cause mismanagement and distress. It has been my experience that there are many varied factors which can cause a breakdown in the early attachment processes. Some of these factors are possible organic, cognitive, muscular, sensory or affective defects *in the child*. On the other hand, the mother's nurturing capacities may be impaired by under-confidence, insecurity or depression from a variety of causes: there may be overbearing relatives or nursing staff, or there may be an unsupportive or absent husband, constant moves from place to place, or an emotionally important relative may have died around the time of the infant's birth. For any of a variety of reasons the mother may be averted from the physical aspects of caring for a baby, or the mother's own infantile experiences and her reaction to them may have made it difficult for her to meet the strains of childbirth and motherhood. A child's psychosis is likely to be the result of an interacting concurrence of some of the factors mentioned above, as well as yet others. A prolonged therapeutic diagnostic procedure is the only method by which some of the interacting strands can be discerned, and help to child and parents given on the basis of these findings. In the relatively unexplored terrain of childhood psychosis, we are constantly discovering new facts and interactions and thus refining our diagnoses.

It is helpful and perhaps indispensable for a therapist who works with psychotic children to have carried out systematic and detailed infant observations. Such observation, over at least the first year of an infant's life, sharpens and makes more subtle our diagnostic observations, as also our therapeutic work itself.

Medical knowledge and opinion are indispensable. This is an area where physiological factors are extremely significant. For example, infants with neurological impairments are likely to be more difficult to nurture and are thus much more liable to fall into 'bottomless pits' and to display psychotic features. In other children, psychological and physiological factors, such as hormonal imbalances, can be so closely intertwined that it is difficult to say which have set into operation the vicious circle of psychosis. In others, nurturant lacks can have occurred so early as to be indistinguishable from constitutional defects. Obviously, a great discretion needs to be exercised in assessing whether a psychotic child is likely to benefit from psychotherapy. However, the few psychotic children who have recovered spontaneously and those who have benefited from psychotherapy must have found some way around physiological impairments, if they existed. As far as psychotherapy goes, it seems very important to start treatment before the age of latency, around five or six years of age.

As diagnosis becomes more sophisticated, we are less likely to fall into distressing errors. In the past misconceptions may have arisen, because in the early mother-infant situation, the nursing couple are such a unity. It is impossible to say whether the mother cuts herself off from her child or the child cuts himself off from the mother. Clinical evidence indicates that all that can be said with any certainty is that the illusion of a bodily flow between mother and infant seems to have been broken in a sudden and catastrophic way and that the child experienced this as a physical bodily break – as an agonizing blow to his sublime belief that the outside world was a continuation of his body, and under his manipulative control.

## The Aims of Psychotherapy

The therapist's task is to try to heal the psychic break between mother and child. Such a therapist does not attempt to come between mother and child, by acting as a mother-substitute or by competing with the mother. Parents and therapist are working together on a difficult task; if it is to have the possibility of a satisfactory outcome, they need each other.

In some cases, over-sensitized modes of communication may have developed between mother and child in an attempt to restore the illusion of unbroken flow, felt to exist before the catastrophic 'break' occurred. This unbroken flow was the guarantee of absolute protection from bodily disaster. But its protective qualities were missed only when it was not there.

A hypersensitized mother and child can be so close to each other that there is no space between them to be bridged by psychological modes of functioning. A father who is effective in his masculine role (and allowed to be so) is important in relaxing undue, interlocking closeness between mother and infant. He also provides protection when the 'absolute' protection of the illusion of an unbroken flow between them is lost.

If such compulsive, panic-stricken closeness between mother and child has developed, professional workers may be able to help by strengthening the father's protective influence in the family. Psychotherapy can also help, for the child will re-enact with the therapist the close tie he has had with the mother and demonstrate some of the reasons for it. With time, patience and skill the therapist may be able to help him to give up the illusory reassurance of an ever-present mother and to pattern his attachment feelings in a more normal way. One of the aims of psychotherapy will be to enable the violence of the child's feelings about frustration to be expressed in a setting in which he is helped to manage and utilize them.

This process does not signify encouraging or allowing the continued and unbridled expression of feelings. Rather it means vigilance and firmness in seeing that they do not wreck the nurturing situation, both at home and in the consulting room. A therapist who protects the possessions and rights of other children who use the room, as well as his own person and right to exist, inspires much more trust in a violent child than one who merely seems so lax as to let foolish things occur. Speaking personally, work with psychotic children has brought me from the misty heights of Cloud-cuckoo-land to a stern realism about the destructiveness that lurks in all of us. The realization has considerably tightened my work with neurotic patients, which has been carried to deeper levels. The outcome has been more effective and creative functioning, as violence was harnessed rather than left to drift around unrecognized and untrapped. Disciplined psychotherapy, however, needs a firm treatment setting to support it. This in an extremely necessary condition.

**Treatment Settings**

To bear the strain of living so close to elemental madness, institutions who care for psychotic children need to be particularly well organized. They need the leadership of a person with deep insight and understanding of the problems arising from the care of such children. Such a person must have qualities of unsentimental compassion and a capacity for good judgment. The staff need to feel protected by the person in charge. They need to feel that the 'buck' of anxiety and panic stops there, to be brought within the orbit of common-sense management and control. It seems to me, that *common* sense is an indispensable quality for all who work with psychotic children, for this is just what these lack.

Under their protective coverings psychotic children have excessively intense feelings. Workers can easily 'pick up' these feelings and be unduly swayed by them. Emotional clashes between workers may arise in which they seem bent on bringing out and seeing the worst in each other. Even sentimental pseudo-relationships, similar to school-girl 'crushes', may arise, in which 'love' rather than 'work' is the dominant theme. The emotional climate of an institution needs to be such that over-intense, entangling relationships are not fostered. Or if they do arise, the participants should be helped to work through them to gain insight, clarity and common sense, without inhibiting their responsiveness. Responsiveness is essential for such work but can lead to some of the difficulties mentioned above.

A psychotherapist who is working in an institution, either day or residential hospital or clinic, needs to be known and trusted by the other workers. In turn the therapist needs to know and trust them. As stated, psychotic children stir up deep feelings in those who are caring for them and can have a very disturbing effect upon relationships. Psychotherapy, or the supervision of another therapist's work with psychotic children, demands particularly strict self-discipline, a firmness in maintaining one's own professional role. In work with such patients it is particularly important to be in possession of oneself, and not to allow the relationship to promise more than it can give. These are some of the realistic safeguards against emotional entanglement among all concerned. Without such professional circumspection work can readily be brought to an irreversible halt, for we will have duplicated a situation which is characteristic of psychosis and which is 'too hot to handle'.

As well as these outward safeguards, the therapists of these children need an organized body of central principles to help them stand the emotional battering they receive. For some, a religious faith, such as Anthroposophy in the Rudolf Steiner Schools, or Judaism, or a Christian or other religion, can provide the psychic support which enables the 'centre' to 'hold'. Others may take the way of self-discovery and self-acceptance. If this is the case, a personal analysis which puts them in touch with deep layers where annihilating destruction lurks is an essential for most. Such personal analysis is likely to be a long one, so that dedication to the work similar to a religious vocation is called for. Equal dedication is necessary from the families and institutions who care for the children.

These are heavy demands and we should be aware of them before committing either ourselves or other people. In my own work, a great deal of which has been in private practice, I have been particularly fortunate in having dedicated support from the parents. Some of these parents were in turn supported by personal analysis, others had the support of skilled psychiatric social workers. The latter support, incidentally, was only provided when the parents asked for it. It was not a condition of treatment.

## Psychotherapeutic Techniques

There are many ways of conducting psychotherapy, and indeed therapists who are ostensibly using the same method often evolve their own individual style. This is as it should be.

Speaking personally, I have found the Kleinian technique I was trained to use has been a very effective one as far as psychotic children are concerned. Melanie Klein knew a great deal about psychotic processes and the entanglements which can result from them. Her technique gives workers an instrument which keeps the therapeutic setting relatively free of contamination from outside sources. Information from the child's case-history or from parents and teachers is not directly used in the therapeutic situation. The therapist's attention is closely focussed on what is going on between him and the child at that moment. He does not allow himself to be either prejudiced or distracted by information from other sources. The Kleinian approach is thus an excellent method of studying psychological growth and the factors which inhibit it, as well as an instrument of therapy.

Furthermore, the child is kept in the same room and does not wander from room to room, as in some other therapeutic methods. Food is not provided, nor are caresses or kisses. In so far as is humanly possible, the room is kept the same from session to session. The simplicity of the setting with its freedom from outside distractions provides a relatively unchanging backcloth, against which the child's and therapist's responses are thrown into high relief.

I have become very appreciative of this technique which, in my less experienced days, I sometimes thought was unduly rigid. I now value and experience it as a reliable hammock in which both child and therapist swing.

## Equipment

In the choice of toys and equipment for psychotherapy with psychotic children, I have evolved my own ideas. For example, a humming-top has seemed to be a useful toy for these children, especially in the early difficult period when contact with them is impossible or fleeting. Almost without exception, they are fascinated by and take notice of it. It links with the spinning which is so characteristic of themselves and can produce a similar hypnotic effect. Nevertheless, although it is so closely linked with their bodily sensations, it is an external object. As such, it is subject to the laws of the outside world and so can be the means whereby these laws are administered to the child in small and bearable doses. In Winnicott's terms it can become a 'transitional object'. This he defined as 'the child's first not-me possession' (Winnicott, 1953). It has possibly, in the first place, been equated with and felt to be a part of their body.

Another object I have found useful is a soft, travelling rug. These children often wrap themselves in carpets or curtains in moments when they feel assailed and vulnerable. The travelling rug is a more appropriate object for this purpose. It is more possible for the therapist to observe and talk to the child when he is enveloped in this more flexible and less unusual covering.

Associated with these items I have found a divan or couch to be a useful piece of equipment. The children lie on it wrapped in the rug, or curl up on it, or bounce about on it.

Water and sand are useful elements, but if the child persists in their use in order to shut himself away from the therapist, it may be necessary to stop him from using them for a time. If stopped, he often graduates to wrapping himself in the rug, and from that to covering his eyes and ears with his hands, and from thence to turning his back on the therapist in the way a normal sulky child would do.

In Klein's technique each child has his own individual drawer, box or cupboard in which his toys are kept. It is unlocked when he comes and locked when he leaves. He has his own personal key for this container for his toys. His private possessions here can include a pencil, rubber, pencil sharpener, crayons, felt pens, paints, a set of family figures, cars and such like objects. String is also a useful provision. Some therapists provide Sellotape and glue.

Of course, psychotic children often ignore their drawer and this disdain can go on for years. Or they may break and dirty their things, so that their drawer is a picture of destructive disorder or uncaring muddle. The use, non-use or misuse the children make of these private possessions is of course revealing and interesting. I see it as the therapist's responsibility to keep the shared objects, such as the rug, the couch, the room and herself, in a good state of repair, for the common-sense reasons stated earlier. Unbridled abreaction is not part of the technique being described here.

This basic technique, used with increasing skill and insight as the years have gone by, combined with dedicated work from co-workers, parents and myself has meant that some psychotic children, who were under five, when treatment commenced, have been enabled to function as relatively normal though still somewhat over-sensitive individuals. Others, who did not come into treatment until well into latency and who were severely psychotic, have been rehabilitated sufficiently for them to live with their families and to hold down a job, although in some ways they are still rather handicapped.

A good example of the second category is Leslie, whose poem was quoted earlier. Leslie, seen in private practice, began therapy aged eight years. He was brought by his devoted mother five times a week for six years at eight o'clock in the morning via a cross-country journey. This mother was greatly helped by her own personal analysis of which she made good use.

Leslie attended a private day school for maladjusted children, which was run by an eccentric but gifted headmaster. When he first came to therapy, his arms and legs were so uncoordinated that some degree of spasticity was suspected. His extremities were quite numb. As the result of this extraordinarily well-supported psychotherapy, his co-ordination became normal – so normal, in fact, that as a young man, many years after therapy had terminated, he passed his driving test 'first shot' (as his mother put it) and became a mini-cab driver. However, after a few months he had to give up the mini-cab as his map-reading was not adequate for the job. He soon found other work and could today support himself on what he earns, if he were not such a spendthrift. He is also a rather solitary boy and does not seem likely to marry.

It is such results as these that I refer to as 'rehabilitation'. I remember that when Leslie first came to see me he was in such a disorganized state that he seemed destined to spend the whole of his life in an institution. I feel that the co-operative work of salvage has been worthwhile. His generous and helpful parents feel this as well: they have a son who can live at home and who can have some of the enjoyments and distresses of normal living.

## Stages in Psychotherapy with Psychotic Children

There are three main stages in a reasonably successful psychotherapeutic treatment of a psychotic child.

In the first stage, it is the 'setting' rather than the therapist which seems 'to get through' to the patient. This is one reason why I have concentrated, in this chapter, on the conditions that have seemed necessary if psychotherapy is to have some chance of success. If, during this stage, the child finds that he is in the hands of someone who understands how he feels when the setting seems 'to let him down', and if this let-down does not occur too often, then he may begin to turn to the therapist.

However, at the beginning of treatment he is normally averted from the therapist as such. He may be mute and as unresponsive as a piece of stone. He may stand still and use nothing in the room. Or he may use a piece of equipment in a compulsive way, such as spooning sand, running the water-taps or spinning the wheels of toy cars and other suitable objects. This non-activity, or canalized, perseverating activity, may go on for weeks. Some other children may talk a great deal, but in a confused, non-communicating kind of way.

The main aim of these kinds of behaviour seems to be to protect the child from feelings of extreme vulnerability and openness to attack. Later, or even at the very beginning, he may wrap himself in rugs or hide under pieces of furniture. Other children may openly caress or tickle themselves. Others again, who show no open auto-erotic behaviour, may secretly suck their tongue or the soft pads of their cheeks, or wriggle their bottom to feel the faeces in their anus. All of these self-comforting activities are to divert attention from the obstinate outside world, from which they fear damaging impingements.

Sensitive people are well aware that it is no good forcing themselves upon such a child who is shying away from outside contact. The psychotherapist is vigilant for any lowering of the seemingly impenetrable protective barriers. Such lowering enables healing intentions to be made manifest in a tactful way.

In this 'wrapped-up' state, the child seems comfortable for most of the time. It is only when the protective wrappings are slipping away that he begins to feel uncomfortable. Some children may arrive in a state of acute discomfort, with very little initial diversionary behaviour.

As the child begins to feel distress and discomfort, he begins also to feel extremely needy and lacking. The sense of lack is invariably expressed in a preoccupation with holes. The preoccupation ushers in the second stage.

In this stage, the emergent child begins to be established. In various ways, he will re-enact the early feeding situation. This re-enactment allows the working over, within the therapeutic setting, of disturbances to the nursing ambience and the setting in train of attachment processes. In normal development, the infant's paucity of discriminating awareness and the mother's 'maternal pre-occupation' (Winnicott) protect the infant from too sharp and harsh an awareness of the lack of an everlasting material connection to the mother. This situation is repeated through transference of these feelings to the therapist. If this lack of connection begins to be tolerated, progressive psychological distinctions and differentiations begin to be made. And this development ushers in the third stage.

Here the 'psychoanalysis proper' can be said to begin – although in fact there has been no modification of the psychotherapeutic technique used with neurotic children, other than such as are imposed by the psychotic child's extremely restricted functioning. At this stage, the work is with a neurotic child beset by psychotic anxieties. An instance of clinical work with a child who had been fully psychotic and who was preparing to move into the third stage now follows.

## Michael

I took over Michael's treatment from a very experienced therapist who retired. The boy was in a day unit attached to the clinic in which I was working. He had been seen twice weekly by his previous therapist for a period of seven years and was now much more in touch with reality than when he first came to the clinic.

I began seeing Michael in October 1971. The session presented occurred on January 25th, 1972 – so that he had experienced one separation from me due to the Christmas holiday. Of course, we had had to do a great deal of work on his feelings about the loss of his previous therapist, with whom he had been able to live through many painful experiences. Michael was now twelve years old.

In the first part of the session Michael had tried to use me in his activities as if I had no life or initiative of my own. I had steadfastly refused to be manipulated in this way. When it became clear that I had kept my integrity and identity in spite of all his attempts to break them down, he suddenly stopped and, drawing his hand around the part of the room on which my desk and table stood, said, 'This is *your* part of the room, isn't it?' I agreed.

He then drew his hand around the rest of the room saying, 'This is mine, isn't it?'

I said, 'Yes, whilst you are here.'

He then pointed to his little cupboard where his toys were kept and said, 'That's mine all the time, isn't it?'

I agreed.

He then crouched in the space of the knee-hole of my desk saying, 'This is a part we can share, isn't it?'

Looking up at the underneath part of the desk above his head, he said, 'It's like a bridge, isn't it?'

I said that he seemed to be accepting the fact that we were separate people, but it was a help to find there was a part that we could share. It seemed to bridge the gap between us.

From this material it seems clear that Michael is beginning to give up the notion that he can have an ever-present bodily link with a nurturing person. He is facing the fact that neither by manipulation nor seductive manoeuvre can he obtain exclusive possession, nor monopolize a permanent place with the mother. There is a gap (a space, a hole, a lack) so far as this unrealistic expectation is concerned. But this hole can be an opening for the development of non-physical ties, which both he and I can share. Michael is on the point of realizing that he can trust me to keep a place in my mind safe for him. This realization will enable him to feel secure enough to tolerate our being apart.

Michael's case material illustrates that this important piece of psychological development can only begin to take place when the child is firmly enabled to become aware of 'me' and 'not-me', of 'mine' and 'thine', and 'having' and 'not-having'. Paradoxically, the sense of lack which comes with awareness of bodily separateness can then become a fountain of psychological possibilities. It is where children's play and adult creative activities have their starting place. If tolerated, it will stimulate the development of skills, techniques and the pursuit of knowledge and understanding. It can be the crucible in which crude, stereotyped instinctual reactions are transformed into the gold of human relationships.

Michael is on the verge of such a development. But the very vista of possibilities which awaits the child who becomes increasingly able to forge psychological links with the outside world throws into relief the poverty in which the psychotic child seems trapped. It is a joy to find that if appropriate conditions for treatment are present, and a sound type of psychotherapy is offered, some of them can be helped to use and to enjoy external possibilities. We nevertheless also have to bear the distress, because appropriate conditions for treatment are not available, or because our present understanding of childhood psychosis is limited, that many of them cannot be helped by psychotherapy.

# Chapter Twelve
## *Freud and Child Psychotherapy*
### by A. C. Reeves

The scene turns now to the beginnings from which child psychotherapy developed, in particular to the work of Freud. We learn how Freud's thinking led him to the idea of unconscious conflict. A summary then follows of those aspects of Freud's theories which are especially relevant to the understanding of this book.

The contributions of the pioneer child analysts, Anna Freud and Melanie Klein, are discussed, showing how each developed and applied Freud's ideas to work with children in somewhat different ways. Mention is also made of some more recent developments in child psychiatry and child psychotherapy by other well-known workers. M.B., D.D.

---

The previous chapters have already described practical applications of the analytic techniques of child psychotherapy in various settings. Inevitably, the reader will have noticed instances of the therapist's intervention by word or act, whose ultimate justification depended on a framework of knowledge beyond the issues presented by the particular case. So we must consider the question – what body of theory supports the practice of analytic child psychotherapy, and how did its principles become established?

I shall begin by highlighting some of Freud's fundamental views on the nature of psychological disorders and their origins in the emotional development of the child. I shall then go on to consider the ways in which Freud's daughter, Anna, on the one hand, and Melanie Klein on the other, developed and applied these concepts to their work with children. Obviously, in a brief survey there will be some over-simplification and loss of nuance. What I hope to show is that, within the framework of theory and practice which owes its origins to the pioneering work of Freud, there continues to be a wholesome diversity of approach, both in understanding the problems of emotional development and in identifying the best ways of meeting them.

## The Unconscious

We can take as a starting point Freud's gradual recognition in the last two decades of the nineteenth century that no psychological theory then prevailing could account satisfactorily for the phenomena exhibited by hysterical patients. One type of theory assigned a physical origin to them; another argued that they were the outcome of suggestions implanted in the minds of over-receptive subjects during a trance-like state. Both kinds of theory assumed that there was an absolute divide between what counted as a physical, and what as a psychological explanation of nervous disorder. The former treated hysterical symptoms as resulting from alterations in the brain mechanisms which underlay human behaviour. The latter saw them as the effect of an influence on conscious thoughts, wishes or intentions.

Freud had several objections to both these types of theory, not least of which was their apparent ineffectiveness in suggesting ways of bringing about a cure. In challenging the conventional dichotomy between physical and psychological causation, through his concept of the unconscious, Freud could at least claim some therapeutic successes. The key to his new method lay in ceasing to regard hysterical and neurotic symptoms generally as states passively endured by the patient, whether as physiological reflexes in his brain, or as thoughts implanted in his mind. Neurotic symptoms were *motivated.* What is more, they were *unconsciously* motivated – that is to say, the ideas which caused them, or rather to which they gave expression, were not ones which the patient consciously entertained among his avowed wishes and purposes. Nevertheless, they were in a real sense meaningful. They did represent at least part of the patient's subjective though hidden aspirations, and were not simply automatisms prompted by peculiar discharges in his brain.

All this reasoning seemed very paradoxical to Freud's contemporaries, for whom 'to intend something' meant consciously to will an outcome. For them a term like 'the unconscious' conveyed (if anything at all) an area of mind governed not by 'the will' but by simple physiological reflexes. To say that neurotic symptoms were 'unconsciously motivated' implied a very much more complex picture of the psychological origins of human behaviour. By treating symptoms as items of behaviour which the individual himself determined, Freud had to demonstrate how and why discrepancies arose between what the subject was secretly wishing and what he was conscious of wishing, and what means were available for bringing his unconscious and conscious wishes into better harmony.

At the start, Freud's theories were largely conditioned by his clinical experiences. The neurotic patients he treated seemed all to be suffering the effects of hidden internal conflict. Once the causes of this conflict were unmasked he found that the neurotic symptoms usually disappeared of their own accord. This led him to argue that within the unconscious area of mind a variety of conflicts of purpose and impulse are rife. Such hidden conflict could be so acute that the individual's daily regimen would be imperilled if it spilled over into conscious thought processes, rather as a government's authority might be undermined if all the departmental lobbying which preceded executive decisions were open to public view. Just as governments habitually impose secrecy on their civil servants, so, in Freud's view, the mind draws a veil of censorship, which he called defence, over the play of forces which shape the eventual form of conscious intentions.

At first, Freud thought of neurotic conflicts as somehow bringing the unconscious into being. The unconscious was simply the area of mind to which the strife over incompatible ideas was relegated through an act of repression from above. Experience, as well as his own self-analysis, soon led him to abandon this simple view. He began to see unconscious conflict as endemic in the mind, and as vitally affecting all activity. Many of the incidental shortcomings of mature human intellectual activity, errors of perception and judgment, slips of the tongue and forgetting, were tokens of the continuing influence of unconscious processes. Dreams in particular were significant, since they revealed the re-emergence of unconscious mental elements in a natural, non-pathological form. What made neurotic symptoms special and pathological, in a way that some other incursions of unconscious mental activity upon human thought and action were not, was that they reproduced unconscious conflicts not properly resolved in the course of the individual's development. Unlike other early, normal resolutions of conflict, in neurosis an extra factor, a psychic trauma, had occurred at a crucial stage in childhood development. This trauma had caused a flawed, partial resolution. As a result, the elements of conflict had become repressed, rather than being resolved. Physical, intellectual and emotional development had now begun to expose the limitations of this partial resolution. Thus, the neurotic symptom was seen as a latter-day attempt on the part of the mind to provide a fresh, but still unavailing, compromise to an earlier state of conflict.

## Infantile Sexuality

So far, I have mentioned unconscious conflict without specifying what mental elements contribute to it. Here again, Freud proposed a set of ideas which his contemporaries found very difficult to accept. He had noted how sexual issues regularly assumed a major part in the conflicts latent in a range of neurotic states. Indeed, he went as far as to assert that different types of neurosis could be distinguished by the way in which they sought to deal with traumatic sexual experiences. Had he been content to maintain that an adult's neurotic conflicts were due to problems over his or her present-day sexual life, his views would probably not have given rise to such controversy and condemnation. As we have just seen, however, he viewed the adult's neurotic symptoms as the revival of an earlier state of conflict having its origins in the patient's childhood. And it was the sexual element in this childhood conflict which he was most concerned to bring into prominence. Before seeing how he explained the existence of infantile sexuality and its connection with unconscious conflict, let us see how his clinical experiences led him to this claim.

As long as Freud's analyses of his patients centred upon the memories of inner conflict and stress which the patient could readily recall from his recent past, little progress was made in alleviating neurotic symptoms. Three things happened, however, when he pressed further. First, the patient, whilst maintaining the wish to be cured, began to display increasing resistance to Freud's probings. Then conflicts over explicitly sexual impulses, which had not hitherto emerged, began to occupy the patient's chain of recollections. Ultimately, some memory of a forgotten childhood sexual episode was revived, one invariably associated in the patient's mind with heightened feelings of disgust, anxiety or remorse. Not only was the recall of such childhood memories accompanied by a degree of resistance in the patient appropriate to the anxiety the episode had originally occasioned, but – and this was the crucial discovery – the neurotic symptoms did not disappear until the childhood memory had been re-evoked.

Clinical discoveries thus alerted Freud to the existence of childhood sexual experiences and their repression. The theoretical problem then confronting him was to explain how and why childhood sexual experiences such as his patients reported should lead to repression, and later to symptom formation. The first explanation which occurred to him was that repression of childhood sexual memories occurred because the feelings associated with them were something the child could not properly master. Sexual feelings had been prematurely aroused in an otherwise latent state. This view, however, he soon abandoned – it was implausible to maintain that neurotic patients had been actively seduced in childhood as regularly as his patients reported. Moreover, the alleged childhood sexual episode was not always remembered either as an instance of seduction or as unpleasurable in itself. The painfulness of the memory appeared to be related rather to the anxiety and guilt feelings it aroused. These feelings of anxiety and guilt seemed to have contributed at least as much to the repression of the original memory as the sexual nature of the episode itself. A still more fundamental consideration caused fresh appraisal of the nature of childhood sexuality and its part in the original unconscious conflict. Freud became aware that the childhood 'memories' whose recall was crucial for the cure of adult neurotic symptoms were not usually factual recollections about historic episodes from the patient's childhood; rather were they phantasy elaborations based upon, and giving expression to, erotic strivings towards significant figures in the child's life, in particular towards his parents.

It took Freud several years to fuse his varied discoveries and reflections into a considered statement about the nature of emotional development and the effects of inner conflict on normal and pathological growth. In *Three Essays on Sexuality* (1905), the emphasis had, on the whole, switched from external to internal factors in the development and resolution of conflict. There were two sorts of instinctual strivings present in human beings from birth. The first set were the precursors of later sexual expression, which he termed 'libido'; the second he called variously the 'ego' or self-preservative instincts (*The Two Principles of Mental Functioning*, Standard Edition, vol. 12, 1911). They differed primarily in that the first were outer-directed strivings, fostering development and contact with figures in the environment, epitomized in the act of sexual union, while the second were inner-directed, aimed at preserving an ideal state of inner equilibrium, in which there would be the minimum expenditure of mental and physical energy. In themselves, the 'libido' and 'ego' instincts were highly abstract concepts, which Freud was to revise more than once in the course of his later writings. He finally came to characterize them as the 'life' and 'death' instincts. Whatever their exact form and denotation, however, he insisted on the presence of a duality of instinctual drives. The importance for us is less in the precise terminology than in the way Freud conceived of the basic psychic material, out of which unconscious instinctual conflict arose.

Conflict in the personality arises basically because of an inbuilt tension between opposing instinctual tendencies, which are partly biological and partly psychological in nature. Sometimes Freud expressed this conflict in a more modern idiom. For example, in *Notes upon a Case of Obsessional Neurosis* (1909) he writes, 'A battle between love and hate was raging in the lover's breast, and the object of both these feelings was one and the same person.' We see here conflict expressed in terms of opposing *feelings* and intimately linked with relationship to a person, the departure point for important developments in psychoanalytic theory. The human animal is distinguished by his capacity to form relationships with others, over and above those required for the fulfilment of his immediate self-preservative needs. The overall circumstances of personality development in childhood, therefore, could be seen as the story of how these potentially conflicting urges – the loving and outward seeking, and the aggressive and self-gratifying – interacted with each other, in relation to the important figures in the individual's life.

## The Oedipus Complex

Since the human infant is so relatively immature at birth, his physical needs are met for a long period through the agency of others, in particular by his parents. Inevitably conflicts between opposing feelings and instinctual drives would be experienced in the unfolding early relationship with the parents. In his *Notes upon a Case of Obsessional Neurosis* Freud became convinced, through his study of the transference phenomena exhibited by his patient, that 'somewhere in the prehistoric period of his infancy, the two opposites [that is, love and hate] should have been split apart and one of them, usually the hatred, has been repressed.' When the opposing elements in such conflict are brought together in consciousness (ambivalence), feelings of anxiety and guilt arise. Every child has to come to terms with his conflictual feelings in relation to each parent and also in relation to the parents as a couple. The culmination of this phase of development was reached in what Freud termed the Oedipus complex. The name was chosen with its allusion to the Greek myth – where the son kills the father and marries the mother – in order to underline its universal character as a stage in human development. The Oedipus complex was thought to be reached around the fourth or fifth year of life. It was a critical point in human development as it marked the full emergence of the child's drive for a relationship, loving and possessive, for the parent of the opposite sex, with all the accompaniments of jealousy, anger, guilt and fear which that entailed towards potential 'rivals', in particular towards the other parent.

It is impossible to elucidate here all that Freud meant by the Oedipus complex and how he justified his concept by reference to his findings about normal and pathological development. For a full discussion of the topic the reader must refer to Freud's own works, particularly to his *Three Essays on Sexuality* (1905) and his account of the resolution of a phobia in a five-year-old boy, the famous case history of *Little Hans* (1909).

I want here to pick out just two points which are relevant to our main topic, that is, the influence of Freud's theories on the development of applications of psychoanalysis to the treatment of children. The child's earliest development could be looked at from two points of view. It could be considered in terms of the way the different instincts competed with each other, the instincts taking different forms and having different 'zones' of dominance as the child developed. Or it could be treated as a series of stages in the development of the capacity for personal relationships, each stage being marked by a new expression of subjective autonomy and objective awareness. Whichever aspect one stressed, the Oedipus complex remained a vital point of development. Thus the stage of the Oedipus complex could be seen as the expression of instinct in a new form, principally in the libidinal investment of the genitals. Or as the stage at which the child was capable of proposing himself as an autonomous individual, to seek and be sought by the parent of the opposite sex as an object of love. The other point is that though the Oedipus complex was the culmination of a phase of development, it was also the beginning of another new and important one.

Around the emergence and resolution of the Oedipus complex there grew in every child an 'infantile neurosis'. Like any neurosis, it had to be resolved. Adult neurotics were individuals who for one reason or another had not successfully negotiated this stage. In referring to the infantile neurosis, Freud did not mean to imply that its effects were necessarily pathological. The conflict it engendered was, he thought, the kernel of those civilizing influences which marked off mankind from the rest of the animal kingdom. By passing through this stage the natural instincts, which in his later writings he habitually denoted as 'the id' (*The Ego and The Id*, 1923), became deflected, and gradually subjected to 'the ego' (the reality sense). Competition with the parents, and particularly with the parent of the same sex, was increasingly replaced by co-operative identification – the boy modelled himself on the father, the girl on the mother. To subjugate the unconscious strivings brought to a head in the Oedipus complex, Freud postulated the emergence of a new structure in the mind, the superego. This was an internal repressing agency, formed from the precipitates of real or imagined parental injunctions. In the guise of a personal conscience, the superego became progressively more autonomous, more capable of influencing the child's behaviour independently of parental admonitions. The effects of the Oedipal conflict and its resolution were apparent not least in the child's developing ability to direct his instincts and intellect to mastery of his actual childhood world. He acquired learning and skills, coming in the process to acknowledge his childhood capacities for the immature endowments which as yet they were, and postponing immediate instinctual gratification for the prospect of future rewards. In short, by passing through this stage the child was able to take the first steps to psychological and social maturity. Whereas, however, the struggles of the first phase were predominantly over the control of instinctual expression (the id), in the second phase arising out of the Oedipus struggle, the problems were primarily over the relative powers exercised by the child's ego and superego. An individual in Freud's eyes was judged mature and relatively less susceptible to neurosis by the degree to which he succeeded in guiding his life by the correct apprehension of reality, through the medium of his ego, rather than by the constraints imposed by his superego on his instinctual impulses.

Freud himself never aspired to be a psychoanalyst of children, however much his theories about adult neurosis and character formation entailed reference to early childhood origins. Enough has been said about some aspects of his general theories, however, to show that they provided both a programme and a theoretical basis for child analysis. It is now time to turn to the application of these principles to the treatment of children, through the work of their two main exponents.

## The Beginnings of Child Analysis

It is difficult nowadays to appreciate the controversies, even among analysts, which attended the first systematic attempts, shortly after the First World War, to treat children according to the principles and teachings of Freud. Basically, there were two sorts of arguments directed against the enterprise. The first was theoretical, the second practical. The theoretical argument centred on the concept of neurosis. This was a term which had become vastly expanded in meaning since Freud had first proposed his psychological treatment of hysteria three decades earlier. Now Freud was prepared to talk of naturally occurring 'infantile neurosis' as a by-product of the Oedipus complex, to which the full-blown adult neurosis harked back. Did the term 'neurosis' have exactly the same sense in the two contexts? If not, was the reference to the 'infantile neurosis' only an analogy with the 'proper' sense of a fully pathological disorder, such as might later develop with the adult? Those who argued that the reference to the infantile neurosis was only metaphorical were also inclined to dispute the necessity of intervening in childhood development when the supposed infantile neurosis was at its height.

This theoretical argument was further supported by practical considerations. Psychoanalysis was a technique specifically designed for the treatment of adults who had a developed capacity for self-reflection and the ability to express themselves through the medium of speech. The child's ego, on the other hand, was immature. He was prone to act upon rather than report his states of feeling. He could not be expected to see the point of communicating his dreams and free associations to the psychoanalyst in the way Freud required of his patients.

It took some courage and perseverance, therefore, for the earlier child psychoanalysts to meet the particular challenges of this sort of work in the face of widespread disbelief from their colleagues that anything valuable could be obtained by it. Anna Freud took the view that disturbances in children which stemmed from unsuccessfully negotiating the stage of the Oedipus complex did constitute neuroses in the full and proper sense. The infantile neurosis was not just a staging post on the way to adulthood, but a site and source of intrapsychic conflict in its own right. At the start she saw the primary task confronting the child analyst as that of helping to resolve the conflicts which arose directly as a result of his Oedipal strivings.

Obviously such a programme did not deny the importance of the play of instinctual dispositions in the child preceding the onset of the Oedipal stage. The way to approach these instinctual dispositions, however, had to be through the different sorts of defences that the ego contrived to master or divert them. The 'id impulses' in their pure form were not accessible to analysis – and children whose ego structures were atrophied were not suitable candidates for this particular treatment technique. Such children had not reached the Oedipal stage, hence were not capable of the complex of guilt feelings which were the necessary prerequisites for neurosis.

Many of Anna Freud's early ideas were expressed in her classic work *The Ego and the Mechanisms of Defence* (1936). In it she pointed to the necessity of modifying the strict canons of adult treatment in the case of children, in view of their greater natural mobility and their diminished capacity for sustaining a purely verbal interchange with a therapist for any length of time. Concessions had to be made, too, to the child's age and circumstances in the matter of interpreting the ego defences he erected against expression of his instinctual drives. The child's play and communications might be valuable indicators of his conflicts – but it did not necessarily mean that the child appreciated them as such, or even that he recognized the existence of his internal conflicts at all. Though such conflicts might actually occasion the child stress, diminish his zest for life and provoke antagonisms in his relationships, it was often someone other than the child – a parent or teacher – who was alerted to the conflicts behind the outward disturbance of behaviour, and who endured its effects. In other words, the primary motive leading the adult patient to seek treatment, the wish to be relieved of an acknowledged stress, could not be assumed in the case of the child. To counter this inherent problem in the treatment of children she suggested that a preparatory phase might be necessary, in which the child could become acquainted with the person of the analyst, could gain experience of the analyst's tolerance, reliability and concern. Although Anna Freud later dispensed with this recommendation, she continued to insist that the success of child analysis, as with that of adults, depended upon working in a treatment alliance with and through the patient's own ego capacities.

In general, Anna Freud started from the premise that the technique of adult analysis could provide a model for work with children. Any technical modifications were dictated by the need to comply with the child's age and relative immaturity. Perhaps the most significant difference between child and adult therapist was that the former had to accept at least an implicitly educational role in the child's life: as an adult confronting the child, it was impossible for the therapist to be altogether exempt from a position of authority in the child's eyes. There was a further corollary to this view. It followed from the condition of childhood that parents and parent substitutes continued to exercise their influence upon the child, and their attitudes and values continued to form the precipitates of his conscience or 'superego'. Consequently, it was unrealistic to expect that the child would transfer on to the person of the therapist the forms and images of his neurosis in the manner expected from adults. Analysis of the transference relationship, therefore, did not play an equivalent role in child and adult analysis. On the other hand, the essential aim of therapy precluded the analyst from interfering with the natural unfolding of the child's conflicts by the use of persuasion, cajoling or admonition - or by providing complex playthings, reading material, and the like - in a way that might inhibit or otherwise influence the nature of the child's communications and obscure the unconscious elements which were particular to him.

It would be wrong to suppose that these observations adequately represent the views and procedures practised by followers of Anna Freud at the present day in all respects. Many details of technique have changed with time - in particular, perhaps, the lessened emphasis on the therapist's educative role and the need for a preliminary stage before the analysis proper could get under way. In the following chapter an account is given of the current theoretical and clinical concerns of child psychotherapists trained according to the teachings of Anna Freud. I have outlined some of her *early* views because I believe they convey in the clearest way something of her overall approach to the psychotherapeutic treatment of children. This approach can be summed up by reference to the central place accorded to the Oedipus conflict, outlined by Freud as the 'nuclear complex' of child and adult neurosis. An important difference between Melanie Klein and Anna Freud hinges on the contrasting way each looked at the Oedipus complex and the emergence of the ego, its timing in the normal process of childhood development and its relationship with the stages of development preceding it.

Melanie Klein, who started her work with children at roughly the same period as Anna Freud, tended to see the child's ego emerging less as the result of repression of instincts than as the result of the action of two much earlier mechanisms, projection and introjection. In essence these terms mean simply the putting outside and the taking inside of things. The earliest *somatic* representation of these mechanisms is the expulsion and absorption of the infant's food. The child's ego formed around its earliest oral experiences. This early formation determined all the later developmental stages, including the way in which the child approached and mastered the Oedipus complex.

Why did Melanie Klein attend so insistently on these very first infantile experiences, before the child had language and thoughts with which to form those experiences as representable memories? There are two parts to the answer. The first concerns the conception of anxiety, the second the nature of instinctual impulses and their psychological (though unconscious) equivalents.

It will be recalled that Freud had not offered a single answer to the question, 'What causes neurotic anxiety?' Instead he had proposed a range of causal factors of ever-widening generality. The immediate cause of neurotic anxiety was a state of conflict in the patient's present life. Behind this lay unresolved conflicts over the Oedipus complex. More fundamentally still, however, one could point to the inevitability of the Oedipal conflict in the duality of instincts universally present at birth. Their early interplay, particularly over the loving and aggressive impulses, determined how the child would negotiate the Oedipal conflict. This was precisely the area, rather than that of the Oedipus complex itself, where Klein felt that the analyst's attention should primarily be directed.

In discussing the nature of instincts and their bearing on the Oedipus complex in Freud's theories, I pointed out that there were two aspects under which the instincts could be considered. Either they could be seen in terms of the drive components and the dominant zones which the instincts centred on in progression – the oral region, the anal region and the genital region – taken together with the particular conflicts over function and expression to which they gave rise, or they could be seen as the preliminary forms of expression of relationship towards the figures who nurtured the child.

At the risk of greatly over-simplifying matters one might say that Anna Freud fastened primarily on the first aspect, Klein on the second. What is certainly obvious from their respective writings is that Klein was much readier to talk about the infant's capacities and overtures for 'primitive relationships' in the earliest phase of life than was Anna Freud. The latter saw the instinctual drives as 'object-relating' rather than 'object-seeking'.

Unconscious anxiety then, according to Klein, is present and palpable in the earliest transactions of the infant with the figures in his environment – indeed, in the infant suckling at the mother's breast. Already the dual instinctual drives, love and hate, are operating and determine the quality of the feeding experience. The infant has no adequate sense of what a person is, but there are some inchoate representations or part-objects which begin to people his earliest unconscious phantasies (Susan Isaacs in *Developments in Psycho-Analysis*, 1952). As the experience of persons is initially fragmented, so is the infant's self-perception. His ability to synthesize his perception of people and to acquire a coherent ego go hand-in-hand. This process of unification, essential to the child's personality growth, is however threatened from the start by the anxiety emanating from his destructive urges. These experiences are not originally felt as coming from within the child himself, but as directed at him from without. The reason here is that his aggressive urges are projected outwards, and are only slowly and painfully accepted back through a process of introjection and assimilation. Klein emphasized two main constellations of feelings and attitudes in this process of development. She called these 'positions' rather than stages, as they do not become superseded but continue to characterize our basic attitudes to others. The first 'paranoid-schizoid' position describes the infant's state during the early months of life when persecutory anxiety is maximal. The baby feels frightened of being annihilated by persecutors. He needs his mother and the good experience he has with her to protect him from pain and from danger. The good and bad experiences are kept quite separate in his mind ('split apart', as Freud said). The emphasis is on the need for self-preservation.

The second 'depressive' position is characterized by concern for the other. It begins to appear in the second half of the first year. Then the baby becomes able to integrate his hitherto unconnected experiences more adequately. He begins not only to differentiate himself from his mother but also to realize that the good loved mother who comforts and feeds is the same as the mother he hates when angry and frustrated. This realization brings feelings of guilt and concern over the aggression felt to have been perpetrated against his loved objects. Concern for the other's welfare begins, at least at times, to supersede self-interest. This is a struggle which originates in infancy but which continues throughout life. Such considerations led Klein to detect tokens of Oedipal conflict and signs of the presence of a superego much earlier in development than was conventional on Freud's original model.

What bearing did Klein's concept of early object-relating have on her technique of treating children? The first, and perhaps most superficial, difference from Anna Freud lay in Klein's readiness to undertake analytic therapy with extremely young children. If Anna Freud appeared an innovator in suggesting that children could be treated by analytic means at all, Klein struck some of her contemporaries as little short of revolutionary when she embarked on her first analysis of a two-year-old child. In one respect, Klein's approach was entirely consistent with her views about the early presence and influence of anxiety, guilt and conflict in the infant. If anxieties were present and palpable, then immediate attempts should be made to deal with them. However, there remained a major technical hurdle to be overcome in applying her concepts to work with such small children. The analytic technique, after all, had been pioneered through the treatment of adults, and relied heavily on verbal communication between patient and therapist. How could very small children communicate information about their internal states of feeling to an adult by verbal means, especially to a therapist who had no other role to play in the child's daily life? And even if such material did emerge, how could the therapist convey insight to the child by means of interpretations in a way that could be meaningful and helpful to the child?

Klein's answer to the first of these questions lay in her conception of play as an expressive communication of the child. She was already alerted to the theoretical importance of infantile phantasies in the formation of conflict. This led her to regard play as a principal means by which children gave symbolic, outward form to unconscious phantasies. In treatment, she relied for her interpretations of the young patient's conflicts on the use he made of the simple toys and other suitable props supplied by the therapist. In accordance with her theoretical conceptions, she interpreted the child's play in terms of the anxieties he might be experiencing over his primitive aggressive and sexual urges. In so doing, she used a directly expressive idiom, which she felt best reflected the concrete modes of thought and speech proper to the young child.

Anna Freud had originally suggested that the child in treatment usually needed a preparatory phase where actual analytic interpretation was at a discount, and where the child was given encouragement to familiarize himself with the conditions of therapy and the personality of the therapist. Klein considered this expedient unnecessary. She noted that children in therapy regularly began to play with the small objects provided, unless they were inhibited by overwhelming anxieties. In either case, she considered it appropriate to attempt immediately to enlighten the child about his behaviour by means of interpretation, feeling that confidence was best engendered by allowing the child to experience the therapist as someone recognizing the unconscious sources of his conflict. Moreover, she maintained that the child did naturally transfer on to the therapist the tokens of his unconscious conflicts, which had hitherto been discharged in a damaging way upon his environment. She regarded the child's play and behaviour in treatment as a symbolic expression of his phantasies, enacted in a sense deliberately in the presence of the therapist. Crashes of objects in play betokened clashes of instinctual impulses within. External destruction meant internal chaos. Attempts at order and mending signified efforts within to redress the destruction perpetrated in phantasy upon the images of parent figures. These actions and reactions had to be interpreted in the context of a transference relationship with the therapist. So universal and extravagant were the phantasies which children regularly revealed in their play, that Klein's clinical experiences at once reinforced her belief about the pervasiveness of early sexual and aggressive instincts, and the terror they induced in the small child. Night-time fears, difficulties about eating, anxieties over separations, the common plight of small (and often older) children, were some of the outward signs of this inner disturbance.

One basic difference between the two approaches makes their variations in technique and practical emphasis especially intelligible. Whilst Klein treated the manifestations of unconscious processes as directly accessible to observation from the earliest days, Anna Freud looked on them primarily as instinctual dispositions, whose organization and intelligibility only emerged by the gradual acquisition of concepts through the use of speech. Whereas for Klein conflict grew between the unconscious urges as such, for Anna Freud the really significant polarization was between the 'id' as the site of unconscious propensities and the 'ego' as the site of perceptual and cognitive order - or, to use another form of words, between the agency of the 'repressed' instincts (the unconscious) and the agency of repression (the preconscious).

From this basic difference of viewpoint flowed the practical variations. If unconscious impulses and phantasies were actual and coherent, as Klein held, then it seemed proper for the therapist to confront them directly and immediately. If, as Anna Freud believed, they were initially unorganized and unavailable as 'raw data' for conscious thought, then the therapist had to be more circumspect. He had first to take account of and to analyse the 'defence mechanisms' constructed by the individual in the course of his development, before the underlying unconscious content could be available for the therapist to recognize and the patient to confront. Correspondingly more stress was therefore placed by Anna Freud on the therapist's need to co-operate with the patient's 'ego capacities', that is, his powers of scrutiny, censorship and active self-regulation. Klein, on the other hand, emphasized the importance of immediate involvement with the patient's unconscious processes, even if this approach met with some resistance initially from the side of the patient's critical or 'rationalizing' functions.

## Child Psychoanalysis and Child Psychotherapy

In the previous section I attempted to set into relief some of the original differences of formulation between Anna Freud and Melanie Klein. At the same time I have tried to show how each could justifiably argue that they were basing themselves on the essentials of Freud's theory and developing particular aspects of it. Of course, it would be a mistake to believe that they and their respective adherents were as precisely and intransigently opposed as my statements of their positions suggest. Klein was by no means exclusively interested in treating small children, nor did Anna Freud and her followers refrain from treating children below the age at which the Oedipus conflict was thought to occur on the traditional paradigm. In practice, a good deal of reciprocal influence took place between the two schools of thought.

Anna Freud, while continuing to insist on the importance of analysing the ego's defence mechanisms and the central position occupied by the Oedipal stage in normal and neurotic development, recognized nevertheless that neurosis in childhood, as indeed with adults, was not absolute and *sui generis*. While psychoanalysis was specifically designed to treat neurotic disorders, it was common for any patient at particular episodes in the course of treatment to display other, more primitive, disorders of thought and feeling. Neurotic conditions, in other words, were frequently intermingled with those bordering upon the psychotic. The value of Klein's work here was that by concentrating upon the earliest phases of emotional development, she had opened up the study of some of the primitive mental mechanisms contributing to the genesis of such pre-neurotic episodes. Certainly the range of conditions which Anna Freud considered treatable by psychoanalytic means was significantly extended over the years. She nevertheless made an important qualification: the earliest processes of thought and feeling in the child were not properly called psychotic when these occurred as part of the child's normal development. Nor, consequently, did they justify psychoanalytic intervention unless they could be shown to be taking deviant forms. It was her abiding conviction that the child's natural capacities for growth and adjustment should not needlessly be interfered with. A major goal of her later researches, carried on in collaboration with her many associates, was to chart the profile of normal stages of psycho-emotional development from infancy to adulthood (*Normality and Pathology in Childhood*, 1966). This profile provided some measure for assessing which were the benign, and which the pathological, forms taken by the sexual and aggressive impulses, and their corresponding defences, at any particular age in the child's life.

Melanie Klein, for her part, partially revised her original, rather austere, view about the overwhelming effect of early sexual and aggressive impulses. Greater importance was now attached to the study of the role which pleasurable experience through good handling played upon the infant's capacity to mitigate the strength of his early aggressive phantasies. These developments are well summarized in Hanna Segal's book, *Introduction to the Work of Melanie Klein* (revised edition, 1973).

Practical issues, too, played some part in modifying some of the more over-enthusiastic recommendations made by some older psychoanalysts about the benefits and possibilities of child analysis. To become a psychoanalyst was a long and arduous task; among this relatively restricted circle of practitioners, the number prepared to devote themselves to child analysis was small. Unless the benefits of treatment were to be the prerogative of a select few, ways had to be found of extending applications of child analysis, both as a form of treatment and as an instrument of education. With time, analytic child psychotherapy became distinguished from child analysis proper, as a form of treatment which did not necessarily require the child to be seen daily. If some children could benefit from less intense and exclusive care, clearly the number of potential patients would be increased significantly.

Another current of thought further emancipated child analysis from its rather rigorous confines and fostered its application in the field of child guidance. The early formulations of child analysis had grown out of Freud's concern to chart the course of intrapsychic conflict and its effects on adult neurosis. It was sometimes felt, not always justifiably, that as a result insufficient attention has been accorded to the effects of the pathology of the parents, or the actual experience with which the child had to contend, when it came to assessing the child's behaviour. At all events, the suffering and dislocation which children (and many psychoanalysts, too) experienced from the circumstances of the Second World War led to renewed practical and theoretical interest in the effects of external circumstances on the child's emotional development. One particular focus of attention was on the reactions of children to the separation or death of the parents. Was it appropriate to consider the pathology of any child exclusively in terms of his instinctual drives and unconscious phantasies, without reference to external factors? Could a child even be treated successfully in isolation? What might the parents' unconscious wishes and impulses have contributed to the child's disturbance in the first place, and how would these be mobilized at the prospect of the child's possible recovery?

Neither Anna Freud nor Melanie Klein had ignored such factors. They faced difficulties, however, in providing a satisfactory way of combining the necessary conditions for successful treatment of the child with simultaneous provision of support and guidance for the parents. If the child did form some transference attachment to the therapist in view of the latter's non-intervention in his daily life concerns, then the gains of the child's treatment could be jeopardized if the therapist now actively involved himself with the parents and teachers in the child's management. The most common solution to this difficulty was to provide the parents with concurrent treatment or support, usually by a psychoanalytically trained colleague or skilled social worker. This practice became standard in the setting up of a number of child guidance clinics, whose rationale was founded on the conceptions of psychoanalytic theory and technique.

This external development was indicative of the increased awareness accorded to the family bond in the psycho-emotional development of the child. Growing attention was placed on the crucial importance of the mother-child relationship in forming and fostering the child's earliest interactions both with his environment and its unconscious counterparts. Much of the pioneer research in this field came, among others, from the work of Bowlby, Winnicott and Spitz. Each was a psychoanalyst by training, well practised in the assessment and treatment of the emotional disorders of children. They helped to widen the clinical perspective by studying the young child in the context of his environment and in situations where the child was deprived of his natural growth supports. Their work, together with parallel research conducted under Anna Freud's own auspices, fostered the applications of psychoanalytic principles into paediatrics, education, social welfare and delinquency.

It is interesting to reflect that the influence of external environmental factors on the psychopathology of the child, which was relegated from a predominant position as Freud developed his aetiology of the neuroses, has recently been the object of renewed attention in the theory of psychoanalytic child psychotherapy. Of course, the way such external influences are nowadays understood as shaping the child's unconscious processes is very different from the conception in Freud's day. It is not the external experience *per se*, so much as the internal response made to it by the child, which is regarded as crucial in the writings of, for example, Winnicott in Britain and Mannoni in France.

Such developments present current psychotherapy with a range of new ideas and new challenges, some of which are reported in this book. It is an indication both of the complexity of the subject matter, and of the suggestive powers of Freud's formulations, that a great variety of standpoints coexist within the general framework of present-day analytic child psychotherapy. Whatever the individual orientation, however, a fundamental tenet continues to unify this diversity. This is that the immediate causes of psychological stress arise from internal conflict, whether understood as conflict between instinctual dispositions, or as conflict between mental agencies regulating such dispositions. Psychological illness is at once the product and the sign of significant failure by the individual psyche to deal adequately with internal conflict. The task of the therapist is to enable the patient first to understand, and then, if possible, to readjust the economy of his strivings. This does not mean that the therapist is indifferent to the environmental influences which bear upon the child and which have possibly contributed as initial occasions for his internal conflicts. Indeed, if these environmental circumstances are too grave and persistent, it is likely that the therapist will not consider analytic therapy as a suitable means of helping the child. It is not part of his task as a psychotherapist, however, to address himself directly to the management of the child's daily life and circumstances. To do so would be to destroy the basis on which alone his analytic work can bear fruit – his presence for the child as a concerned but non-participant interpreter of intrapsychic conflicts.

# Chapter Thirteen

# *Some Comments on Clinical Casework*

## by Sara Rosenfeld

Sara Rosenfeld had agreed to write a chapter for this book before her tragically early death in 1973. Because she was unable to complete the chapter, it was decided to include instead an already published paper. We hope this will serve as a memorial to the creativity of her work, the richness of her psychotherapeutic insight and the inspiration of her teaching. This paper gives a detailed overview of work conducted by Mrs Rosenfeld's colleagues at the Hampstead Child Therapy Clinic and elsewhere. It provides a useful counter-balance to the next chapter, which is a Tavistock description of an alternative training in child psychotherapy. M.B., D.D.

---

This chapter evaluates some aspects of clinical casework as conducted by a group of child psychotherapists. The survey is confined to the experience of my colleagues and myself at the Hampstead Child Therapy Clinic; there is therefore emphasis on one clinical and theoretical standpoint only. However, we recall that Freud stated there can be no monopoly in the field of psychotherapy. He reminds us: 'There are many ways and means of practising psychotherapy. All that lead to recovery are good.' (Freud, 1905)

At the time the Hampstead Clinic entered the field of psychoanalysis, certain shifts in emphasis had already taken place. Psychoanalysts were not so much concerned with infant psychopathology as with child analysis as a source of information for understanding and treating adult neurosis.

The existence of infantile sexuality was accepted, and indeed was already beginning to influence methods of child rearing in our generation. The contribution of infantile sexuality to the establishment of an infantile neurosis which proved to be universally present in neurotic adult patients was also established fact.

A further shift from the focus of interest on the id to the dynamics and operation of the ego had already taken place. This was crystallized in Anna Freud's book *The Ego and thee Mechanisms of Defence.* It established beyond doubt that childhood neursis existed in its own right and showed a similar development to adult neurosis. That is, in the child as in the adult, conflict was followed by regression to earlier fixation points. These regressive aims aroused anxiety, which was warded off by defences, and resulted in a compromise solution in the form of symptom formation.

Anna Freud defined the task of psychoanalysis as follows: 'To acquire the fullest possible knowledge of all three institutions of which we believe the psychic personality to be constituted and to learn what are their relations to one another and to the outside world. That is to say, in relation to the ego, to explore its contents, its boundaries and its functions and to trace the influence in the outside world, the id and the super-ego by which it has been shaped and, in relation to the id, to give an account of the instincts, i.e. of id-contents, and to follow them through the transformation which they undergo.' (Freud, A., 1937)

Stress placed upon the central role of the ego has at times been thought to indicate emphasis on reality and education at the expense of the exploration of the patient's phantasy life and inner world. Indeed, in his book *The Question of Lay Analysis*, Freud spoke of child analysis as 'a treatment that combines analytic influence with educational measure' (Freud, S., 1926).

Moreover, many child analysts have been, from the outset, preoccupied with application of the discoveries of psychoanalysis to education. The *Journal for Psychoanalytic Pedagogy* bears witness to the many aspects of education discussed. While it is of fundamental importance that educational methods are influenced by psychoanalytic findings, the tie between psychoanalytic techniques of child analysis and education became burdensome. It only gradually diminished, and it might be interesting, on some other occasion, to discuss just how far subtle educational attitudes still persist in our technique today.

The stress laid upon the ego was not, however, a means of distracting from the phantasy life and inner world of the child. It was rather to draw attention to the fact that the ego plays a specific role in adaptation by means of mediating between the instincts, the super-ego and the environment. It is as well to be reminded of the basic unity between ego and id. The ego is evolved primarily as a helpmate to the id in that it searches for the best possibilities for the gratification of pleasure and the avoidance of pain. For this purpose a variety of defence mechanisms and defensive character formations are evolved.

## Classical Childhood Neurosis

A distinct difference exists between children and adults, in that the ego of the adult neurotic will remain relatively intact. In the immature personality of the child the ego cannot stand firm against instinctual pressures and may regress more readily. The well-defined neuroses which we sometimes find in children are likely to occur in patients whose ego development is unusually good and where secondary autonomy of the ego has been established at an early date.

The following brief accounts of three cases will illustrate our present approach and understanding of childhood neurosis, as well as the extension of our approach to a wider group of patients than we could formerly reach in treatment. The first case is that of Simon, aged nine (Elkan, 1963).

Simon was a depressed boy with an obsessional character structure. It was confirmed in sessions that he had reached the phallic stage of the Oedipus complex, but had regressed to earlier levels of libido development with marked fixations at the oral and anal levels. As described by Elkan, Simon's sleeping and eating difficulties began at the age of eighteen months, following the birth of a baby sister. They were also associated with a series of separations from his mother. Simon's acute anxiety was defended by silence and withdrawal, by joking and a compulsive need to control the therapist.

The underlying conflicts seemed to be centred around anxieties related to different phases of development. Feelings of distrust and of being abandoned seemed to be associated with castration fears. His conviction, for example, that he was stupid or mad was felt as a punishment for his overwhelming feelings of aggression of which he feared to lose control. Analysis was experienced as seductive. The threat of being overwhelmed by sexual as well as aggressive feelings contributed to a severe resistance. It was largely as a result of working through these anxieties and his defences against them that a particular kind of transference situation developed, in which he seemed to be repeating early fears of being abandoned, of loss of love and of rejection. In response to interpretations of these feelings he burst into tears, saying, 'Sometimes I wish I had never come to the clinic.' His ability to experience emotion in the transference was crucial to the work with this child.

This very brief summary seems to illustrate the existence of conflict within a well-structured personality, with symptom formation and neurotic character structure being compromise solutions against pressures from the id.

The anxieties described are primarily related to fear of castration, of abandonment and loss of love. The extent to which this anxiety manifested itself, and coloured the phallic conflicts, must be seen to be related to the persistence of much earlier anxieties belonging to the oral and early anal phases of development (Sandler and Joffe, 1967). Even if we had not known from external sources that Simon had actually experienced the loss of his mother at the height of the separation-individuation phase, we would have reconstructed the emotional loss of a love object at about that time (Mahler, 1963). Castration anxiety was preceded and its nature determined by the child's experience of earlier emotional losses. These caused acute pain against which the toddler probably had to defend himself with aggression directed against the source of his pain – the mothering object. Projection, introjection and displacement being the relevant mechanisms of this period of development, it would follow that Simon's internal world, his representations of objects as well as his self-representation, would be coloured by these primitive aggressive impulses and his defences against them. We know that Simon had little trust in the object and his self-image was that of an unworthy and stupid boy. Here again we see that the basis for such low self-esteem and the underlying narcissistic vulnerability was laid long before he entered the phallic phase.

## The Role of Transference

Assessment of clinical work in child analysis today points to the central position of the treatment relationship. Transference phenomena will occur, which range from fleeting manifestations of transference to an established transference neurosis. To by-pass feelings lodged within the treatment relationship – of whatever transference status – and to refer them back immediately to the original objects can hinder and block the analytic process, so playing into the patient's resistances. In any case, to ignore the patient's feelings for his analyst, his positive longings and curiosities, as well as his anger and rage, will be experienced as a rebuff, a 'not being understood'.

An example is seen in a declaration of love made to me by a boy patient at the end of a week's analysis. He said he hoped to meet me in the main road near the clinic to say hello or to go swimming with me. To allow himself the expression of positive emotion was in itself a sign of progress in this suspicious, untrusting, defensive child. To have referred his feelings to his father (to whom they actually belonged) would at that moment have confirmed the boy's feelings of being misunderstood and added to resistance. Later it was of course possible to take the feelings back to their original objects. In my own view, analysis must always work from the here and now, dealing first with the emotions aroused in the treatment relationship.

In 1951 Fraiberg still maintained that transference neurosis was non-existent in child analysis, though she has since modified her view. Berta Bornstein argued that there is no need for the child to develop a transference neurosis, since he still possesses his original objects.

These views triggered off my own researches (Kut, 1953). I put forward the opinion that transference does exist in child analysis in different forms and can, at times, assume the appearance of a transference neurosis quite independent of the physical external presence of the parents. This view differs from the one advanced by Molly Mason (1970). She is closer to the opinions expressed by Bornstein (1945) and Fraiberg (1951), in that she expresses doubts about the development of a transference neurosis in child analysis: 'They are still attached to and dependent on the original love objects, the parents.'

It seems that the dependence on the external parent has to be weighed against the degree to which processes of internalization have been built. These will exist in a rudimentary state in the young child, although the existence of developing mental representations has to be acknowledged even in under-fives. As the child develops, objects and self-representations become ever more firmly established. Their existence relates directly to the manner in which conflicts are internalized, which in turn dictates the technique appropriate to a particular case. Moreover, it seems that the therapeutic relationship does not only deal with aspects of conflicts extended into the treatment relationship. A situation develops which closely resembles that of the adult transference neurosis. The therapist is made aware of such a state of events when resistances have to be interpreted and worked through specifically within the transference. Thus we find that 'regressed conflicts, once they had been worked through in relation to the original objects, were repeated in the analysis with the therapist as the central object, and only resolved and finally given up when these were interpreted.' (Kut, 1953) There is no contradiction between the establishment of mental representations which will contribute to the child's increasing psychic independence and the continued need for actual physical and emotional care derived from his real, external parents.

For a description of the central role of transference in the Kleinian approach, we turn to a paper by Dina Rosenbluth (1970). She clearly indicates the fundamental divergence from the views of this chapter.

## The Developmental Viewpoint

An important aspect in the understanding of childhood neurosis, or for that matter emotional illness in children and adults alike, is demonstrated in Simon's analysis. It concerns the manner in which neurotic disturbances are now viewed in depth. The assumption that this is in any way a novel mode of approach may be questioned by some. It may be pointed out that not a few workers in the field have always maintained the importance – and, in fact, the overriding relevance – of the pre-phallic phases, more especially the oral phase and the first year of life.

What is missed here, in my opinion, is the emphasis on the developmental viewpoint. This concerns itself with the progression and regression from phase to phase in terms of development of libido and aggression, set against the total background of the maturational processes. The infant and growing child experience the impingement of the environment according to the particular phase within which they find themselves at any particular moment. Thus they may react in a wide variety of ways producing a specific mode of functioning, perhaps only in one small area. Moreover, the view leaves room for the possibility that the earliest phases of development were not in fact interfered with and that conflict arose at later stages of development. While fixation points may be created in the oral phase, I am personally in no way convinced that this has always to be the case. My view does not mean that the interaction between infant and mother in the first year of life is not of the utmost relevance for the shaping of the style of the later personality, and its mode of functioning.

Kris (1956) refers to the relevance of pre-verbal phantasies belonging to this period of life and states: 'We take it for granted that the impact of such pre-verbal imprints may determine the modes of later reactions to environmental stimuli.' In a fine paper he pays tribute to Melanie Klein 'who has enlarged our vision of the psychic content of early pre-verbal stages of development, thus contributing to the deeper understanding of our clinical work today'. Kris also, however, points to the divergences between Kleinian theory and those pursued by myself and my colleagues, referring principally to a disregard for maturational processes.

Moreover, the concept of regression in its many senses (regression in drive development, regression in ego development, normal and pathological) has no meaning, in my view, unless understood in terms of developmental stages the child passes through in its entire personality development.

**Some Clinical Examples and Technical Considerations**

Twenty-one years ago clinical work was almost exclusively confined to patients whose psychopathology was predominantly neurotic – that is, whose disturbance was primarily due to conflict. We learnt the techniques associated with the recognition and understanding of the sources of anxiety, such as fears of loss of object love, which would indicate that the conflict was still largely external to the child. These anxieties referred to the super-ego, or perhaps to the conflict between opposing drives or opposing trends – masculinity-femininity, activity-passivity. It did not mean that all the children seeking help were confined to this particular area of disturbance. Cases which did not conform to this diagnosis were disposed of in other ways – for example, by special teaching methods or placement. Some children did not come to us at all. They may have been diagnosed as mentally subnormal and thus beyond the scope of psychotherapy.

Greater clarity and increased knowledge of the map of child development has come to serve us as a more precise tool. We can diagnose disturbances which lie beyond those of neurotic conflict and which hitherto were inaccessible to psychotherapy. To find an approach to these patients became a therapeutic challenge. It promised to open up new hope to children suffering a variety of disturbances: in particular, to those suffering illnesses caused by arrest at or regression to early phases of development, and children with minimal brain damage and congenital effects such as blindness (Wills, 1965). It also offered hope to all those cases where the environment was lacking in one specific ingredient necessary for the healthy growth of the child. Here we would include mental or physical handicap in a parent, or a severely crippling disturbance in object relationships which made it impossible for the mother to act as the appropriate object at specific stages of development. I am thinking here particularly of Colin, aged four, whose mother withdrew emotionally at the beginning of his second year and who was unavailable as a love object through subsequent phases of development.

The manner in which Colin experienced his mother's withdrawal was crucial for the development of his feelings about the self. He regarded himself as wholly bad. In an attempt to protect the object from his rage, he turned aggression against himself with disastrous results. Moreover, when he entered the phallic Oedipal phase, still in search of an object, he experienced his mother's inability to respond to him (due to her own psychopathology) as a further narcissistic blow, which confirmed his idea of himself as a bad and worthless child. Later in treatment Colin verbalized these feelings by referring to himself as 'Mr Nobody'. He threatened to kill himself. The degree to which he turned aggression against the self did in fact endanger his life and brought him into treatment. This boy is still considered to belong broadly to the neurotic group, for whom psychoanalytic treatment is the therapy of choice. It may be added that Colin's analysis indicated beyond doubt the relevance of the treatment relationship and the existence of states within the transference which signified the presence of a transference neurosis. However, the emotional 'absence' of the mother also complicated transference development, in that attempts to use the therapist as a real object often predominated, working against the establishment of transference. The therapist's skill is taxed to the utmost in negotiating a path between these two opposing trends.

A type of disturbance still further removed from the classical model of infantile neurosis, but on investigation revealing a degree of internalization enabling one to speak of conflict, is that of Jo. Scoring an I.Q. of 58 on referral, it was first thought that he was either defective or brain-damaged. However, he had formed a positive tie to a male teacher. This indicated considerable capacity for object relatedness. Trust in the object had in turn stimulated improvements in behaviour and ego functioning. Jo was therefore taken into daily treatment.

Jo was a child who had been exposed to very early traumatization, through accidents which were in part due to the mother's inability to provide what Winnicott calls 'the good enough holding environment' (1958). In addition the mother had displaced on to this boy the hostility and disappointment she felt towards her husband. Thus the child had become the symbol of all that was rejected, hated and unwanted in his father. The father was unable to support her emotionally and created in her a feeling of being unloved and rejected. She appeared to treat Jo and her other children as she felt she was being treated. One might assume, along with

Novick and Hurry (1969), that the mother's choice of this husband had already been determined by a deep-seated feeling about herself as an unwanted, damaged object.

Jo's personality development was characterized by primitive modes of behaviour, particularly in drive control and frustration tolerance. He still demonstrates a severe intellectual impairment which places him in the bracket of the mentally subnormal. He has frequent outbursts of temper, bizarre and unpredictable behaviour, and a mechanism of reversal which can be seen in a continuous rather imbecile smile. It has become clear that Jo is defending against the upsurge of primitive aggressive drives, which are projected. Projection, identification with the aggressor and reversal of affect point to the existence of conflict. However, it seems that the conflict is not yet predominantly between id and superego. The anxiety which is defended is still lodged in the external real object. That is, the conflict is largely between Jo and the environment. The existence of forerunners of superego introjects does not in any way contradict this assumption. It also has to be borne in mind that Jo is still exposed to frequent physical attacks from his father. These are a continuous threat to his masculine intactness and beyond it to his life. No doubt the effect of these events is reinforced by the memory of earlier ones. In the analysis we can now see the transfer of his suspiciousness and anger with the object more clearly. Further work will help to clarify this area.

The first part of the analysis was occupied with Jo's need to act the hurt, devalued aspect of himself. By turning passive into active, he was doing to others – and more specifically now in the transference – what he felt was being done to him. But he also externalized his 'no good' aspect of self representation. He denigrated me in a variety of ways, proving that I was no good as a therapist and he beyond hope. Jo, as in the case of Tommy described by Novick and Hurry (1969), shows severe narcissistic disturbance 'with mental pain and conflict rooted in the acceptance of the devalued self and the inability to integrate positive aspects with his conscious self representation'.

With Simon, Colin and Jo, we can in each case observe a basic narcissistic vulnerability expressed in their feelings about themselves: 'I am a bad child.' The three boys are, however, still accessible to the techniques of child analysis.

Through analysis it is possible to explore the roads which have led to this devastating feeling of being unworthy and unlovable.

The manner in which these boys communicated their emotional state to the therapist differed in each case. Simon's material was brought primarily in verbal form. Colin's was a mixture of verbal and non-verbal. Jo's, to date, appears in predominantly non-verbal form. The point to make is that non-verbal material ranks equal with verbal in the understanding of conflicts. Non-verbal behaviour can of course occur in a context of full speech – but speech can be temporarily inhibited, or be inadequate for the discharge of tension. The aim, however, is to help the patient to reduce the discharge of his feelings into action or acting-out, in favour of verbalization. Thus I consider that the material currently being presented by Jo in non-verbal fashion should subsequently be worked through again in verbal form. Nonetheless, the attitude we now have towards non-verbal material in patients, who have nevertheless developed 'inner speech', contrasts with the attitude of some earlier analysts, who regarded the ability to communicate via speech almost as a necessary condition for an analysis.

The technique of psychoanalysis is certainly aimed towards verbalization. In cases where the capacity for verbal expression is either inhibited or retarded, the therapist's verbal communication may have to be brief and very much to the point. If, however, impulsive action is to be regarded as a communication, one could perhaps resort to other, more concrete methods of allaying or containing the patient's anxiety. Thus, after Jo had transferred his suspicious hatred on to me, minor details of the condition of the treatment room, such as a hole in the wall, aroused frequent outbursts of panic states. Verbalization of the content underlying the panic, or of the defensive nature of the behaviour, was not effective. One day, therefore, I resorted to an entirely different approach. Together we papered over the offending hole. I did not expect this activity to be any kind of substitute for interpretation, but it helped to create the conditions for interpretation.

Jo and I both knew that the damage to the wall had not been repaired, but that we had only covered it up. We also knew the extension – that 'covering up' Jo's own 'hole', in other words the frightening feelings of emptiness and being damaged, would not be really helpful. But Jo was nevertheless relieved. It seemed that my acknowledgment of the relevance of the cavity in the wall for him was a non-verbal acceptance of his anxiety and the fact that we were both involved in it together. Equally, then, it meant that together we might be able to master both the feelings and the thoughts which gave rise to the overwhelming states of panic anxiety.

Twenty-one years ago Jo might easily have escaped the diagnostician. A very low I.Q., accompanied by withdrawal from objects, together with bizarre and impulsive behaviour, would have made him an obvious candidate for a mental deficiency hospital.

## Borderline Psychotic Disturbances

All who have attempted to work with psychotic and near-psychotic children have faced a disturbing and complex situation quite unlike that presented by neurotic children. In other writings M. Sprince and myself have tried to spell out the precise nature of the overwhelming impact of these chaotic children on the therapist (1963, 1965). We point out that in order to understand these children, we must in some measure follow the children into their world of psychic chaos and accept its reality. We find this world so frightening that we attempt to impose order on to it. That step can result in greater manageability of the child and a reduction of our own anxiety.

We become aware of our ignorance and limitations, both within our professional discipline and in ourselves as individuals. Yet the fact that we are involved on a level of interaction not usually found in the treatment of neurotic patients offers us also opportunities for further development within ourselves and in the technique we try to apply.

With psychotic children we work under other disadvantages also. A patient suffering from a neurotic disturbance comes to us with an initial diagnosis which allows us to sketch a treatment plan. True, it may have to be revised. But still, we have an initial feeling of familiarity and confidence. With psychotic children, in spite of much that has been written, we are not yet clear about the origins and development of the condition. We lack even precise diagnosis. What we have to go on are some very broad divisions of psychopathology, and a conviction that the origins of all these conditions are to be found in the first year of life.

Ruth Thomas has described in detail the picture presented by some of our patients at the outset of treatment and the changes brought about in therapy (Ruth Thomas *et al.*, 1966). It is clear that in spite of arrest or regression to primitive stages of development, part of the child's personality has moved forward. It is precisely this imbalance of arrest and development that we find even in the most severe cases, and which adds to our theoretical confusion. We are often further puzzled by, and at a loss to recognize, the emotional retardation, since its primitive state is hidden within a more mature body with some age-adequate ego functioning.

The authors mentioned clearly demonstrate that we have to become familiar with a new kind of language. It is a language of feelings and thoughts belonging to stages of development where primary process is readily accessible. This access influences the imagery of the patients. When one of the girls was angry with her therapist she said, 'Don't want feeling doctor. Want dentist. Don't talk about feeling. Talk about teeth, upper teeth, lower teeth, baby teeth.' Anger was often experienced by this girl as 'a splinter in her throat'.

Frances Tustin has further added to our insight and understanding of these patients with her original and lucid comments on their primitive anxieties. She writes of her fourteen-year-old patient, David: 'He provided a working demonstration of those states of relatively minimal differentiation and of well-nigh absolute terror, when he felt in imminent danger of collapse. It is obvious that it is only when autistic states of inhibition and non-communication are over that patients can communicate about what it was like.'

These states were most pronounced at impending holiday breaks. David and his therapist were linked together by what Tustin called 'the ever-present umbilical cord'. This was to keep them in constant touch. The cord was part of a telephone which David himself had made of plasticine. It signified the bodily communication which was to bridge the gap between himself and his therapist. A boil on his finger became central to the working-through of the feelings of separation. Tustin tells us: 'Later, he cupped his hands and said that it was a mouth.' Then wagging the finger on which he had the boil he said, 'It's you – a puppet-midget – my tongue – I mean my finger.' Here we see the equation of his hands with his mouth and the illusion that the therapist was a bad part of his body, just as his boil was. The delusion that the therapist was so malleable that he could 'twist her round his finger', turned her into something bad (Tustin, 1969).

I find myself in agreement with Frances Tustin when she describes the child's experience of separateness. This includes the notion of a nameless dread, that is, death or annihilation, the source of which is attributable to a particular perception of the mother. However, some clarification is perhaps called for. One needs to distinguish here between the state described as one of fluctuation between differentiation and non-differentiation, and the developmental phase of non-differentiation (see Edgcumbe and Burgner, 1971). Anna Freud noted that this earliest period could be described as one oscillating between moments of 'darkness' and moments of 'light'. The latter would be called forth by means of experiences of satisfaction and pleasure. Around these pleasurable 'light' moments other experiences collect and constitute the beginnings of 'me'. The whole then gradually develops into the nucleus of what we call the 'inner world'. All other experiences which do not fit or jell with these collected moments of primitive pleasure, well-being and safety are relegated to the outside, the soon-to-be-differentiated external world.

Anna Freud suggested that one factor contributing to borderline and outright psychotic states may indeed be the failure to experience pleasure with the object, or with the help of the object. In this context it may again be useful to be reminded of the developmental standpoint. We tend to confuse states of development and the appropriate ego mechanism transposing them on to each other. Processes such as internalization, externalization, projection, object relations and so on can only come into operation after some differentiation between self and object, between inner and outer reality, has taken place. In the study of borderline psychotic children we are particularly exposed to this kind of error. For the patients we have studied show coexistence and overlapping of phases of libido and ego development, without the primacy of any one phase, which we are accustomed to in neurotic children.

This enlarged picture of childhood disturbance has repercussions on analytic technique. Though it is thought by some workers in the field that the very early narcissistic injuries, sustained for whatever reason, are accessible to analysis, there is the reservation that some alteration in technique is called for. This may involve the use of parameters which relieve and possibly reverse the original injury. One such factor is mentioned by Martin James (1970). He speaks of providing 'environmental therapeutic action'. My own experience with psychotic children has not as yet borne out this view. It has seemed to me that certain traumatic experiences, whether of a cumulative or a devastating kind, occurring within the first year of life, leave a specific residue within the personality which manifests itself in an undue narcissistic vulnerability and an object hunger which may persist despite analysis.

It may be that it is necessary to reconsider the frame of reference in which we approach the treatment of atypical children. Ventures into unexplored territories can act as a testing ground for the theories with which we have hitherto worked and so point up their shortcomings and limitations (Kris, 1956). Rigid adherence to the aims and methods of psychoanalytic therapy specifically designed for psychoneurotic patients may cloud our view. It may impede our judgment to the detriment of the patient's therapeutic gain. The concept of treatment gain may have to be restricted and drastically reformulated.

Patients I have known have adapted to a more circumscribed form of living within a protective environment, which provided feelings of safety and relative freedom from conflict. I am here referring to conflict aroused as a result of their inability to conform to expectations and ambitions of their environment, which may well have included the therapist. The emotional plateau achieved enabled them to derive satisfaction and pleasure from limited, sometimes artistic, achievements and from their friendships, which were frequently characterized by their childlike nature.

A total rethinking of the aims and goals of treatment which would influence the technique of management of patients beyond neurosis might then bring us nearer to the state referred to by Freud regarding the suitability of patients for analysis. He excluded psychotic patients – but qualified his statement: 'I do not regard it as by any means impossible that by suitable changes in the method we may succeed in overcoming this contra-indication, and so be able to initiate a psychotherapy of the psychoses.' (Freud, 1905) It seems that we may be moving towards this possibility today.

The classical technique includes a variety of non-analytic devices such as those described by Anna Freud (1965) and Ralph R. Greenson (1967). Amongst these are abreaction, clarification, suggestion, reassurance and manipulation. Abreaction refers to the relief of affects associated with a traumatic experience within the analysis. Indeed, the analyst's ability to tolerate the patient's expression of affect without being overwhelmed is frequently an essential feature of the treatment relationship, particularly with children. Clarification is part of the analytic work of interpretation, which includes confrontation, interpretation and working through (Greenson, 1967). Suggestion is the aspect least acceptable to the analyst, but nevertheless present and requiring to be analysed. An element of reassurance is unavoidable in the analytic approach, but need not be understood in terms of an actual verbal reassurance. For example, the continued contact with the analyst in the face of a patient's feelings of unworthiness can in itself act as a reassurance. So does an appropriate and well-timed interpretation. To remain silent, either to allow the unimpeded emergence of emotion or to comply with a patient's demands, as I have done in the case of Jo, constitutes manipulation on the part of the analyst. The compliance with Jo's demands occurred at moments in treatment when I knew that he could not bear the strain of frustration – or indeed when I was unable to stand the full brunt of his physical attack.

These so-called 'non-analytic' devices have to be seen against the backdrop of a continuous relationship. The one-to-one nature of the relationship is in itself taken for granted. One cannot say what opportunities occurring in this reliable and predictable contact may not affect the child in a therapeutic manner.

## Psychotherapy

Freud's remark that all psychotherapies which lead to recovery are good was cited earlier. In the same paper he warns against the ill use of psychotherapeutic techniques, reminding us that the patient may well sustain an injury, 'for it is not easy to play upon the instrument of the mind'. The existence of the Association of Child Psychotherapists is evidence that therapists, too, support that sentiment.

Divergent views exist about the differences between adult analysis and adult psychotherapy. Very little, however, has been written about children. Heineke has studied the relative effect of weekly and daily psychoanalytic child psychotherapy in two groups of children (Heineke, 1965). He concentrated on the changes which occurred as a result of these two types of schedule. However, he did not really examine the techniques employed, nor describe the differences, if any, in the process.

In an ideal situation one would have the choice of psychoanalysis or psychotherapy - whichever was more suited to the patient and his illness. The conditions of work of most of our members, however, preclude this ideal choice.

The immediate clinical aim of psychoanalysis is to relieve the patient's illness by means of interpretation of the transference and resistances. By tracing these to their genetic roots the personality is permitted to unfold and grow. An additional factor enters in child analysis. Here there is the attempt to re-establish the patient along age-appropriate developmental paths so that maturation can once more proceed smoothly.

Psychoanalytic child psychotherapy is an adaptation of the classical psychoanalytic technique. Along with other forms of psychotherapy with children, it is valuable and clinically relevant so long as the therapist is alive to the necessary differences, and modifies his technique in line with both the limitations and advantages of the situation.

Although there are differences of opinion among child psychotherapists, it is my view that the central focus will be on the relief of symptoms, more so than in classical analysis. By placing the symptom in more central place, one's global aims of complete transformation of personality are necessarily limited.

In clinical terms, the immediate concern would be for the child-patient's capacity to bear and contain anxiety. Attention would need to be focussed on the patient's tendency to act out rather than to report verbally, which of course must influence the handling of the case.

The state of the child patient's ego must be examined

carefully, with a view to dosing the amounts of interpretation. If one recalls that an interpretation consists of four aspects, even a confrontation – the first stage towards interpretation – can precipitate high degrees of anxiety. The degree to which a patient's ego can participate in the analytic work is a further crucial factor. It influences the establishment of a treatment alliance. An awareness of the need for treatment (automatically present in the adult seeking help) is a prerequisite for classical analysis that may be absent in the child. Anna Freud has discussed this important point (1945).

Perhaps the principal difference between child analysis and child psychotherapy is not in such matters as the dosing of interpretations, but rather in the recognition that the patient has to do a good deal of the working through without the immediate help of the analyst. We are speaking of the capacity to experience, to contain and to evaluate painful affect such as anxiety or depression. At such points one may offer extra sessions or a telephone contact to the patient. Still, one must carefully evaluate also the repercussions of any such move. Offer of extra help might represent a gratification which could play into the patient's resistance towards treatment. Or it might support a wish to manipulate and control the therapist and the therapeutic process. A wish for closer and more intimate contact with the therapist might be 'merely' an aspect of regression to an earlier, more infantile stage. All these and many other meanings may accrue to such an offer on the analyst's part.

Inherent in this situation is the nature of the treatment relationship, which comprises both reality and transference features. In psychoanalytic treatment the opportunity exists to follow through in detail just what such manipulation might mean for the patient. The conditions exist for the re-experiencing of regressive states or early traumas with their accompanying emotion. In psychotherapy the reliving of early states of emotional stress presents a far greater strain on the patient. It is for this reason I have made reference to the relative intactness of ego organization.

Transference and resistance, the two cornerstones of psychoanalysis, remain of the utmost importance in weekly psychotherapy. I am of the view, however, that they cannot there unfold as comprehensively as they do in full analysis. This limits the data we are likely to gather in terms of understanding and will confine the area of conflict to be worked through. Conflicts producing predominantly negative transference or regressive transference may not be amenable to weekly therapy. They should therefore be skilfully circumvented by the therapist. Lesser factors, such as abreaction and suggestion, may be more prominently placed.

It is clear that the skill, insight and experience required by a therapist in once-weekly sessions is considerable. In full analysis, however blind and deaf we as therapists may be, the relevant material will eventually present itself. Although the continuity of material is of course maintained in once-weekly therapy, one cannot see the material in the depth described earlier.

The roots of child psychotherapy are in child analysis. Ideally, I think all therapists should have at least one child in full analysis. In this way one is afforded the broader view of childhood pathology and has the opportunity to pursue 'in depth' the kind of matters we have been discussing.

Based on a paper read to the Association of Child Psychotherapists (Non-Medical).

# Chapter Fourteen

# *The Tavistock Training and Philosophy*

## by Martha Harris

The following is an account of one of the three trainings in child psychotherapy which currently exist – that of the Tavistock Clinic. The two alternative trainings are undertaken at the Hampstead Child Therapy Clinic and the Society of Analytical Psychology.

The Hampstead course has its theoretical orientation briefly described in the previous chapter by Sara Rosenfeld. The newly inaugurated training at the Society of Analytical Psychology is not described in detail here. It is a Jungian course, and the writings of Michael Fordham form a very relevant introduction to that training.

To describe and compare all three of these trainings in detail would go beyond the scope of this book. We have therefore included one full account only. This is of the Tavistock training. In it we are shown vividly the process of self-discovery that the child psychotherapy student there undergoes. It is believed that something of this process is also experienced in the other available trainings. Anyone seriously attracted to this work will of course wish to investigate the alternative approaches to discover the one most suitable for them personally.

One of the points made by the author of this chapter is worth emphasizing: many child psychotherapists, while feeling they owe to their training schools the gift of the basic equipment of their profession and the beginnings of their own self-development, feel that their individual style of working has in time diverged from the strict letter of their original training. This is a sign, perhaps, of an ability to work freely and creatively. It means that child psychotherapists cannot be narrowly labelled – and that in the practical day-to-day work of child therapy some of the various individual approaches may come much closer together in their common aim of understanding children. M.B., D.D.

---

This chapter begins with a brief note on the history of the Tavistock course and its present position in a rapidly changing social framework. I shall try also to describe some of the thinking which has shaped and continues to shape this training, although the responsibility for the views expressed must remain my own. There is some description and discussion of aspects of the content of the course and of our teaching methods. However, no attempt is made to give a detailed account of the syllabus. An up-to-date prospectus can, of course, always be obtained from the Tavistock Clinic itself.

## The History of the Course

The Tavistock training in child psychotherapy began life in 1948 in the Department for Children and Parents, under the direction of John Bowlby. He saw the need for an analytical training for non-medical personnel practising psychotherapy in clinics. The organizing tutor during the first eleven years was Esther Bick, who set a high standard of learning from precise and detailed observation. This has continued to influence both students and tutors long after Mrs Bick's retirement.

For a number of years applications for this training were relatively few. This was no doubt due to the infancy of the profession, the degree of commitment required and the expense entailed. The current position is very different: despite the expense and commitment, which have not decreased, applications are many and our resources for training are strained. Although the Tavistock Clinic and Institute have expanded greatly and the teaching staff increased, we are able to meet only in a small way the demand for trained therapists.

## The Place of the Course

The Tavistock is an amalgam of organizations and disciplines accountable to different governing bodies. The Clinic itself is within the National Health Service, which supports the bulk of the training of child psychotherapists, as well as the post-graduate training of psychiatrists, psychologists and the advanced training of social workers. Nevertheless it is at present necessary to ask students to pay fees in addition to their personal analysis, as part of the training is supported by the Tavistock School of Family Psychiatry and Community Mental Health.

Although the Tavistock is multi-disciplinary, varies in its aims and speaks with many voices, there is nonetheless a certain consensus of ultimate goals and beliefs. These give it coherence as an institution. People who study and work there have over a period of time the opportunity to gather a rather wide experience of the way in which different disciplines and departments set about trying to implement their aims.

I think all would agree that we are concerned with the promotion of healthy growth in the individual, the family and society. In this aim we pay attention not only to illness but also to the conditions which seem to permit developmental change. We are averse to fostering privilege, although oriented to allowing individual growth and eccentricity. We are aware of the responsibility we have to share with the community at large the knowledge and insights, which we as privileged individuals acquire in pursuing our work. We believe that change is initiated by the enthusiasm of individuals and small groups, enabled by the very process of close observation of inter and intra personal relationships. We recognize that the possible quality and range of that observation has been radically affected by psychoanalysis, which obliges the observer to scrutinize himself, his feelings and motivation, the counter-transference which may be used to enrich or to distort what he sees.

## Organization

The training is organized in two parts. Minimally it comprises a four-year full-time period. Circumstances may arise, however, which make it desirable or necessary for a student to take some aspects on a part-time basis, and in this case the total course exceeds the four years. Students have to complete both parts of the training in order to be recommended for membership of the Association of Child Psychotherapists. The teaching is geared throughout to on-going professional work; in the first two years that work takes place in an institution outside the Tavistock.

Students are employed in a variety of roles with children, families or young people. Teaching during the first two years takes place in the evenings, so that it is possible for students to work full-time if necessary, but this would ordinarily be undesirable - preparation and writing of observations, together with the necessary reading and attendance at seminars themselves should occupy around twenty hours a week during this section of the course.

Students are responsible for finding their own jobs during this two-year period. They are accountable to their employers for the work they do. Nevertheless, we are often approached with a request for someone in training to undertake certain work, and are therefore often able to make suggestions to students about suitable employment. The kind of tasks which students are able to undertake during the first part of the course tends increasingly to be determined by their previous training or qualifications. It is likely that in the future the Tavistock will be required to evolve a more official relationship with the employing bodies, but it is unlikely that any tutorial or supervisory role which it has with students could extend to taking responsibility for the work they do with these employers.

Of the several essential seminars which run throughout the first section of the course, two are now described.

## The Work-Study Seminar

Seminar members, who are working in varied settings with children, adolescents and families, take turns to present detailed accounts of some aspect of their work. This presentation almost always includes aspects of the interaction between themselves and their 'clients'. The presentation is discussed by the rest of the group, led by a psychotherapist experienced in analytic work with children and adolescents, although not necessarily in the particular work-roles of the group members.

No particular technique is taught in these seminars. The members are encouraged to consider and discuss appropriate ways of dealing with the situations and material described after the possible 'meanings' have been explored. The aim of the seminar is to sharpen perceptions and to enlarge imagination, to understand more fully the underlying dynamics of the personality interactions described. Our belief is that education in sensitivity and awareness is a gradual process which takes place through working and discussing work with a more experienced colleague, through a close study of individuals and groups, and of one's own role and responsibility.

As a leader of one such seminar my task would be to elicit as fully as possible the details of the case, the problem, the situation concerned. It takes a little time to do this. Time is also required to allow the other seminar members to feel their way into the situation and to ask questions. The questions can sometimes cause the presenter to remember details he had not registered as important. It then takes further time to consider and to try to link together apparently disparate elements in the presentation, in ways that can make it more immediate and meaningful to the participants.

I consider it important to pay attention to the emotions evoked by the case presented, both in the actual work and in the seminar group. Further, to consider these as relevant to the understanding of the material – and whether, in fact, the emotion evoked in us is the one we are meant to feel. In this way one tries to encourage the worker to make use of his own feelings, recognizing that these are a valuable part of imaginative perception without which any relationship and any attitude to work is two-dimensional.

It is vital, conversely, to recognize when some of the feeling evoked is not a true response to something actually communicated by the child, but an arousal of inappropriate emotions connected with unresolved infantile conflicts in the worker himself. These may be projected in ways that distort the perception of the child's real message and individuality. When projection is taking place it seems to me inappropriate to comment upon it in any *personal* way. It is appropriate, however, to try to make the members of the seminar aware as we go along that such distortions of perception happen at times with us all. It is a possibility that has to be kept constantly under review. Projections may be examined and understood by renewed scrutiny of the situation in question, by discussion with colleagues, or by self-questioning. The personal analysis is of course the place in which the student has the possibility of fuller examination of personal motivation, and of disturbances and blocks in the capacity to see and feel for the object.

The exchange of experiences in different work settings helps students to feel for the problems which other students encounter and to respect the work which they do. I shall single out for mention here the task which a number of students have undertaken in the past five or six years, that of working with small groups of children in primary schools.

This work arose initially out of the request of various head teachers for someone willing to take charge of small groups of children unable to benefit from ordinary class teaching. These were children with behaviour and learning difficulties. Licence was given to the group worker to engage the children in any kind of activity which seemed profitable. This would at least give the class teacher some respite from coping with one or more children whom she found a source of trouble or despair. With these fairly free terms of reference, and despite great difficulties with chaotic and unmanageable children, as with others who began as inert 'lumps' and only then went through periods of volcanic and destructive behaviour, many students found this an invaluable learning experience. It was for them, and I think for many of the teachers, both surprising and illuminating to watch the emotional and intellectual development of such a group of children, usually from chaotic and deprived homes. These were often thirsty for the interest and attention shown, relieved at the acceptance of their more unacceptable behaviour and at the opportunity to translate them into more constructive means of communication.

In some of these small groups the children achieved a stage of deep intimacy and trust. This made it possible for a rich spectrum of the most intense emotions of infantile dependence, sadness and loss, jealousy and rage, to be talked about and lived through with the worker. Children who were formerly drawn together only in collusive, thug-like alliances learned to show interest, friendliness and attentiveness to each other. Such behaviour would have seemed unthinkable in the chaotic early days of a group. Beneficial developments within the group invariably carried over to some extent, sometimes dramatically, into the child's relationships in the wider areas of school life.

There is much to learn from these small groups concerning interpersonal relationships. The parts and roles played by members of the group can be seen to be operating within the individual personality. The experience of taking a group has often helped the therapist of the individual child to describe and talk to these different parts of the child's personality.

Since the work study seminar runs parallel to the infant observation seminar, which I shall describe next, there is some cross-fertilization between the two. It may in the future be possible for seminar leaders to initiate more formal and organized ways of making links between relationships and patterns discerned in the work experience and those seen in the baby-mother-family observations. At present we do this where we can and hope that students will be encouraged to integrate the variety of their own experience in a manner which may lead on to further fields of enquiry.

**The Mother-Infant Observation Seminar**

This seminar was initiated by Esther Bick at the outset of the course in 1948. All the current seminar leaders at the Tavistock have at some time or another taken part in one of her seminars and have made observations themselves. I mention this not only to acknowledge the debt of those of us who have found this a unique method of learning about the fundamentals of personality development, but also to emphasize that this kind of observation does require the help of trained and experienced people if it is to become meaningful.

For most people other than the mother concerned the movements of a small baby are chaotic and fairly meaningless, except in generalized behaviour terms. One has to allow oneself to come close to the baby in order to see and retain details, and to cope with the emotional impact and struggle with a great deal of uncertainty in oneself before understandable patterns begin to emerge. At a distance one baby (or one person) is much like any other.

This particular seminar more than any other is valuable in helping students to discover the value of being, and themselves becoming, a receptive observer. In this exercise there is no obligation to *do* anything beyond observing – indeed, one has to learn to refrain from action. The mothers are asked if they are willing to have an observer who, although he may be a professional worker with children and may even be a parent himself, would like the opportunity to learn by observing for one hour each week how an infant grows and develops within a family. The mother is also told that it will be helpful and interesting for the student to be informed of any changes and developments which she has noticed in the baby during the intervening week. Her thoughts and feelings about the baby are welcomed, and one often finds that the interest of the observer seems to encourage the mother to take more notice of the baby as a developing individual.

In some cases of course – where for instance there is another child below school age, or where the father is at home when the observer visits – the process also becomes a family observation. If it is possible to learn to retain and record complicated details of interactions and conversations, the observation affords a very rich experience to study and ponder over. Tentative interpretations and hypotheses about current family interactions may be checked when ensuing weeks offer further data.

Most people who undertake this exercise find that the closeness to the infant and mother arouses in them extremely intense feelings deriving from their own infancy. These are not always readily recognizable as such, but even when recognized, not to be explained away. Clearly, it is important for the seminar leader to recognize when such feelings are aroused, in herself as well as in other seminar members. She must encourage them to feel both for the mother and for the baby, not to over-identify with one or other. By allowing himself to feel his own counter-transference, by trying to contain it and refrain from action or interference, the observer may learn to comprehend the impact on the mother of the responsibility of the baby. He may feel the change and vulnerability evoked in her by her own aroused infantile feelings. He may learn how her sensitivity to the baby and his needs does indeed spring from her capacity to be open to reverberations of his gropings and disturbances, to learn to differentiate among messages by feeling and responding appropriately to them. This, rather than to do what she has learned or been told she ought to do by precept, hearsay or academic psychology.

Not every mother is able to respond in this way. In some the necessary learning comes only slowly. There is every possible variation in degree and in areas of responsiveness and blindness between mothers, and at different times within each mother, as within all of us.

The seminar affords an opportunity to study these personality aspects over a period of two years, together with an opportunity to see the thrust for development in each infant, varying in strength in each case but present in all who live. One can observe the way in which trust and love and a capacity to form object relationships grows in the child through recurrent experiences of being understood. In these ways the student has the opportunity to introject selectively an experience which he can continue to draw on as a model and source for his own development as a therapist with patients.

The observation experience helps the student to endure 'living in the question' (as Keats put it) with his patients, to struggle till he can discern the implications of his first-hand, detailed impressions rather than to flee to premature application of theory. It helps him to see the infant both in the child and the adult, and in his analytic work to stay with that infant and aid him in his arrested or distorted development. It helps him to distinguish movements that are leading towards healthy rather than spurious or superficial growth. It helps to alert him to the significance of minute behavioural indicators and signs of emotion which, when taken into account, add dimension to the quality of his later work.

I think observation also helps some of us in our analytic work to avoid premature, anxiety-ridden interpretation and intervention. It helps relax undue therapeutic zeal, allows us to learn to feel and to respect the drive towards development in every patient, as in every baby. It cannot be hurried. It can be facilitated, encouraged and protected, but it cannot be created or forced. One acquires something of this feeling from observing the wise mother who has learned not to push the baby on prematurely. She knows that it is illusory to believe that, if she is good enough, she can help him grow up without any frustration. She therefore allows him to struggle with what is within his compass.

It is possible to note and discuss in this seminar the general tendency at times to find fault with the mother. (Or, in another context, the other therapist or caretaking person.) To believe, surreptitiously, that one could do so much better oneself. One may see how this tendency lies behind the recurrent urge to find psychopathology in everything, the voyeuristic eye that looks to criticize rather than to empathize. One also sees the defences against this same tendency – the projective identification with and idealization of the mother-baby, and blindness to the difficulties with which they are struggling or failing to struggle. These impediments to accurate observation manifest themselves in every group at times. They are important to note and to be taken into account as material for the seminar. As in other working groups, their full significance for the individual student and his contribution towards them are matters for further comprehension within the privacy of the personal analysis.

One further point about this seminar. As it is a discussion of observations, not of *work* undertaken by the participants, a standard not only of detailed but also of freer and more honest reporting is facilitated. In seminars and meetings where individuals present clinical work and results, there is tremendous pressure to trim up, to leave out longeurs, confusions, mistakes, and to organize presentation in a way that pre-empts criticism. The opportunities for mutual learning can be restricted by this desire to present oneself as above reproach. One cannot do away with competitiveness and the need to appear well in the eyes of authority, whoever that authority may be. We are all so tempted. But this seminar focusses attention on the material itself, rather than upon that comparison and measurement of individual performance, which so inhibits honesty and spontaneity in describing one's own work.

## Training in Psychoanalytic Psychotherapy

The heart of the course, although not its ultimate goal, is the training in the techniques of psychoanalytic psychotherapy. Three cases - a very young child, a child in the latency period and an adolescent - are seen on an intensive basis, optimally five times a week. During this part of the training the majority of the students have a sessional appointment at the Tavistock within the National Health Service. Very few spend all their time at the Tavistock, however, as most are working also at some other clinic, where they usually have been given a full-time post and seconded by the Authority concerned for training at the Tavistock. In this way we are able to train more people than the limitations of space and paid establishment at the Clinic itself would permit.

For their three intensive cases students have three different supervisors. This arrangement helps to give them some experience of the ways in which different therapists think and work. They also see a number of children and young people whom they treat by the same general techniques on a less intensive basis. They have the opportunity to learn casework with parents and in some instances to conduct analytic psychotherapy with them, when this seems appropriate.

This brings us to the often asked question: what is analysis and what is psychotherapy? Is analysis treatment of a patient on a four or five times weekly basis? And is what one does less intensively while using the same basic approach termed psychotherapy? One could use an arbitrary definition, and say that analysis is the method of treatment practised by members of psychoanalytic societies when they say they are practising analysis - however varied their ideas of this may be, and indeed are. I myself shall call analytic psychotherapy the analytic technique which our students are helped to grasp and to apply five times weekly or less. This is the analysis of the processes set in motion by interpretation of the transference relationship, enriched by private attention to the therapist's counter-transference (Meltzer, 1967). Its essence consists in the provision of a setting in which the patient is encouraged, through attention to and interpretive descriptions of his total behaviour, to bring increasingly to the therapist unknown and hitherto unacceptable parts of himself. These are experienced in the relationship with the therapist. They are scrutinized together, and hopefully understood and integrated. This brief statement, as will be appreciated, is necessarily an oversimplification of a complex process.

On the whole, the therapists at the Tavistock employ this analytic technique whether the patient is seen five, four or even one session a week. The criteria for frequency of sessions remain a matter of constant debate and exploration. One of the simplest criteria is that of sheer expediency. If a therapist has a vacancy for an intensive case at a particular time, and if parents are willing and able to bring the child so frequently, or if it is a question of a child or adolescent of an age and sufficiently motivated to bring himself, the intensive help may be offered. I think this proves a better criterion than it may seem, especially if it turns out – as it sometimes does – that the patient's willingness to attend indicates a willingness also to invest in analytic work. Nonetheless, there are some children who receive five times weekly therapy who could have benefited significantly from less. On the other hand, there are some who for a variety of reasons cannot be seen more than once a week – but for whom one may feel this is totally inadequate. There are many fewer of these children, I suspect however, than is generally believed by those who have not had experience in working under clinic conditions.

There is general agreement that, whether therapists after their training wish to work intensively or not, the training work on a five times weekly basis is a necessary and valuable core experience. In it students discern and gain conviction of the intensity of infantile transference to the therapist in analytic therapy. As a rule the transference manifests itself most clearly in the rhythm of the five days sessions and the two days weekend. A recurrent experience is afforded of time with the therapist, then time away. When the infant in the patient comes to trust the experience of being closely held by the therapist's attention, he then has to cope with the break, the absence. We then see what he is able to retain of that previous experience of togetherness. The situation gives the student the most leisurely possibility of being able to study in the analytic therapy what has been glimpsed earlier in infant observation: how the infant may learn to trust, to love and to let go, optimally and desirably through gradually introjecting and assimilating the experience of togetherness which he is given.

It might in some ways be more accurate to state that analytic therapy is very largely concerned with studying in the transference the factors which militate against the possibility of internalizing – 'learning from experience' (Bion, 1962). This study always includes oneself as well as one's patients, for no development in therapeutic skill can take place without continual re-examination on the part of the therapist.

In a field where resources are infinitesimal and need is great, the criteria of selection for frequency of sessions, or indeed for analytic treatment at all, concern all psychotherapists. We have come to realize increasingly that participation in diagnosis and assessment is an essential part of the therapist's traiining. It is likely to play an increasing part in the work he does and in which he can sefully co-operate with psychiatric and other colleagues, utilizing the experience that is accumulated over the years from investigating in depth the developmental potential of the individual.

In the later stages of their training, or after qualification, psychotherapists are given the opportunity to be supervised on short-term consultative work with self-referred adolescents in the Young People's Consultation Centre and thereby begin to gain some experience of the possibilities and the limitations of this kind of work.

## Supervision of Clinical Work

During the first part of the course there is, as a rule, no individual supervision of students' work unless it is specifically requested. Students, however, may go to their personal tutor to discuss general work problems and programme. If it seems vital that they should receive more support than can be given in the work discussion seminar groups, attempts are made to supply it. During the second part of the course, however, in addition now to individual supervision, students have three weekly clinical seminar groups. Here they have the opportunity to present, and to listen to others presenting, material from the treatment of children, young people and parents.

Throughout the second stage students are recognized as being responsible for the cases with which they are working, in conjunction of course with the relevant senior colleagues in their place of work. The role of the supervisor in this training is similar to that of the seminar leader, but more personally oriented. The personal supervisor helps the student to think about and better understand the material he is presenting. Equally, to understand the processes of communication, or failure to achieve communication, between him and the patients with whom he is working. The supervisor aims to help the student to sketch tentative maps of the patient's personality and development. He encourages him in alternative ways of thinking about problems, and sometimes raises questions when all seems too clear or pat.

As teachers we ask ourselves questions. How much should we feel we have to tell the student what to say? How far should we go in teaching him to make actual interpretations, and how far should we encourage him to formulate these for himself? It can be appropriate to do both at different times. Even if one is quite convinced that a student recurrently fails to comment upon or even see material that is asking for attention, one can be useful only by trying to approach the material again and again – by describing it ever anew from different angles as it recurs in different contexts. Just as in working with a patient one has to do precisely that when trying to illuminate some blind spot. Undoubtedly the attitude of the supervisor can affect the attitude of the student-therapist to the particular case. A mother who is having trouble with her baby is often confirmed in her own inadequacy by some 'well meant' advice *de haut en bas*. In the same way the student struggling with his own inadequacy in practising therapy can be crushed by over-knowledgeable interpretations of the supervisor, which take no account of his feelings and his struggles.

A supervisor can do much to strengthen or melt away the illusion that there is a 'way' which those who have inside information know about. One may arouse feelings of envy and inadequacy, not by genuine and useful attempts to link material together meaningfully, but by hinting rather nebulously about areas where the student is not in touch and 'hasn't got it quite right' – yet without offering a helpful alternative. In short, in implying a criticism without being able to document it clearly or to teach otherwise. I suspect that when we so act we are failing to shoulder our own uncertainties. We are failing to recognize or admit how we all have to struggle in the dark towards some glimmer of light.

On the other side is the problem of the student who cannot bear to be wrong. He is touchy about being taught and having his work illuminated by someone else. That is his personal problem, with which he has to wrestle in his analysis. The supervisor may discern it and may have to take it into account. I do not think it is necessarily his job to draw attention to the student's attitude, unless it is intractable. We have a constant task in trying to improve our methods of supervising, just as the student has his in learning how to remember, to record, to present material and ask the questions which can help supervisors to be useful.

## Written Work

We try to present students with the opportunity of describing and evaluating what they are learning and the teaching they receive. They are required to write descriptive papers on their observation and work experiences in each of the first two years of the course. If they go on to take the second part of the training they are asked to prepare further presentations and to write papers on some of their cases.

## The Place of Theory

During their training and general reading the students encounter a variety of theoretical approaches and orientations. They are encouraged to make for themselves meaningful links between the work they are doing and the theories they study.

The basis of formal teaching in the course is that of psychoanalytical theory, as developed by Freud in his clinical work and writings and his own self-analysis, which helped him to evaluate this more accurately and to deepen the field of his enquiry – in short, to explore the unconscious in himself and in others. In addition, students study in particular Karl Abraham and the theories developed by Melanie Klein and her followers. If Freud discovered the child within the adult, then Melanie Klein revealed the possibility of seeing the infant within the child and the adult.

Her work has contributed to our depth of knowledge of ways in which development, through truthfully based object relationships, may proceed in a healthy form. And, of course, of ways in which perversity and psychopathology originate and distort or impede growth (Klein, Meltzer, 1973).

The Tavistock course is one which is inevitably known as the Kleinian course in child psychotherapy. Yet it seems a disservice both to the pioneer spirit of Freud and of Melanie Klein herself to label it such. As the years have gone by, many of us who have been intimately involved in the work have come to feel increasingly that the future of psychoanalysis depends not on the learning and propagation of even the most valuable or 'respectably' documented theories, but on attention to the conditions in which the observations may be made. These allow each student of human nature to realize, and to note in others and in himself, the phenomena on which theories have been based. The furtherance of the work of Freud, of Melanie Klein and of other inspired contributors to the science or art of psychoanalysis, depends on each student living through in his own way that path of discovery – of the interaction between the internal and the external world, the influence of the unconscious upon conscious activities. The journey is made a little easier by using the maps of those who have crossed the wilderness before. But maps read in the cosy safety of home are no substitute for the journey itself. Such cosiness prevents not only further inroads into unknown territory, but the maintenance of ways that have already been cleared.

## The Personal Analysis

Personal analysis is a requirement for every student who decides he wishes to proceed with the second part of the course. He is asked to have about a year's experience of analysis himself before undertaking analytic cases of his own. Some candidates may have had a personal analysis before they apply, but we do not require students to be in analysis during their first year with us. This is a time of mutual exploration and selection between tutors and students. Our experience over the last few years has shown that many people are able to develop in themselves to varying degrees an enquiring approach of considerable imagination and depth towards the work they are doing, without the experience of being analysed themselves. Many people, when given encouragement to utilize and examine their own emotional responses rather than discard them as unscientific, probably improve greatly the quality and range of their work in the field of personal relationships. Some people who have never had a personal analysis may indeed already be richer and more subtle human beings than others who have. The analyst cannot *create* the individual, any more than the parents create the baby in that sense.

Nevertheless, even the most gifted individuals, capable of extensive learning from experience, do have unknown areas in themselves which can prevent them learning from experience in particular areas. These unknown or hived-off areas may be discovered and integrated by analysis. The analysis is not part of the course in the way the seminars and discussions are. It remains a private affair. Its purpose is to put the student more fully in possession of himself. Hopefully it will give him the courage to submit himself more completely to observations and experiences from which he may learn, while tolerating degrees of anxiety and pain which he could not tolerate before.

Analysis should increase the student's fellow-feeling for the children with whom he works. Many of these will be quite crushed and stunted in their growth: in order to proceed in their development they need compassion and understanding from an adult, who knows what it is to be in pain or fear – but, importantly, also knows how to struggle through it.

During the personal analysis it is hoped the student will experience more fully the infant and the child in himself; learn step by step how to contain and educate them; and resolve residual infantile grievances and distortions of perception. He should eventually be more free to fully address himself to his patient's similar problems but unique personality.

## Qualities Desirable in the Therapist

The qualities of the good therapist are notably hard to define. In the past we have tried a variety of methods of selection for the course. These included group procedures, individual interviews and reference to people who know the applicants well. We have never been entirely happy about the effectiveness or fairness of any method. Because of the inherent difficulties of selection we have tried, by dividing the course into two parts, to give individuals the opportunity for self-selection. In this way the candidate can obtain gradual, realistic experience of the kind of work he will be expected to do, the kind of training offered and his own responses to it. However, there has unfortunately still to be some selection even at the preliminary stage, as the demand for training in child psychotherapy continues to grow. Up to a point we work on the basis of first come, first served. Nonetheless, there is no objection to anyone not finding a place making a further application in a succeeding year.

Many applicants come in their early twenties before they already have an established profession. Others come at a later point in their careers, when they envisage this training as furthering the development of interests arising from their previous work. Any group of students profits from the inclusion both of younger and of more mature individuals from a variety of backgrounds. It is especially enriched in the present case by the inclusion of some from fields outside that of mental health – the humanities, for instance. An education which has afforded the opportunity to specialize in imaginative literature encourages a dimension of perception which may be dismissed as unscientific in many courses of academic psychology. That training takes cognizance of the reality of the inner world of feeling, imagination and values, with which psychoanalysis must be concerned. Such contributions help psychoanalysis not to surface into shallower fields of behaviouristic description, nor the aridities of Talmudic precept and argument over theory. The future of psychoanalytic work depends on the unswerving realization that the inner world of feeling and imagination is also a matter for scientific study and description.

It is important for the profession that it should contain a living core of workers who are devoted to the study itself, but who bring into their consulting room a depth and wisdom from the accumulating experience of their own lives. From the private existence – both external and internal – comes the individual richness of experience. This enables one to be aware with greater sensitivity and precision of the more subtle shades of the patient's communications and behaviour, more likely to bring about a meeting of minds than an explanation derived from a library of previously learned interpretations.

It is equally important for the quality of the therapist's work, however, that he should live in it and be fed by it, as well as by his private and personal life. It is doubtful whether, in the long run, any fundamental benefit can be derived from a contact between two people which does not benefit both parties. The child psychotherapist, nevertheless, has to acquire the capacity to delay, or rather to refrain from asking for, immediate satisfaction from the patient himself. He has to learn to contain and to struggle with just such qualities which militate against contact and comprehension, both in himself and in the child.

In order to be able to learn from experience, and to be able to utilize that wisdom to help others to bear themselves better, a reasonable degree of intelligence is necessary. As a rule, the acquisition of an honours degree guarantees the presence of this. But the possession of intelligence by itself is not enough. Method and motivation for using it are vital. We all use our intelligence, to some extent, to find ways of managing ourselves and the world, ways which help us to avoid feeling small and inadequate. It is a more serious and questionable matter, however, when we use it to make ourselves big at the expense of others.

The child psychotherapist has to be able to tolerate feeling small and in the dark, because this is the way a child often feels. This is what the child in *us* must often feel if he is to remain alive to the wonder and adventure, as well as the hazards, of the world.

Although the therapist's private and professional life need to feed each other, at times they seem to interfere with each other. For instance, although there is now an increase in the number of male applicants, and increasing recognition of satisfying career prospects for men in child psychotherapy, work with children and young people is likely to continue to have particular appeal for women – especially, perhaps, for young women already married, or likely to marry and have children themselves. It is not, however, enough to love one's own children. One needs to have enough feeling and generosity to extend this to other people's children (who represent in the depths of the unconscious one's mother's babies). For a time, when one's own children are young, it may be difficult to find the emotional resource to make the necessary extension. It is, however, an extension which needs finally to be made in the field of work itself. It is not enough, and not in the interests of our own patients ultimately, if our preoccupation with them is so exclusive and intense that we ignore the existence of many others – those others, that is, who do not have the benefit of our special attention, however imperfect that may be.

If the benefits of psychotherapy as an art-science are to be shared, it must concern itself with society as well as the individual. As analytical psychotherapists we must realize that it is a privilege, as well as a task, to be able to offer or receive an educational resource so rare and so costly in time and money. It is therefore an obligation, if we have so benefited, to continue to consider how the attitudes which we have found to be essentially life-promoting may be encouraged in others, especially those who have a hand in the rearing of children. For this reason students are encouraged during their training, or shortly afterwards, to take part in a teaching or consultative project, provided by the Tavistock for workers in the social and educational fields. Many participate in small group discussions in the course for teachers and others engaged in aspects of education.

## The Philosophy of the Training

My own preference is to regard this course not as a training where students are encouraged to model themselves like apprentices on their teachers, even on the best of them, but to see it as an opportunity for education in the field of inter and intra personal development. In this the students are encouraged to work from their own observations of themselves and of the young people with whom they work. They can be helped to organize their observations by psychoanalytical theory; but they must find and draw upon their own style of working within the psychoanalytical technique.

We try to follow an approach which enables the study of links between intra psychic development and inter personal family and group relationships. We try to consider the extent to which the individual child seems able to develop by introjecting, assimilating and growing from within – as distinct from the spurious progress made by projecting oneself into unassimilated persons and knowledge. The difference, that is, between the three-dimensional creative growing which proceeds from introjective identification, as opposed to the two-dimensional socializing or the 'being grown-up' which stops at projective identification. The latter is the 'living in someone else's shoes'; the former the still more impoverished mimicry that clings to surfaces and the appearance of things (Klein, 1946; Bick, 1968).

Our method of teaching, as I have already indicated, is essentially through small seminar groups and individual supervisions. These aim to direct the attention of the student towards increasingly close observation of the details of interaction between himself and the individuals he is studying. The course intends to increase the student's capacity to tolerate uncertainty; to contain, to think about and to use his counter-transference, thereby becoming more sensitive to emotional as well as cognitive communication. It aims to help him respond in practice with less certainty of ever having the final answers, but with greater hope of learning, with the help of the patient or client, the direction in which to proceed. This attitude with patients will tend to take the form of interpretations that describe and bring together data in a way that leads on to further enquiry – and not to the kind of explanations that are conversation stoppers.

Theoretical teaching and seminar discussion would aim to present theories not as sacred or final, but as convenient. They should illuminate methods of organizing observations, of naming and generalizing, and bring order out of chaotic experience – yet leave the space and freedom to admit new data.

At the end of training one hopes that the student does not emerge feeling 'qualified' with a certificate giving him the right to practise psychotherapy, or armed with a method and technique that gives him the edge over other trainings and techniques. One hopes, certainly, he has learned something tangible. But more importantly, that he has learned how to bear uncertainties and difficult questions. One hopes he retains a deep sense of wonder at the infinite diversities of human nature, together with a great fellow-feeling for his patients. I would hope he has gathered some experience of the ways in which he may continue to explore the split-off or repressed aspects of mental functioning; how to bear the pain of struggling, sweetened by hope derived from hard-won experience.

Some of the former students of the course have extended the age range of their clients to work also with adults, an extension which is increasingly taking place within the course.

We are also concerned with the wider issues of personality development in families, schools and societies. We hope as therapists to do something towards breaking down the barriers of resentment about the privilege enjoyed by those who receive and practise psychoanalytic treatment. These barriers are erected, understandably, by some of those workers who have responsibility for the many needy not in a position to be helped in this way.

We see the training in analytic psychotherapy as a foundation rather than an end, a foundation from which further researches into the infinite variety and complications of the individual and his relationships may proceed. We believe that it is necessary for a stream of analytic work to continue more deeply and more widely, not only because of its therapeutic value but because of its necessary fertilizing effect on all studies of human relationships.

## Post-Graduate Developments

Ours is a course which owes its existence to the discovery of psychoanalysis. This, however fallible its practitioners, is essentially concerned with the self-realization and striving after truth in every human being. The quality of the teaching and of the work done by anyone who undertakes training in the psychoanalytic method ultimately rests on the way in which he continues to maintain that striving in his own heart; and further, tries to foster it in the patients whom he treats and the colleagues with whom he works. It can be kept alive only by the individual working as best he can, not by his following precepts set by supposedly superior authorities, not by remaining a child who wishes to please the parents, but by working through the crisis which any truly developing adolescent has in finding his own mind, identity and style of life. To do this he has to question himself as well as what his parents have taught him, in order to find his best way of realizing in practice the values and experience that stand the test of scrutiny ... of promoting and protecting what he loves.

In saying this I am aware that it is the exceptional individual who is able to stand alone, who is confident enough about what he thinks and feels in the light of his own experience. The quality of his judgment reflects the capacity to internalize selectively, based upon some fairly clear discrimination between true and false. For most of us it takes a long time to reach a position of relative independence fortified by inner strength; we are often tempted lazily to give up the struggle and settle for our equivalent of the ten commandments, which give at least a sense of knowing how to avoid giving offence to whatever our particular representatives of God or Authority are – feared or idealized, or both.

Most of us need help, support and stimulation long after we are trained and 'qualified' to practise psychoanalytic therapy. This is not necessarily the help of further personal analysis – which has its parasitic temptations. We do need the protection of some group within which work may be discussed with colleagues of varying degrees of seniority and experience. It seems to me that such groups should see themselves as gatherings to promote mutual exchange and development, rather than to monitor or judge. Otherwise they may become, as the families of adolescents sometimes do, a restriction, rather than a nurturing resource that allows for and tolerates mistakes made in the struggle for identity and self-responsibility.

Analytical work inevitably brings the therapist into continual close contact with the relationships and constitutional factors which impede growth. To wrestle with these he has to tolerate the projection of a great deal of frustration, pain and sometimes hatred and reproach from his patients. Like parents who care for their wayward and troublesome children, therapists are also very vulnerable to criticism from the 'neighbours' – that is, their own colleagues.

It seems to me that as a professional group our health and strength depend upon the capacity of each one of us for self-scrutiny as well as devotion to the work. When we are genuinely able to shoulder the burden of trying to keep our own house in order (a never-ending task), we are more likely to be able to feel for, and to be good neighbours to, our colleagues. There is no group solution for work which is essentially individual. It is also a problem in this field, as in others, for a professional group to maintain an *esprit de corps* without becoming élitist or heresy-hunting.

The problems with which psychotherapists struggle are likely to be slightly different at different times in their careers. As practitioners and teachers we are, in growing older, bound to face encounters with our younger colleagues and students. These are the kind of anxieties that middle-aged parents face when threatened by the growing-up of their children, and by their challenge. Such threats may encourage a dangerous tendency to shore up uncertainties by the collecting of followers or admirers, by using them to further one's ideas through variations of the patronage system. Anxieties about the future of one's work and profession can increase fear of change, and promote that kind of conservatism which looks always to be reminded rather than informed.

The psychic demands of this work can make it difficult to steer between the narrows of complacency and self-righteous criticism and the whirlpool of disorganization. If we are able to face the demands however, it seems to me that the work may continue to be rewarding in a personal sense into old age, and always conducive to strength and wisdom. As long as we do not surface into clichés, we are continually wrestling with 'the enemies of promise', with the foe within. Where else, as Shakespeare so well knew, can death be defeated but in the inner world? (Sonnet 164)

# Appendix
# *Doubly Deprived*
## by Gianna Henry

This additional case study gives an account of psychotherapy with a patient very different from others described in this book. In fact, the doubly deprived patient described by Gianna Henry belongs to a group of children often considered inaccessible to psychotherapy. Mrs Henry, however, gives an impressive and hopeful account of how she patiently made contact and progress with a boy at first almost impossible to reach. M.B., D.D.

---

I intend to present some aspects of the first two years of treatment of an adolescent boy whom I saw once a week for just over a year and then on a twice weekly basis. Martin was referred to the clinic because of considerable learning difficulties (he was nearly fourteen when he started treatment and his reading age was six), aggressive behaviour and stealing. Two years prior to referral he had made a suicide attempt when he tried to jump from a second floor window.

### History

Martin is the illegitimate child of West Indian parents. His mother died when he was seven years old, but she had had no contact with him after the age of two months, when he was placed in residential care. His father had disappeared at the beginning of the mother's pregnancy. Martin had three placements up to the age of two, when he was fostered by an

English couple with a child of their own, a boy four years older than Martin. He was with the foster parents for ten years, until fostering broke down. Martin was at that time twelve years old. It seems that the foster parents found Martin increasingly unmanageable because of his stealing and defiant behaviour. They felt that they were no longer able 'to accept him or have any trust in him'. There is no indication of the impact that the attempted suicide (one year before the breakdown of fostering) might have had on the foster parents and how it might have contributed to their feeling of inadequacy. They discontinued contact with Martin after he left the foster home to return to a children's home.

**Identification with the 'Vain Mother'**

When Martin started treatment, he had spent just over a year at the children's home and was attending a large secondary school. The most alarmed and alarming reports came at first from the school, where Martin had become dangerously aggressive towards other children. In spite of careful daily inspections, he had developed a talent for smuggling knives into the school and suddenly flicking them open, terrorizing other children. On one occasion he had pointed a knife at a child's throat and the child had very nearly fainted with fear. Martin did not seem to react to punishment or reproach. He provoked extremely violent emotions in others, but he appeared himself, most of the time, devoid of feelings. As he was to tell me some months later: 'A teacher in school said that I am the only person he has come across who has no feelings.'

When I first met Martin, I too perceived an alarming quality of numbness in him, as if, although his suicide attempt had failed, he was really only going through the motions of being alive, through the motions of coming for treatment, very regularly and punctually (he was invariably early), but without being in the least in touch with his motivations for coming. The environment was indeed highly motivated and, at that time, carried the weight of all the feelings Martin was not experiencing himself.

There was only one thing that Martin seemed to invest with enoromous importance and that was his appearance. Before he started treatment, I had heard that he often took more than an hour getting ready to go out, and the care he took over details showed at first sight. Although there was always a feeling that he was not totally present, which made it very difficult to establish contact with him, I gradually came to realize that there was a very specific mood attached to the lack of contact. While not listening, or treating what I had said as if it were a remote sound, he appeared totally absorbed in some detail of his appearance; at times it might be something very minor, like removing tiny specks of dust or fluff from his jacket; at times his movements became very feminine, almost caricatured. For instance, using his sunglasses as a mirror, he would spend long periods smoothing his eyebrows with his finger tips; or he could become totally absorbed in the care of his nails. Once he actually came to his session wearing nail varnish on the nails of both hands. On such occasions, he would treat my attempts to reach him as if they were disturbances from an annoying child or as a noise in the background; I should not distract him while he was busy with something so much more important than anything I could possibly say.

One particular session provided a vivid example of the type of projective identification involved. Martin was wearing a parka with a fur-trimmed hood. He pulled the hood over his head, took a comb out of his pocket, and started combing the long fur around his hood as if he were curling it with long, sensuous and very feminine strokes. He behaved as if he perceived himself inside someone else's skin. The impact of his behaviour was heightened by the fact that he was wearing, as he often did, menacing rings on his right hand, though he seemed completely oblivious of them.

In this and other sessions, there were some verbal responses to my attempts to reach him, in the nature of: 'Yes, what is it you wanted to say?' 'I have got no time for your rubbish', 'Tough, you have got to suffer', 'You are talking to a brick wall'. His tone of voice, on those occasions, was cold, contemptuous and very hard. Indeed, it *was* like talking to a brick wall, and after some trial and error, I realized that this was the most important quality of Martin's communication. He had to put me in the position of a child trying to make contact with somebody who had no time to listen, a hard and vain mother who, while curling her hair, says: 'Tough, you have got to suffer,' and treats with scorn and contempt the weakling who is trying to get her attention. I am referring to an *internal* image but, from later material, this appeared to be the phantasy that Martin had formed about the reason why his mother had left him just after his birth. She was too vain, self-centred and hard to care for a small baby. He saw her as vain even after her death: 'She is having a lovely holiday pushing up the daisies,' he said once, bitterly, close to one of my holiday breaks.

The purpose of Martin's unreachable attitude was then, as it had probably been many times in the past to split and project into somebody else both the feelings he could not tolerate and a part of himself, the needy child he had to disown, while he identified himself with the unavailable mother whom at this time he idealized. He felt completely at one with her and thus in control of her.

When I told Martin that I thought he behaved with me as if I were a nuisance child, trying to talk to a mother who is only interested with the reflection of her face in the mirror and can't be bothered to listen, a very hard mother, like a brick wall, he answered: 'There is only one way to find out whether you are a brick wall or not. You hit your head against a brick wall, if it hurts, you are not.' The implication of this statement is very enlightening in terms of the development of Martin's defences. He appeared to be saying that the only way not to get hurt, if you have this sort of mother, is to identify with her, become a brick wall yourself and leave the hurt to someone else.

At this time Martin put enormous pressure on me to give up trying, to give up any hope that he might be reached. I think that the very forceful impact he had on people in this respect must have deprived him many times of positive experiences. He had developed a talent not only for hardening himself, but for hardening people around him and making them deaf to the real nature of his needs. Any further deprivation and experience of external hardness was reintrojected, and it cemented the hardness of his internal image.

**The Pakistani**

One can understand Martin's dread of getting in touch with feelings of dependency, for inside himself he had a very insensitive internal mother and he had often helped to harden people around him. His profound contempt and hatred of a split-off and needy part of himself was a recurrent theme in treatment: it was initially known to us as 'The Pakistani'.

Although Martin is coloured himself, his prejudice against Pakistanis was fierce and sanctimonious, and he often chose Pakistani children as the target of his attacks in school. He used to say: 'They can't fend for themselves, or they wouldn't have come over here for help, would they? They are inferior, they are savages, not like us British.' This inferior and needy savage not only had to be despised, but crushed and obliterated. 'Oh I love Pakistanis,' Martin said once, 'you hit them and they come back for more and more and more until you kill them', and he menacingly caressed the knuckle rings which covered all the fingers of his right hand. This is probably what he felt would happen to the weakling, the fool who kept hitting his head against an insensitive hard mother; he would not survive for long. Subsequent material has brought much more into the open regarding Martin's anxieties about death, but he was certainly projecting the fear of death into the children he terrorized in school with knives. This type of acting out fluctuated, but it completely ceased at the beginning of the second year of treatment, when signs of integration of this split-off part began to emerge. One day Martin told me: 'I'm not after all the Pakistanis in the world, I'm not man-hunting, I am just after one bloke'. He started scribbling then, on the side of his box, he wrote his own name, address, and telephone number.

## Grievances

As Martin, gradually and very tentatively, began to realize that the Pakistani he had been bashing, despising and depriving of the help he needed, was inside himself, and when he caught the first glimpses of insight into this area of need, of wanting me to retrieve him when he lost touch (the address and telephone number), he began to reproach me increasingly for hardness, coldness and negligence and for failing to provide what he needed. He could idealize the aloof, detached, narcissistic quality of the 'vain mother' only as long as he kept the needy child completely split off. While he used this defence, he *was* the insensitive mother and completely identified with her. The feelings that she evoked had to be felt by the despised, trampled Pakistanis, not by him. As he began to perceive his feelings of need, he also got in touch with his grievances. His appearance very strikingly mirrored his change of attitude and the shift in his identifications. At times he would come to the clinic wearing trousers that were too short for him, a torn jumper, holes in his socks. In the session previous to a holiday break he was wearing a very thick 'second skin' (Bick 1967): a shirt, two jumpers, a cardigan and his parka, although it was not a very cold day. As soon as he sat down, he touched the radiator as if shivering and said: 'Call this central heating? Cold water running through a mass of metal.' When I linked this reproach for coldness and his holding himself together with many protective layers to the forthcoming holiday break, Martin moved to an eroticized and much safer area of grievances: he said I was such a cold person, because I came from a cold country (he was convinced I was Polish) and all we have in Poland is snow and ice, while he came from Africa where they have beautiful tropical fish and sunshine. While saying that, his attitude became very seductive, as if he wished to imply that he had all the warmth, the passion, the glamour of Africa, as opposed to me: a metallic object with cold water in my veins (the mass of metal with cold water running through it).

On occasions the grievances had a marked defensive quality to them and Martin appeared to go to great lengths to put himself in a position in which he could reproach me for neglect. For example, he often arrived early for his sessions, and when I met him at the prearranged time, he looked very sullen and resentful and treated me as if I had kept him waiting. On one occasion he said: referring to the previous session: 'You were half minute late last time'.

I think that the main defensive purpose of the grievances was that Martin felt more comfortable in a known situation, confronted by someone he did not value, someone who could be of no use to him, somebody not worthy of trust. He could move with great ease in this familiar dimension. He had never really trusted anybody in his life, he was not prepared to take chances. His defences, for instance his identification with the insensitive internal mother, had an enormous advantage over a relationship with any living external object as it could be conjured up at any moment, it was always available and Martin felt in full control; while he could not fall back on my help all the time. In fact he could only do so, at first, for fifty minutes out of all the hours of the week. I wondered about a possible reference to the seven days of the week, when he told me that he had 'seven layers of skin that covered the soft spot'. Not just a 'crust of the week-end' but a 'crust of the week'.

When I was able to offer him an extra session, he reacted with very mixed feelings. At first he insisted that he should be allowed to choose the day and time himself. When he settled for my offer, he conveyed the feeling that these 'miserable fifty minutes' extra as he called them, were experienced by him as a cruel tantalizing game. If I could give him a little more, then why so little?

I doubt that he would have expressed no grievances had I been able to offer him, as I wished, five 'miserable fifty minutes' sessions a week. He brought to one of the sessions an advertisement for a restaurant that was open 'most hours of the day and night', providing me with a model of how things should be. He told me, after I had referred to myself as 'mother' in a transference interpretation that 'there are no mothers in a place like this' (he referred to the clinic and, I expect, just as much to a children's home). 'Only people doing their job and getting paid for it, there might be some mothers, but that means that they have got children at home'. Reproach for being no more than yet another part-time person in his life was recurrent. It always appeared to imply that if I put him in touch with a feeling of need, if I was responsible for his knowing that he had a soft spot *inside* himself and not lodged in some Pakistani, then I could help him only by offering the actual mothering he had been deprived of, or deprived himself of and a very idealized, always available mothering. I should not expose him to the pain of knowing what he had missed without providing it, in the present, if not in the past. Whenever I fell short of those expectations (and I was bound to all the time), I was felt to be playing a cruel tantalizing game.

## Physical and mental violence

I came to understand only later that Martin's repeated accusations of my wanting to make him cry were, at least partly, serving the purpose of turning me into the executioner and himself into the victim, who was only fighting in self-defence and was thus immune to guilt.

Towards the end of the first year of treatment while reproaching me for cruelty, Martin threatened me with physical violence on several occasions. Once, just before our first Christmas break, he complained about the rain on his way to the clinic and, referring to the doll's house (an open plan one) in the corner, said: 'That house is no good: it would let the rain in.' He put his head out of the window, it was still raining, and wiped his face when he pulled his head back. When I said that he seemed to be talking about getting his face wet with tears, that he felt that like the doll's house I did not provide enough protection against the rain-tears, Martin caressed his knuckle rings with a smile, as if getting ready to punch me, and said: 'You can get your face wet with rain, with tears, with blood, and yours is going to be wet with blood before mine is wet with tears.'

It might be relevant that the risk of physical violence being acted out or, better, 'acted in' in treatment (Meltzer, 1967) coincided with the end of aggressive behaviour elsewhere. The problem came to be gathered more in the transference. Although physical violence did not actually occur, I think that Martin needed to generate a situation in which I would take very seriously the possibility that it could occur and bear the feelings that this aroused.

When he threatened me with knuckle rings or suddenly flicked open a knife and stabbed his box ('We'll have to get a new box: we'll have to get a new Mrs Henry'), he did not seem to experience any guilt feelings, because *I* was supposed to feel all the guilt for wanting to make him cry, as his mother had wanted to make him cry. I was confronted with the grievances of a lifetime: he behaved as if he were either phantasizing attacks or threatening physical violence in self-defence.

When the threat of physical violence receded, the impact of the violence did not diminish, however; it remained as mental violence, but it became to a certain extent easier to work with. It is difficult to gather one's thoughts and interpret when a knife may appear out of nowhere (the element of surprise was central).

Martin let me know that this type of danger was over in a

manner that was typical of his way of showing that he had gained a piece of insight; he would give it back to me in a patronizing way. I was quite unaware of moving my hands while talking. Martin touched one of my hands with a finger, gently pressing it towards the table and said: 'We can just talk, you don't need to use your hands.' *I* had suddenly become the acting-out patient.

On this occasion I also think that eroticization of the relationship (touching my hand, the seductive behaviour, the innuendo in Martin's words) had been used as a defence: in this case against tender feelings.

Martin found any feelings of warmth, closeness or tenderness so painful that he had to dispose of them very quickly. Either he eroticized them and turned them into excitement or he had to 'execute' them. 'My hurt is not my business. I execute it,' he said once while cutting in half with a sharp movement a piece of string he was holding in his hands. I think that this sign language provides a very good example of the 'attacks on linking' described by Bion (1959), which have formed the core of mental violence in Martin and, possibly, one of the greatest sources of his deprivation and learning difficulties.

Using the model proposed by Bion to summarize the most frequent 'attacks on linking' that occured in Martin's treatment, I must refer first to his attempt to empty the meaning, and therefore the feeling, out of a piece of insight he had just acquired: *attacks on links within his mind.* He used this method as the quickest remedy against any painful feelings, as he much preferred to be in a muddle than to be in pain. He could achieve this by taking a word out of context and 'executing it'. For example, after he had emerged from one of his delusional identifications with the vain mother and, for a moment, seemed really to feel and to understand how little sustenance she could provide for him, there was an abrupt change of mood; he took out of context the word 'character' which I had just used in connection with the vain mother, and said: 'Character, character? Oh yes, I like carrots.' It was as quick and sudden as a knife flicking open; in no time the meaning and the feeling were executed, the part of Martin that knew where it hurts and why it hurts was executed, and the consequence was a loss of *contact between his mind and my mind.*

This loss of contact is the second type of 'attacks on linking' to which I wish to refer. Martin was very much in need of a container (Bion, 1952) for the feelings he could not bear himself and of the experience that they could be survived, understood and filtered for him by somebody else. Bion suggests that a very extensive use in treatment of this type of 'projective identification', a stepping stone in development, probably implies that patients have been cheated out of the use of this mechanism in infancy. It is very likely that this might be true of some children cared for in institutions. But the reaction to being given what has been needed for so long is often accompanied by very painful feelings. As Bion (1959) points out: 'The patient feels he is being allowed an opportunity of which he had hitherto been cheated: the poignancy of the deprivation is thereby rendered the more acute and so are the feelings of resentment at the deprivation.' I think that the rapid 'execution' of feelings of being understood, of being in touch, and the consequent loss of contact with me were defences against this painful experience.

A third type of attack, intimately connected with the first two, was aimed at *disrupting links within my mind.* Martin expressed very openly his intolerance of my being anything more than a passive container for his projections. 'You are just a big dustbin stuffed with rubbish. Dustbins don't talk.' Or, 'I want to overwork that little man that runs round your head putting together all the data.' 'Why don't you throw him out the window and let him have a bit of fresh air?' He often interrupted me, if I started a sentence with the words 'I think that ...' 'You think everything don't you? You are a brain box.' If I stopped talking (silence was undoubtedly preferable to a battle of wits) he would say: 'Come on – proceed – what is it you were trying to say? Can't you remember?' Indeed this behaviour was also a meaningful communication, for Martin was once again telling me about a very destructive part of himself, another version of the 'Paki-basher' that was paralysing *his* capacity to think and showing me how it happened. The whole painful issue of the impaired use of his mind, of his incapacity to retain knowledge ('Can't you remember?') to link and to learn was being put across and he had been confronted daily with this self-inflicted deprivation, fortunately a reversible one.

**Wish to be Retrieved**

During the second year of treatment, especially in the second half, there were many indications that Martin relied on my work to re-establish links when they were broken, so that he would not get lost in his muddle or otherwise drift away. He told me, for instance, 'You can put a piece of rope to all sorts of good uses: you need it to tie a boat to the shore, so that it doesn't drift away, or you can tie the rope to a buoy'. He laughed as soon as he became aware of the double meaning of the word (boy – buoy) and said, 'I know what you are going to say.' He showed me in the same session, using the string for pulling the curtains, a very safe knot used by mountain climbers which he tied round both his legs. He said that even if he threw himself out of the window he wouldn't fall, he would just hang by his legs. The reference to his attempted suicide was striking, but, as Martin never mentioned it, I did not refer to it in my interpretations. There was plenty of material in the sessions that put us in touch with his suicidal impulses and, at this stage, with his fear of them. Martin had often asked me why I didn't just 'let him rot in peace', 'six feet underground is such a peaceful place, the brain only stops working when you are dead.' 'Dead people lose life, but they gain death.' He also said: 'If I were to kill myself I know the quickest way of doing it. You jump out of a window, head first.' Very often his 'attacks on linking' during a session, his throwing his feelings out of the window and the deadening of his mind, had a suicidal quality of brutal anesthesia. I could talk about the suicide, while it was happening.

I do not think that Martin could have dared me to let him drift away into madness or actual death without having developed some trust in a parental figure that could protect him from the 'Paki-basher', the most destructive part of himself. The development of a more trusting relationship in the transference was probably fostered by external events that made Martin feel very much at risk. He was supposed to leave the children's home when he was sixteen, and he had often told the house parents in the past that he wished to join the army. He had brought to the sessions a great deal of material about the meaning the army had for him. At first it was a 'licence to kill'; later more clearly, it was a 'licence to be killed', 'a passport to death', as Martin called it. Although he felt much less motivated to join the army, which would obviously have meant the end of treatment, many people in his environment had felt initially that this would be the best course of action. Martin had made good progress from the external point of view and his learning difficulties had considerably diminished; if he could pass the exams and join the Regulars, it seemed to make sense that he should. He brought the problem quite openly to his session when he asked me 'so what's going to happen when I am sixteen?' He also brought to the clinic, at this time, a picture of one of the homes where he had stayed as a small child. On another occasion he brought a leaflet from the Local Authority Council and Related Services, and he browsed through it. He pointed at 'Territorial and Army Volunteer Reserve' and said 'we don't want that, do we?' He looked at length at the page listing Child Care and Child Guidance.

I think it was important for Martin to know that other people in the clinic were concerned with the factual arrangements of his life and, fortunately, a suitable placement could be found and treatment was not disrupted. If Martin were to feel that I was in any way involved with practical, external arrangements for him, he would probably have perceived my change of role as very confusing and tantalizing. Because of the extent of his deprivation and his craving for the full-time mother he will never have in external reality, I felt that I protected him from unnecessary psychic pain by keeping the boundaries of our relationships very firm. If any change were possible, then he could start hoping that I might, at some stage, make up for all that he had missed in life – while I could only mitigate the extent of his *double* deprivation by helping him lessen the extent of the one deriving from *internal* sources, e.g., from the crippling defences he had developed which made him an orphan inwardly as well as outwardly.

I felt it was hopeful, for instance, that rather than opting for a 'licence to kill' or 'to be killed', Martin appeared to be able to stand on the side of his real need and ask for some more 'Child Care and Child Guidance'. It seemed an indication that he was in touch with parents *within* himself who could treat his needs with respect and ask that they be taken seriously: a role which he had completely left to me in the past.

It cannot be denied, however, that Martin had also been

deprived of something by his treatment. The previous changes of placement had probably been relatively painless. He let himself be moved like a suitcase, a fairly empty one, and left the tears to someone else. About the time of his sixteenth birthday, two weeks before his move from the children's home to his new placement, the prospective foster parents came to take him to their house for a week-end, and they found him very cosily tucked up in bed with the blanket up to his nose, engrossed in reading a book. He said that he would prefer the break to be final, go to their house and stay there, he did not want to come and go. He was asked whether he would accept going to them if he could bring something that mattered with him. As he was so engrossed in reading, would he like to bring that book; Martin answered that he would go only if he could take all 'his family' with him. Fortunately, it was possible to arrange regular contacts with the house parents after he left, but it is undeniable that this move was yet another loss in his life and he had shed, by then, some of the protective layers that had made him immune to feelings of loss. Early in treatment he had told me very proudly: 'I never miss anybody – people miss me'. I could understand Martin's puzzlement and reservations when he seemed to be asking me in so many ways: 'If it hurts, how can you call it getting better?'

# *References and Further Reading*


**Chapter 1: The Contribution of the Child Psychotherapist**

Ainsworth, M.D.S. and Bell, S.M. 'Mother-Infant Interaction and the Development of Competence' in *The Growth of Competence*, ed. K. J. Connolly and J. S. Bruner (Academic Press, London, 1974).

Bentovim, A. 'Handicapped Pre-School Children and their Families', *British Medical Journal*, 1972.

Bentovim, A. 'The Impact of Malformation on the Emotional Development of the Child and his Family' in *Teratology. Trends and Applications*, ed. C. L. Berry and D. E. Poswillo (Springer-Verlag, Berlin, Heidelberg, New York, 1975).

Bion, W. R. *Learning from Experience* (Heinemann, London, 1962).

Boston, M. 'The Effect of External Circumstances on the Inner Experience of Two Child Patients,' *Journal of Child Psychotherapy*, vol. 2, no. 1, 1967.

Bowlby, J. *Maternal Care and Mental Health* (W.H.O. Report, 1951).

Bowlby, J. *Attachment* (Hogarth Press, London, and Institute of Psychoanalysis, 1969).

Burt, C. *The Subnormal Mind* (Oxford University Press, London, 1937).

Chazan, M. and Jackson, S. 'Behaviour Problems in the Infant School: Changes over Two Years', *Journal of Child Psychology and Psychiatry*, vol. 15, no. 1, 1974.

Davie, R., Butler, N. and Goldstein, H. *From Birth to Seven* (National Children's Bureau, Longmans, London, 1972).

Douglas, J. W. B. *The Home and School* (Panther, London, 1964).

Douglas, J. W. B., Ross, J. M. and Simpson, H. R. *All our Future* (Peter Davies Ltd, London, 1968).

Foss, B. *New Perspectives in Child Development* (Penguin Books, Harmondsworth, 1974).

Graham, P. and Rutter, M. 'Psychiatric Disorder in the Young Adolescent' A follow-up study, *Proceedings of the Royal Society of Medicine*, vol. 66, no. 12, 1973.

Menzies, I. 'Thoughts on the Maternal Role in Contemporary Society', *Journal of Child Psychotherapy*, vol. 4, no. 1, 1975.

Newson, J. 'Towards a Theory of Infant Understanding', *British Psychological Society Bulletin*, June 1974.

Pringle, M. L. K., Butler, N. R. and Davie, R. *11,000 Seven Year Olds* (Longman Green, London, 1967).

Richards, M. 'The One Day Old Deprived Child', *New Scientist*, March 28th, 1974.

Richman, N. 'Depression in Mothers of Pre-school Children', *Journal of Child Psychology and Psychiatry*, vol. 17, no. 1, 1976.
Richman, N. Stevenson J. E. and Graham P. J. 'Prevalance of Behaviour Problems in Three Year Old Children: An Epidemiological Study in a London Borough', *Journal of Child Psychology and Psychiatry*, vol. 16, October 1975.
Robertson J. and J. 'Young Children in Brief Separation: A Fresh Look', *Psychoanalytic Study of Child*, vol. 26, 1972.
Robertson, Joyce 'Mother-Infant Interaction from Birth to Twelve Months. Two Case Studies', in *Determinants of Infant Behaviour*, III, ed. B. Foss (Methuen, London, 1965).
Rutter, M. and Graham, P. 'Psychiatric Disorder in Ten and Eleven Year Old Children', *Proceedings of the Royal Society of Medicine*, vol. 59, 1966.
Rutter, M. and Graham, P. 'Epidemiology of Psychiatric Disorder' in *Education, Health and Behaviour*, ed. Rutter, M., Tizard, J. and Whitmore, K. (Longman, London, 1970).
Rutter, M. *Maternal Deprivation Reassessed* (Penguin Books, Harmondsworth, 1972).
Rutter, M. 'Why are London Children so Disturbed?', *Proceedings of the Royal Society of Medicine*, vol. 66, 1973.
Rutter, M. 'A Child's Life', *New Scientist*, June 27th, 1974.
Wedge, P. and Prosser, H. *Born to Fail* (Arrow Books, London, 1973).
Winnicott, D. W. *The Family and Individual Development* (Tavistock, London, 1965).

### Chapter 2: Working with Small Groups of Children in Primary Schools

Barnes, Gill Gorell 'The Potential for Growth: The Parents', N.A.M.H. Inter-Clinic Conference, 1973.
Boxall, Marjorie 'Multiple Deprivation: An Experiment in Nurture', Occasional Paper Two, Spring 1973, Division of Education and Child Psychology of the B.P.S.
Boxall, Marjorie 'The Potential for Growth: The Children', N.A.M.H. Inter-Clinic Conference, 1973.
Boxall, Marjorie 'Nurture Groups' and Barnes, Gill Gorell, 'Work with Nurture Group Parents', *Concern*, no. 12, Summer 1973.
Institute of Group Analysis, Mimeographed report circulated to members of the Institute, 1974.

### Chapter 5: The Child Psychotherapist in a Day Centre for Young Children and Parents

Bentovim, A. and Boston, M. 'A Day Centre for Disturbed Young Children and their Parents', *Journal of Child Psychotherapy*, vol. 3, no. 3, 1973.

### Chapter 6: Working in a Hospital

Burton, L. (ed.) *Care of the Child Facing Death* (Routledge & Kegan Paul, London, 1974).
Klein, H. S. 'The Use of Analysis in a Child Psychiatric Clinic', *Journal of Child Psychology and Psychiatry*, vol. 1, no. 4, 1961.
Meltzer, D. 'The Differentiation of Somatic Delusions from Hypochondriasis', *International Journal of Psychoanalysis*, vol. 45, 1964.

Mundy, L. 'Psychotherapy in a Hospital Clinic', *Journal of Child Psychotherapy*, vol. 1, no. 3, 1965.
Radford, P. 'A Case of Anorexia in a Three and a Half Year Old Girl', *Journal of Child Psychotherapy*, vol. 2, no. 3, 1969.

**Chapter 8: A Study of an Elective Mute**

Adams and Glassner 'Emotional Involvement in Some Forms of Mutism', *Journal of Speech and Hearing Disorders*, vol. 19, 1954.
Browne, E. *et al.* 'Diagnosis and Treatment of Elective Mutism in Children', *Journal of American Academy of Child Psychiatry*, vol. 2, no. 4, October 1963.
Doris, J. and Solnit, A. L. 'Treatment of Children with Brain Damage and Associated Problems', *Journal of American Academy of Child Psychiatry*, vol. 2, no. 4, October 1963.
Halpern, W. L. *et al.* 'A Therapeutic Approach to Speech Phobia: Elective Mutism Re-examined', *Journal of American Academy of Child Psychiatry*, vol. 10, no. 1, January 1971.
Pustrom E. and Speers, R. W. 'Elective Mutism in Children', *Journal of American Academy of Child Psychiatry*, vol. 3, no. 2, April 1964.
Von Misch, A. 'Elektver Mutismus in Kindersalter', *Z. Kinderpsychiat.*, 19: 49-87, 1952.
Wright, H. L. 'A Clinical Study of Children Who Refuse to Speak in School', *Journal of American Academy of Child Psychiatry*, vol. 7, no. 4, October 1968.
Wyatt, G. L. 'Treating Children with Non-Organic Language Disorders', Restricted Circulation, N.I.M.H., Washington, U.S.A., December 1964.

**Chapter 9: Beginnings in Communication: Two Children in Psychotherapy**

Fordham, M. *New Developments in Analytical Psychology* (Routledge & Kegan Paul, London, 1957).
Rubinfine, D. L. 'Maternal Stimulation, Psychic Structure and Early Object Relations', *Psychoanalytic Study of the Child*, vol. 17, 1962.
Spitz, R. *Psychoanalytic Study of the Child*, vol. 10, 1955.

**Chapter 10: Play and Communication**

Bion, W. R. *Learning from Experience* (Heinemann, London, 1962).
Freud, S. *Analysis of a Phobia in a Five-Year-Old Boy*, Standard Edition 7 (1905).
Freud, S. *Beyond the Pleasure Principle*, Standard Edition 18 (1920).
Klein, M. 'The Technique of Child Analysis' in *The Psychoanalysis of Children* (Hogarth Press, London, 1950).
Klein, M. *Narrative of a Child Analysis* (Hogarth Press, London, 1961).
Meltzer, D. *The Psycho-analytical Process* (Heinemann Medical Books, London, 1967).
Meltzer, D. 'The Theory of Psychosexual Development' in *Sexual States of Mind* (Clunie Press, Perthshire, 1973).
Winnicott, D. W. *The Maturational Processes and the Facilitating Environment* (Hogarth Press, London, 1965).
Winnicott, D. W. *Playing and Reality* (Tavistock, London, 1971).

**Chapter 11: Psychotherapy with Psychotic Children**

Balint, M. 'Trauma and Object Relationship', *International Journal of Psycho-Analysis*, vol. 50, 1969.
Bick, E. 'Notes on Infant Observation in Psycho-Analytic Training', *International Journal of Psycho-Analysis*, vol. 45, 1964.
Bion, W. R. 'A Psycho-Analytic Study of Thinking', *International Journal of Psycho-Analysis*, vol. 43, 1962.
Bion, W. R. *Learning from Experience* (Heinemann Medical Books, London, 1962).
Bowlby, J. *Attachment and Loss*, vol. 1 'Attachment' (Hogarth Press, London, 1969; Basic Books, New York, 1969).
Docker-Drysdale, B. *Therapy in Child Care* (Longman, London, 1971).
Freud, S. 'Formulation on Two Principles of Mental Functioning', *Standard Edition of Complete Psychological Works of Sigmund Freud*, vol. 12 (Hogarth Press, London, 1911).
Freud, S. 'Beyond the Pleasure Principle', Standard Edition, vol. 18, 1920.
Klein, M. 'The Psychotherapy of the Psychoses', *Contributions to Psycho-Analysis* (Hogarth Press, London, 1930).
Klein, M. 'Notes on Some Schizoid Mechanisms', *Developments in Psycho-Analysis* (Hogarth Press, London, 1952).
Mahler, M. 'On Sadness and Grief in Infancy and Childhood Loss and Restoration of the Symbolic Love Object', *Psychoanalytic Study of the Child*, vol. 16, 1961.
Meltzer, D. *The Psycho-Analytical Process* (Heinemann Medical Books, London, 1967).
Milner, M. *The Hands of the Living God* (Hogarth Press, London, 1969).
O'Shaughnessy, E. 'The Absent Object', *Journal of Child Psychotherapy*, 1964.
Spitz, R. 'The Primal Cavity, A Contribution to the Genesis of Perception', *Psychoanalytic Study of the Child*, vol. 10, 1955.
Stroh, G. 'Psychotic Children' in *The Residential Psychiatric Treatment of Children*, ed. Barber, Philip (Crosby Lockwood Staples, London, 1974), pp. 178-204.
Tischler, S. 'Observations Based on Psychotherapy with Psychotic Children', *Selected Lectures, 6th International Congress of Psychotherapy* (S. Karger/Based New York), 1964.
Tischler, S. 'Clinical Work with Parents of Psychotic Children', *Psychiatria, Neurologia, Neurochirurgia*, vol. 74 (Amsterdam), 1971.
Tustin, F. 'A Significant Element in the Development of Autism', *Journal of Child Psychology and Psychiatry*, vol. 7 (Pergamon, Oxford, 1966).
Tustin, F. *Autism and Childhood Psychosis* (Hogarth Press, London, 1971; Science House Inc., New York, 1972).
Winnicott, D. W. 'Transitional Objects and Transitional Phenomena', *International Journal of Psychoanalysis*, vol. 34, 1953. Reprinted in *Collected Papers* (Tavistock, London, 1958).
Winnicott, D. *Collected Papers* (Tavistock, London, 1958).

**Chapter 12: Freud and Child Psychotherapy**

Bowlby, J. *Attachment and Loss*, vols. 1 and 2 (Hogarth Press, London, 1969, 1973).
Freud, A. *The Psychoanalytical Treatment of Children* (Image, London, 1946).
Freud, A. *The Ego and the Mechanisms of Defence* (Hogarth Press, London, 1937).
Freud, A. *Normality and Pathology in Childhood* (Hogarth Press, London, 1966).

Freud, S. *Three Essays on Sexuality*, Standard Edition 7 (1905).
Freud, S. *Analysis of a Phobia in a Five-Year-Old Boy*, Standard Edition 9 (1909).
Freud, S. *Notes upon a Case of Obsessional Neurosis*, Standard Edition 10 (1909).
Freud, S. *Five Lectures on Psychoanalysis*, Standard Edition 11 (1910).
Freud, S. *Introductory Lectures on Psychoanalysis*, Standard Editions 15 and 16 (1915-17).
Freud, S. *The Ego and the Id*, Standard Edition 19 (1923).
Freud, S, *New Introductory Lectures on Psychoanalysis*, Standard Edition 22 (1933).
Jones, E. *The Life and Work of Sigmund Freud*, 3 vols (Hogarth Press, London, 1953-7) and abridged version, 1 vol. (1962).
Klein, M. *The Psychoanalysis of Children* (Hogarth Press, London, 1949).
Klein, M. *Narrative of a Child Analysis* (Hogarth Press, London, 1961).
Klein, M. *et al. Developments in Psychoanalysis* (Hogarth Press, London, 1952).
Mannoni, M. *The Child, His 'Illness', and The Others* (Tavistock, London, 1970).
Segal, H. *Introduction to the Work of Melanie Klein*, Revised Edition (Hogarth Press, London, 1973).
Smirnoff, V. *The Scope of Child Analysis* (Routledge & Kegan Paul, London, 1971).
Spitz, R. *The First Year of Life* (International Universities Press, New York, 1965).
Winnicott, D. W. *Collected Papers* (Tavistock, London, 1958).
Winnicott, D. W. *Playing and Reality* (Tavistock, London, 1971).
Wollheim, R. *Freud* (Fontana, London, 1971).

**Chapter 13: Some Comments on Clinical Casework**

Bornstein, B. 'Clinical Notes on Child Analysis', *Psychoanalytic Study of the Child*, vol. 1, 1945.
Braithwaite, D. and Edgcumbe, R. 'Interactions in the Treatment of a Child and Her Mother', *Journal of Child Psychotherapy*, vol. 2, no. 1, 1967.
Edgcumbe, R. and Burgner, M. (1971) 'Some Problems in the Conceptualisation of Early Object Relationships'. As yet unpublished.
Elkan, I. 'Sources and Management of Resistance in Child Treatment', *Journal of Child Psychotherapy*, vol. 1, no. 1, 1963.
Fraiberg, S. 'Clinical Notes on the Nature of Transference in Child Analysis', *Psychoanalytic Study of the Child*, vol. 6, 1951.
Fraiberg, S. 'Further Considerations of the Role of Transference', *Psychoanalytic Study of the Child*, vol. 21, 1966.
Freud, A. *The Ego and Mechanisms of Defence* (Hogarth Press, London, 1937).
Freud, A. 'Indications for Child Analysis', *Psychoanalytic Study of the Child*, vol. 1, 1945.
Freud, A. *Normality and Pathology in Childhood* (International Universities Press Inc., New York, 1965).
Freud, S. *On Psychotherapy*, Standard Edition 7 (1905).
Freud, S. *The Question of Lay Analysis*, Standard Edition 20 (1926).
Greenson, R. R. *The Technique and Practice of Psycho-Analysis* (Hogarth Press, London, 1967).
Heineke, C. M. 'Frequency of Psychotherapeutic Sessions as a Factor Affecting the Child's Developmental Status', *Psychoanalytic Study of the Child*, vol. 20, 1965.
James, M. 'Changing Concepts of Infantile Neurosis and their Effects on

Theory and Technique'. Read at a meeting of the European Psychoanalytic Society, 1970.
Klein, M. *Contributions to Psychoanalysis* (Hogarth Press, London, 1948).
Kris, E. 'The Recovery of Childhood Memories in Psychoanalysis', *Psychoanalytic Study of the Child*, vol. 11, 1956.
Kut, S. 'Changing Patterns of Transference', *Psychoanalytic Study of the Child*, vol. 8, 1953.
Kut Rosenfeld, S. and Sprince, M. P. 'An Attempt to Formulate the Meaning of the Concept "Borderline"', *Psychoanalytic Study of the Child*, vol. 18, 1963.
Kut Rosenfeld, S. and Sprince, M. P. 'Some Thoughts on the Technical Handling of Borderline Children', *Psychoanalytic Study of the Child*, vol. 20, 1965.
Mahler, M. S. 'Thoughts about Development and Individuation', *Psychoanalytic Study of the Child*, vol. 18, 1963.
Mason, M. 'Transference in Daily and Weekly Treatment', *Journal of Child Psychotherapy*, vol. 2, no. 4, 1970.
Novick, J. and Hurry, A. 'Projection and Externalisation', *Journal of Child Psychotherapy*, vol. 2, no. 3, 1969.
Rosenbluth, D. 'Transference in Child Psychotherapy', *Journal of Child Psychotherapy*, vol. 2, no. 4, 1970.
Sandler, J. and Joffe, W. 'The Tendency to Persistence in Psychological Functioning and Development', *Bulletin, Menninger Clinic*, vol. 31, no. 5, 1967.
Thomas, R. *et al* 'Comments on Some Aspects of Self and Object Representation in a Group of Psychotic Children', *Psychoanalytic Study of the Child*, vol. 21, 1966.
Tustin, F. 'Autistic Processes', *Journal of Child Psychotherapy*, vol. 2, no. 3, 1969.
Wills, D. M. 'Some Observations on Blind Nursery School Children's Understanding of Their World', *Psychoanalytic Study of the Child*, vol. 20, 1965.
Winnicott, D. W. *Collected Papers* (Tavistock, London, 1958).

**Chapter 14: The Tavistock Training and Philosophy**

Bick, E. 'Notes on Infant Observation in Psycho-analytic Training', *International Journal of Psychoanalysis*, vol. 45, no. 4, 1964.
Bion, W. R. *Learning from Experience* (Heinemann, London, 1962).
Bion, W. R. *Attention and Interpretation* (Tavistock, London, 1970).
Bion, W. R. 'A Theory of Thinking', *International Journal of Psychoanalysis*, vol. 43, 1962.
Klein, M. *Our Adult World and its Roots in Infancy* (Tavistock London, 1960). Also published in *Our Adult World, and Other Essays* (Heinemann Medical Books, London, 1963), pp. 1-22.
Klein, M. 'Some Theoretical Conclusions Regarding the Emotional Life of the Infant' in Klein, M. *et al.*, *Developments in Psychoanalysis* (Hogarth Press, London, 1952), pp. 198-236.
Klein, M. 'Notes on Some Schizoid Mechanisms' in Klein, M. *et al.*, *Developments in Psychoanalysis*, op. cit., pp. 292-320.
Meltzer, D. *The Psychoanalytic Process* (Heinemann Medical Books, London, 1967).
Meltzer, D. *Sexual States of Mind* (Clunie Press, Perthshire, 1973).
Shakespeare, W. Sonnet 146.

**Appendix: Doubly Deprived**

Bick, E. 'The Experience of the Skin in Early Object Relations', *International Journal of Psychoanalysis*, vol. 49, 1968.

Bion, W. R. 'Attacks on Linking', *International Journal of Psychoanalysis*, vol. 40, 1959.

Meltzer, D. *The Psychoanalytic Process* (Heinemann, Medical Books, London, 1967).

# Index

(Authors' names appear in list of references.)

For Product Safety Concerns and Information please contact our EU
representative GPSR@taylorandfrancis.com
Taylor & Francis Verlag GmbH, Kaufingerstraße 24, 80331 München, Germany

www.ingramcontent.com/pod-product-compliance
Ingram Content Group UK Ltd.
Pitfield, Milton Keynes, MK11 3LW, UK
UKHW022206190926
475702UK00003B/224
* 9 7 8 0 3 6 7 0 9 9 5 5 8 *